DIRECTORY GUIDE

OF

EUROPEAN SECURITY AND DEFENSE RESEARCH

Edited by
LUC REYCHLER
ROBERT RUDNEY

Published jointly by
LEUVEN UNIVERSITY PRESS
and
PERGAMON-BRASSEY'S
International Defense Publishers

C.I.P. KONINKLIJKE BIBLIOTHEEK ALBERT I

Directory

Directory guide of European security and defense research / edited by Luc Reychler, Robert Rudney. — Leuven: Leuven University Press, 1985. — 326 p.; 22 cm.
ISBN 90-6186-164-0
SISO 399.25 UDC 355(4-15)

Onderwerpen: Ontwapening; Bewapening; Veiligheid [Internationale]; Krijgskunst en -kunde — Onderzoek

Publishers:
Leuven University Press V.Z.W.
Krakenstraat 3
B-3000 Leuven/Louvain (Belgium)

PERGAMON-BRASSEY'S
International Defense Publishers
1340 Old Chain Bridge Road, McLean, Virginia 22101 (USA)

© 1985 L. Reychler and R. Rudney

No part of this book may be reproduced in any form, by print, photoprint, microfilm or any other means without written permission from the publishers.

D/1984/1869/8

Omslagontwerp: W. Platteborze

DIRECTORY GUIDE OF EUROPEAN SECURITY AND DEFENSE RESEARCH

PREFACE

This directory guide is designed for all those interested in the security, defense, and disarmament debate in Western Europe. The directory itself includes reference material on over 200 research centers in 19 countries of neutral and NATO Europe.[1] For most of these institutions, we were able to compile detailed information on : (1) organization and objectives; (2) personnel; (3) research projects in progress; (4) periodicals and other publications; and (5) collaborative efforts with foreign institutions. We have also included introductory descriptions outlining the state of research in each country. It is our hope that, through the dissemination of this book, we will encourage other research centers to provide substantive information, so that the next edition of the directory (in 1986) will be even more complete. The absence of communication and cooperation among European research centers has greatly inhibited the development of a distinctly European consciousness on defense questions, and this deficiency has often reduced the defense debate to the level of oversimplification and mythologizing on all sides.

We believe that well-respected, serious research organizations can best serve as "outside catalysts" to encourage more intelligent public discussion, to provide expert critiques of official policy, and to lay the foundations for future consensus on European defense and

---

1. Austria, Belgium, Denmark, Federal Republic of Germany, Finland, France, Greece, Iceland, Ireland, Italy, Luxembourg, Netherlands, Norway, Portugal, Spain, Sweden, Switzerland, Turkey, United Kingdom.

disarmament issues.² In a previous article, we found that, despite tremendous progress in recent years, the European research sector still suffers from fragmentation. This fragmentation is the consequence of the fact that the research objectives are determined by multiple, relatively small and inadequately funded centers whose national and transnational interactions have stayed limited.³ For these reasons, it would be more accurate to speak of a "scatter-brained" Europe than of a European "brain trust".

The project on European security and defense research was initiated through the Division of International Relations, at the Catholic University of Leuven (Louvain), Belgium, and supported by grants from the Ford Foundation, NATO Research Program, and the Royal Higher Institute of Defense Studies, Brussels. In addition to the directory, we will submit a report assessing the structure and impact of the research sector to the Ford Foundation this spring, and we anticipate that the report will be available shortly thereafter in monograph form. We are also designing a computerized data bank for easier classification and access to this bibliographic material. Because of publishing time lags, the present directory may contain some dated information on research projects in progress. These delays are inevitable and will eventually be rectified through the data bank. We have

---

2. The term "outside catalyst" was first coined by David Abshire in his article, "Twenty Years inside the Strategic Labyrinth", <u>The Washington Quarterly</u>, Winter 1982, pp. 83-105.

3. L. Reychler and R. Rudney, "Toward a More Efficient Organization of European Security and Defense Thinking", <u>Studia Diplomatica</u>, Vol. XXXVI (1983), N°3, pp. 289-310.

---

tried to be as non-partisan and impartial as possible and take full responsibility for the accuracy of all material printed here.

Very few publications exist concerning European institutions involved in security- and defense-related research. Consequently, we have undertaken an extensive questionnaire survey of all countries to collect this information, and we have supplemented the survey results with material gathered through telephone and personal interviews. In the next edition, we would like to expand the directory to include parliamentary and government documents in the field, foreign affairs and defense publications that are independent of research centers, and individual researchers who have no formal institutional affiliation. It should also be noted that nearly all institutions listed here are public policy research organizations. In Europe, there exists a minimum of outside research on the "hardware" aspects of defense or the operational dimension (unlike the case in the U.S.).

We would like to acknowledge the assistance of a number of experts in the compilation of this reference book : Jan G. Siccama, Ursula Fellner, Malcolm Spaven, Lawrence Freedman, Jan Jakob Floryan, Niels J. Haagerup, Kari Möttölä, Hans Günter Brauch, Norbert Ropers, Gerhard Wettig, Gebhard Schweigler, Virgilio Ilari, C. Wiebes, Antonio Sanchez-Gijon, Daniel Frei, Thanos Veremis, Seyfi Tashan, Unto Vesa, Ake Sparring, Alvaro Vasconcelos, Gunnar Gunnarsson, and J.F. Guilhaudis. We would also like to thank all those who contributed their time and thoughts during our interviews. The Nordic Cooperation Committee for International Politics generously permitted us to use some of their material for those countries. Harry Zubkoff was very helpful in providing research sources from the United States. At Leuven, Mark Riga and Jorg Leenards made important contributions to the project. Linda Beyens did a superb job working the Kaypro word processor.

                                          Luc REYCHLER
                                          Robert RUDNEY

                                          Division of International Relations
                                          Department of Political Science
                                          Catholic University of Leuven
                                          Van Evenstraat 2B
                                          3000 Leuven, Belgium

AUSTRIA

AUSTRIA

Austria's military occupation terminated in the autumn of 1955 when American, Soviet, British, and French forces left the country, and formal Austrian sovereignty was reestablished. The country's constitution guarantees a policy of perpetual neutrality, based on a refusal to join military alliances or permit foreign military installations on Austrian territory. The Austrians are allowed an armed forces (<u>Bundesheer</u>) of 50,000 men for territorial defense and are prohibited from possessing atomic weapons or missiles. As a neutral country, Austria plays a unique role as a link between East and West, hosting Soviet-American summit meetings (most recently, the Brezhnev-Carter encounter of 1979 for the signing of the ill-fated SALT II agreement). Vienna has been the site (since 1973) for the Mutual and Balanced Force Reduction (MBFR) talks between NATO and the Warsaw Pact, and is the headquarters of OPEC and the International Atomic Energy Agency. The Austrian government has been active in the Conference on Security and Cooperation in Europe and in peace proposals for the Middle East crisis. Though politically non-aligned, Austria is a member of the United Nations, the European Council, the European Free Trade Association, and the Organization for Economic Cooperation and Development.

As might be expected, the study of neutralist policy and small states' roles in international relations predominates in Austrian research centers. The largest such organization is the Oesterreichisches Institut für Internationale Politik, located at Laxenburg (near Vienna). The Institute functions as the primary channel for academic research to reach policymaking circles. One project now in progress examines the political relationship of three neutral states (Austria, Sweden, and Switzerland) with the European Community. The best-known Austrian journal on international affairs, <u>Oesterreichisches Zeitschrift für Aussenpolitik</u>, is published by the Oesterreichisches Gesellschaft für Aussenpolitik und Internationale Beziehungen. The journal also contains chronologies and lists of official documentation on Austrian foreign policy. Unfortunately, because of financial difficulties, the Society's research center has suspended its activities.

Peace research is undertaken by the Austrian Institute for Peace Research and the Vienna University Center for Peace Research. The former organization has a major education and information program on peace activities, but also is engaged in a study of Austrian neutrality and peace policy. One focus of the University Center is on the relationship between the churches and the peace movement. Another group of researchers studying Austrian neutrality policy is located at the University of Graz.

The Austrian State Treaty of May 1955 was one of the first augurs of detente during the Cold War years. From the very start, then, the Austrians have had a vital stake in the relaxation of East-West tensions and in the control of the European arms race. The doctrine of neutrality is generally accepted, and the postwar Austrian economic expansion has benefited from many of the advantages of Austria's position as a "bridge" in Central Europe.

DIRECTORY CODE NUMBER : 1

Name of Institution : Austrian Institute for Peace Research

Address : 7461 Stadtschlaining - Burg

Telephone : (3355) 24-98

Founding Date : Sept. 1982   Founding Place : Wien

Type of Organization : National Public

Objectives : (1) conduct and coordinate peace research;
            (2) promote international scientific and political
                dialogue in peace research and peace-related
                subjects;
            (3) undertake educational and information efforts to
                spread the idea of peace.

Director : Dr. Gerald Mader

Total Staff : 5

Number of researchers on security and defense issues : 2

Projects in Progress : Title
                                Name(s) of Researcher(s)

Neutrality and peace policy in Austria.
                          Josef Binter/Wilfried Graf

Library services provided for outside researchers : yes

Comments : Yearbook and proceedings of seminars are forthcoming
           publications.

DIRECTORY CODE NUMBER : 2

Name of Institution : Austrian Society for Foreign Affairs and
                      International Relations

Address : Palais Palffy
          Josefsplatz 6
          1010 WIEN

DIRECTORY CODE NUMBER : 3

Name of Institution : Institut für Strategische Grundlagenforschung
                      an der Landesverteidigungsakademie

Address : Stiftgasse 2A
          1070 WIEN

Telephone : (222) 93-84-87

Founding Date : 1969   Founding Place : Wien

Type of Organization : National Public

Director : Brig. Gen. Franz Freistetter

DIRECTORY CODE NUMBER : 4

Name of Institution : Institut für Völkerrecht und Internationale
                      Beziehungen

Address : Universität Graz
          Hans-Sachs-Gasse 3/III
          8010 GRAZ

Telephone : (316) 31581

Type of Organization : University

Objectives : Education (teaching, seminars) in international law
             and international relations within the law curriculum;
             research in international law and international
             relations.

Director : Prof. Konrad Ginther

Total Staff : 7

Number of researchers on security and defense issues : 2

Projects in Progress : Title   Name(s) of Researcher(s)

Contemporary Austrian neutrality and peace policy.

        Dr. Wolfgang Benedek
        Dr. Hubert Isak

Publications (since January 1983)

Hubert Isak, "War and Peace - Observations on the Present Discussion in view of International Law" (in German), in Joseph Marko and Kurt Salamuns (Eds.), <u>Conditions for a Constructive Concept of Peace</u> (in German), (Graz : Edition OeH, 1983).

Library services provided for outside researchers : yes

DIRECTORY CODE NUMBER : 5

Name of Institution : Institut für Völkerrecht und Internationale
        Beziehungen

Address : Universitätsstrasse 2
    1090 WIEN

Telephone : (222) 42-92-86

Type of Organization : University

DIRECTORY CODE NUMBER : 6

Name of Institution : Oesterreichische Gesellschaft für Aussenpolitik
und Internationale Beziehungen

Address : Favoritenstrasse 15
1040 WIEN

Telephone : (222) 65-09-197

Founding Date : 1960   Founding Place : Wien

Type of Organization : National Private Non-Profit

Objectives : Encouragement of understanding of the problems of
foreign policy and international relations.

Director : Dr. Georg Fürstenberg

Total Staff : 3

Regular Periodicals : Title	Founding Date	Issues Annually
Oesterreichische Zeitschrift für Aussenpolitik	1960	4

Comments : The Association's research institute is inactive due to
lack of funds.

DIRECTORY CODE NUMBER : 7

Name of Institution : Oesterreichische Gesellschaft für Politische-
Strategische Studien

Address : Schwarzenbergplatz
1010 WIEN

DIRECTORY CODE NUMBER : 8

Name of Institution : Oesterreichische Gesellschaft zur Förderung der Landesverteidigung

Address : Stiftskaserne
Mariahiferstrasse
1150 WIEN

President : Prof. Günther Winkler

DIRECTORY CODE NUMBER : 9

Name of Institution : Oesterreichisches Institut für Internationale Politik

Address : Schlossplatz 13
2361 LAYENBURG

Telephone : (2236) 71575

Founding Date : Dec. 1978   Founding Place : Vienna

Type of Organization : National Private Non-Profit

Objectives : The chief task is to provide public information on problems of international politics and assistance to decision-makers on different aspects of Austrian foreign policy. To this end the Institute undertakes policy-relevant research and other activities addressing both professionals and the general public.

Director : Ambassador Dr. Hans Thalberg

Total Staff : 12

Number of researchers on security and defense issues : 3

Projects in Progress : Title
                       Name(s) of Researcher(s)

1. Nuclear disengagement and the nation - state.
   Heinz Gärtner

2. Political aspects of Austria's, Sweden's and Switzerland's relations to the European Community.
   Paul Luif

3. Soviet policy towards Israel and the Palestinians.
   John Bunzl

Publications (since January 1983)

1. Karl E. Birnbaum (Ed.), <u>Confidence Building and East-West Relations</u>, March 1983.

2. Heinz Gärtner, <u>The Structures of Hegemony and the Causes of War</u> (in German), May 1983.

<u>Library services provided for outside researchers</u> : yes

DIRECTORY CODE NUMBER : 10

<u>Name of Institution</u> : Oesterreichisches Ost- und Südosteuropa-Institut

<u>Address</u> : Josefplatz 6
            1010 WIEN 1

<u>Telephone</u> : (222) 52-18-95

<u>Comments</u> : While not doing specific projects on security and defense, the Institute undertakes economic and social research on Eastern Europe and the USSR which has security implications.

DIRECTORY CODE NUMBER : 11

Name of Institution : Universitätszentrum für Friedensforschung

Address : Schottenring 21
1010 WIEN

Telephone : (222) 31-25-44   x. 248

Founding Date : 1973   Founding Place : Wien

Type of Organization : National Private University

Objectives : Organization of lectures, symposia, congresses and research discussions on the topics of peace research, peace education, arms control, disarmament, confidence-building measures and East-West dialogue.

Director : Prof. Rudolf Weiler

Number of researchers on security and defense issues : 2

Projects in Progress : Title
                       Name(s) of Researcher(s)

1. Analysis of peace and conflict research in Austria from 1900 to the 1980s (structures and tendencies).
   Dr. Christoph Gütermann

2. Development of Catholic theories on the topic "War and Peace".
   Dr. Hubert Mader

Regular Periodicals : Title	Founding Date	Issues Annually
Wiener Blätter zur Friedensforschung	1973	4

Other Publications (since January 1983)

1. <u>Christians and Marxists in a Peace Dialogue</u> (series of symposia).

2. Smaller publications on various similar topics.

<u>Library services provided for outside researchers</u> : yes

BELGIUM

BELGIUM

Belgium is a small, business-like country of only ten million people, yet it is an important nodal point in the international diplomatic, economic, and strategic network. For some, Belgium recalls Flanders fields, the Battle of the Bulge, the headquarters of the European Community and NATO, the Concours Queen Elisabeth (in music), or the strife between the francophone Walloons and Dutch-speaking Flemings. It is a country whose national self-definition seems to be the object of a perpetual revision.

Overall, Belgium is one of the most economically sensitive and vulnerable countries in the world. In 1981, the Gross National Product was 3607 billion Belgian francs. The export of goods and services amounted to 2685 billion (or 74 % of GNP), and the import bill was 2838 billion (or 79.1 % of GNP). Belgium is dependent on other countries for 84 % of its energy supply. It is not surprising that in the threat perception of the Belgians, the economic dimension occupies a very significant place.

The two organizations whose effective functioning is considered of strategic importance are the European Community and the Atlantic Alliance. The European Community is instrumental in defending Belgian economic and political interests in the East-West, North-South, and West-West contexts; the Atlantic Alliance in the East-West military context. In 1949, NATO was considered the best possible course for Belgian postwar policy. Today, in spite of a considerable range of criticism, NATO has retained this position. The Atlantic Alliance is generally considered a sine qua non for the realization of Belgian national security. Nevertheless, there is no longer the unquestioning support of the Alliance that there once was.

A just impression of the Belgian defense scene reveals a stark contrast between its serious defense efforts and the embryonic state of the security- and defense-related research. Belgium has several small research units; some are documentation centers, others are concerned with teaching or organizing colloquia or seminars, while a minority does real research work. There are two institutions at the national level. The oldest "flagship" is the Royal Institute of International Relations. It has hosted colloquia about security and defense issues, and distinguishes itself through its lecture series about international relations in general and security and defense issues in particular. The second national institution, the Defense Studies Center, is dependent on the Ministry of Defense and was created in 1978 to contribute to the study of security and defense issues; the permanent formation of staff officers; the dialogue between military officers and civilians; and the enhancement of public discussion about defense and military problems.

In Flanders, security and defense issues are being studied mainly at two locations. In past years, the University of Leuven (K.U.L.) has done research about Belgian defense policy and international peace-keeping. During the late 1960's, the Division of International Relations created courses about peace research and strategy. These activities were subsequently reinforced by the creation of the Center for Strategic Studies in 1979 and the Center for Peace Research in 1983. The Center for Polemology at the Free University of Brussels (V.U.B.), established in 1972, focuses its studies on peace research in general, arms control and disarmament, and non-violent defense alternatives. In addition, the International Peace Information Service (IPIS), a documentation and education center, is located in Antwerp.

In the francophone part of Belgium, there are four centers. The Centre de Sociologie de la Guerre (Université Libre de Bruxelles) is currently undertaking research projects on the defense decision-making process and on pacifism in Belgium. There are also two centers which cater predominately to the peace movement. The most prolific in terms of publications has been the Groupe de Recherche et d'Information sur la Paix (GRIP). Recently, a new defense-oriented center, the Institut Européen pour la Paix et la Sécurité, has been formed by General Robert Close. The objective of this institute is to be an information center on Western security problems and global issues.

In addition to the Belgian organizations, a number of international research organizations have established themselves in Brussels. Two of these organizations examine security problems. The Centre for European Policy Studies was created in 1982 through the initiative of the Ford Foundation, the European Cultural Foundation, and the King Baudoin Foundation to provide a uniquely European research perspective on global problems, including defense questions. The Centre is now engaged in a major study of European policy with respect to nuclear non-proliferation issues. The North Atlantic Assembly is essentially a forum for NATO parliamentarians to discuss topical security and defense subjects, but it does publish regular reports and texts of proceedings of the Assembly.

DIRECTORY CODE NUMBER : 12

Name of Institution : Centre de Sociologie de la Guerre

Address : Institut de Sociologie
Université Libre de Bruxelles
44, avenue Jeanne
1050 BRUSSELS

Telephone : (2) 649-00-30   x. 3326
                                 3373

Founding Date : Jan. 1967   Founding Place : Brussels

Type of Organization : National Public University

Objectives : Multidisciplinary study of peace and the prevention of war.

Total Staff : 2

Number of researchers on security and defense issues : 2

Projects in Progress : Title
                             Name(s) of Researcher(s)

1. The Reappraisal of pacifist movements in Europe.
                              Nadine Zubelski-Bernard

2. Sociological analysis of a stratification process and political integration : the results of decisions concerning national defense in Belgium.
                              Philippe Manigart

Publications (since January 1983)

1. N. Zubelski-Bernard, "Pacifism in Belgium", in West European Pacifism and the Strategy for Peace (London : Macmillan, 1984).

2. P. Manigart, "The Evolution of Military Expenditures in Belgium since 1900" (in French), Courrier Hebdomadaire du CRISP, N°1009 (1983), 25 pp.

3. P. Manigart, "The Evolution of the Demographic Structure of the Belgian Armed Forces since 1900", (in French), <u>Courrier Hebdomadaire du CRISP</u>, N°1012 (1983), 31 pp.

4. P. Manigart, "Military Manpower Management in Belgium : Problems and Alternatives". Paper presented at the 1983 Conference of the Inter-University Seminar on Armed Forces and Society, Chicago, Oct. 1983, 22 pp.

Collaboration with Foreign Study Centers

1. Professors World Peace Academy in Europe on "West European pacifism and the strategy for peace".

2. Conference of Peace Research in History (USA).

3. Department of Sociology, University of Chicago (USA).

DIRECTORY CODE NUMBER : 13

<u>Name of Institution</u> : Centre for European Policy Studies

<u>Address</u> : Rue Ducale 33
            1000 BRUSSELS

<u>Telephone</u> : (2) 513-40-88

<u>Founding Date</u> : 1982   <u>Founding Place</u> : Brussels

<u>Type of Organization</u> : International Private Non-Profit

<u>Objectives</u> : To encourage the study and discussion of public affairs in the European Community and the rest of Western Europe.

<u>Director</u> : Dr. Peter Ludlow

<u>Total Staff</u> : 23

<u>Number of researchers on security and defense issues</u> : 1

Projects in Progress : Title   Name(s) of Researcher(s)

1. New approaches to non-proliferation - a European approach.
   Harald Müller et al

2. Euro-South relations.
   Robert Cassen et al

Regular Periodicals : Title	Founding Date	Issues Annually
1. CEPS Papers	1983	occasional
2. CEPS Working Documents	1983	occasional
3. CEPS Books	1984	occasional

Other Publications (since January 1983)

1. Simon May, "On the Problems and Prerequisites of Public Support for the Defence of Western Europe", CEPS Papers, N°4, March 1984, 32 pp.

2. Jean-Marie Soutou, "For a Western Policy with Respect to the Soviet Union" (in French), CEPS Working Document, Sept. 1983.

3. Antonio Armellini, "The Nature of the Soviet Regime and its Fundamental Objectives", CEPS Working Document, Sept. 1983.

4. Walter Stützle, "The Politico-Military Situation at the Beginning of the Eighties : Problems and Tasks", CEPS Working Document, Nov. 1983.

Collaboration with Foreign Study Centers

Institutes from seven European countries are participating in the non-proliferation project.

Library services provided for outside researchers : yes

Comments : CEPS was established to meet "the comparative shortage of high quality, policy-orientated research into the fundamental, medium and long-term issues facing Europeans in general".

DIRECTORY CODE NUMBER : 14

Name of Institution : Centrum voor Polemologie

Address : Vrije Universiteit Brussel
Pleinlaan 2
1050 BRUSSEL

Telephone : (2) 641-20-24
641-20-28

Founding Date : 1972   Founding Place : Brussels

Type of Organization : National Public University

Objectives : (1) To conduct peace research;
(2) to coordinate courses on polemology at the university:
(3) to provide public information.

Director : Prof. J. Niezing

Total Staff : 5

Projects in Progress : Title	Name(s) of Researcher(s)
1. NATO-procurement policy and Belgian media.	P. Stouthuysen
2. Risk-analysis as a contribution to Peace Research.	L. Beek/J. Niezing
3. Social Defense.	G. Geeraerts

Regular Periodicals : Title	Founding Date	Issues Annually
1. "Publications of the Polemological Centre of the Free University of Brussels"		occasional
2. Pole-papers		occasional
3. Bijdragen tot het Vredesonderzoek		occasional

Other Publications (since January 1983)

Patrick Stouthuysen, "The Political Identity of an Ecologist Movement. Case Study : The Flemish Green Party Agalev", Pole-papers (1983), 30 pp.

Library services provided for outside researchers : yes

DIRECTORY CODE NUMBER : 15

Name of Institution : Centrum voor Strategische Studies

Address : Katholieke Universiteit Leuven
Departement Politieke Wetenschappen
Afdeling Internationale Betrekkingen
Van Evenstraat 2B
3000 LEUVEN

Telephone : (16) 22-83-44

Founding Date : 1979   Founding Place : Leuven

Type of Organization : National Public University

Objectives : Promote research in security and strategy.

Director : Prof. Luc Reychler

Total Staff : 4

Projects in Progress : Title
                               Name(s) of Researcher(s)

---

1. Belgian Defense Policy.
                    L. Reychler/J. Leenaards/
                    R. Vrankx/A. Boeykens

2. The organization of European security and defense research.
                    L. Reychler/R. Rudney

3. Straight and crooked strategic thinking : identification of the requirements for objective strategic analysis.
                    L. Reychler

Publications (since January 1983)

---

1. Reychler L., "Towards a More Systematic Research of Belgian security and defense policy" (in Dutch) in B. De Clercq et al, Political Instruments for Control of Crises, (Louvain, University Press, 1983, pp. 171-201).

2. Reychler L., "Belgian Defense Policy", in The Neglected and Neglectful Small Northern Allies, (Paris : Atlantic Institute, to be published in 1984).

3. L. Reychler, R. Rudney, "Towards a more Efficient Organization of European Security and Defense Thinking", in Studia Diplomatica, 1983, N°3, pp. 289-310.

4. R. Rudney, "European Defense Think Tanks", National Defense, November 1983, pp. 30-35.

5. R. Rudney, "Mitterrand's New Atlanticism : Evolving French Attitudes Toward NATO", Orbis, Spring 1984.

6. R. Rudney, "Mitterrand's Defense Concepts : Some Unsocialist Earmarks", Strategic Review, Spring 1983, pp. 20-35.

7. L. Reychler, "Peace, Morality, and Science" (in Dutch), A.I.B. Papers, 1983 (2).

8. L. Reychler, "The Future of European Security" (in Dutch), A.I.B. Papers, 1984 (1).

Collaboration with Foreign Study Centers

Atlantic Institute for International Affairs on defense study of NATO northern allies.

DIRECTORY CODE NUMBER : 16

Name of Institution : Centrum voor Vredesonderzoek

Address : Katholieke Universiteit Leuven
Departement Politieke Wetenschappen
Van Evenstraat 2B
3000 LEUVEN

Telephone : (16) 22-83-44

Founding Date : 1983 (1967)   Founding Place : Leuven

Type of Organization : National Public University

Objectives : (1) To increase contact with national and foreign peace research centers to cope more efficiently with peace research problems;
(2) to stimulate and coordinate peace research on a broader scale than simply problems of arms control;
(3) to make peace research more accessible for students in all universities;
(4) to clarify peace problems for people outside the university and non-specialists.

Director : Prof. V. Werck

Total Staff : 5

Projects in Progress : Title
                              Name(s) of Researcher(s)

---

1. Handbook on peace and security (with videotapes).
   L. Reychler/A. Boeykens
   Y. Bormans/C. Huybrechts

2. The Soviet Union and European security.

Regular Periodicals : Title	Founding Date	Issues Annually
Cahiers van het Centrum voor Vredesonderzoek	Dec. 1983	6-8

Other Publications (since January 1983)

1. P. van de Meerssche et al, Security and Development : How Do We Gain Peace (in Dutch), (Leuven : Davidsfonds, 1983).
2. V. Werck, "Crisis Management in International Relations" (in Dutch), in B.J. De Clercq et al, Political Instruments of Crisis Management (in Dutch), (Leuven : University Press, 1983) pp. 203-213.

Collaboration with Foreign Study Centers

The Graduate Institute of Peace Studies, Kyung Hee University, Seoul, Korea.

Comments : Peace research began at the University in 1967-68 in the Division of International Relations under the direction of Prof. Victor Werck. The Center was formalized in 1983 to support and coordinate the research activities.

DIRECTORY CODE NUMBER : 17

Name of Institution : Comité international pour la Sécurité et la Coopération européennes

Address : 42, rue Dautzenberg
1050 BRUSSELS

Telephone : (2) 649-55-70

Founding Date : June 1972   Founding Place : Brussels

Type of Organization : International Non-Profit

Objectives : (1) Inform the general public of the implications of the Final Act of the Helsinki Conference on Security and Cooperation in Europe;
(2) encourage discussion of the Final Act among governments and the general public.

DIRECTORY CODE NUMBER : 18

Name of Institution : Defense Studies Center

Address : Royal Higher Institute for Defense
Kortenberglaan 115
1040 BRUSSELS

Telephone : (2) 243-31-71

Founding Date : Nov. 1978   Founding Place : Brussels

Type of Organization : National Public

Objectives : (1) Study of security and defense issues on national and international levels;
(2) formation of staff officers;
(3) involvement of military officers and civilians in the study of an optimal defense policy;
(4) improvement of the public information process;
(5) improving the quality of the policymaking process;
(6) keeping up with major news events.

Director : Col. Hollants van Loocke

Total Staff : 5

Projects in Progress : Title
                              Name(s) of Researcher(s)

1. Religious aspects of nuclear weaponry.
                              C. Franck/E.H. Herr

2. International legal aspects of security zones, demilitarized zones, and nuclear-free zones.
                              M. Bossuyt

3. Investigation of the image of the armed forces.

Regular Periodicals : Title	Founding Date	Issues Annually
1. <u>Acta</u>		occasional
2. <u>Veiligheid en Strategie/ Sécurité et Stratégie</u>	Dec. 1981	4

<u>Library services provided for outside researchers</u> : yes

<u>Comments</u> : The Institute has an extensive program of lectures, seminars, and colloquia. The 1983 annual conference covered subjects like "The Media and Defense", "Non-Military Aspects of Defense", and "Problems of European Defense".

DIRECTORY CODE NUMBER : 19

<u>Name of Institution</u> : Groupe de Recherche et d'Information sur la Paix (GRIP)

<u>Address</u> : Avenue Maréchal Foch, 22
1030 BRUSSELS

<u>Telephone</u> : (2) 241-80-96
241-84-20

<u>Founding Date</u> : 1978   <u>Founding Place</u> : Brussels

<u>Type of Organization</u> : National Private Non-Profit

<u>Objectives</u> : To study, research, and inform on all problems of peace, defense, and disarmament.

<u>Director</u> : Bernard Adam

<u>Total Staff</u> : 11

Projects in Progress : Title
                                Name(s) of Researcher(s)

1. Belgian arms trade.
2. Arms economy and the defense budget of Belgium.
3. Belgian diplomacy with respect to the defense of Europe, the Euromissiles, and East-West force levels.

Regular Periodicals : Title	Founding Date	Issues Annually
1. Gyroscope	1982	4
2. Revue de presse sur les problèmes de paix et de défense		6
3. Notes de synthèse		10
4. Travaux de recherche		occasional

Other Publications (since January 1983)

1. Report of GRIP on the Problem of the Euromissiles (in French), (Brussels, 1983).
2. Memo on the Euromissiles (in French), (Brussels, 1983).

DIRECTORY CODE NUMBER : 20

Name of Institution : Institut Européen pour la Paix et la Sécurité
                     (IEPS)

Address : 31, rue du Champ de Mars
          1050 BRUSSELS

Telephone : (2) 511-56-23

Founding Date : June 1983   Founding Place : Brussels

Type of Organization : National Private Non-Profit

Objectives : Non-partisan research and information center concerned with the preservation and strengthening of peace and security in Europe and the world.

Director : Maj. Gen. Robert Close

Projects in Progress : Title
                      Name(s) of Researcher(s)

1. Civil defense (to appear in Oct. 1984).

2. Defense of Europe.

Publications (since January 1983)

"The Europeans in the Atlantic Alliance Confronted with 'Star Wars'" (in French), June 1984.

DIRECTORY CODE NUMBER : 21

Name of Institution : International Peace Information Service (IPIS)

Address : Kerkstraat 150
         2008 ANTWERPEN

Telephone : (3) 235-02-72

Founding Date : Nov. 1980   Founding Place : Antwerp

Type of Organization : National Private Non-Profit

Objectives : (1) collect information and documentation about peace problems;
             (2) strive for objectivity concerning information on peace policy;
             (3) provide the information and documentation service to as wide a public as possible.

Director : Mark Heirman

Total Staff : 5

Projects in Progress : Title   Name(s) of Researcher(s)

---

1. Security and human rights.
                                 Mark Heirman

2. Eastern Europe and human rights.
                                 Dirk De Haeck

3. Churches and peace.
                                 Mark van Rompaey

4. Non-violence.
                                 André Vermeulen

5. Security and polemology.
                                 Luc De Smet

6. Arms trade.
                                 Wim Willems

7. Peace education.
                                 Jan Gauderis

8. Arms trade in Belgium and the Netherlands.

9. Relationship between security, human rights, and development in Belgium and the Netherlands.

Regular Periodicals : Title	Founding Date	Issues Annually
IPIS-Informatief	1983	4

Other Publications (since January 1983)

"Eastern Europe in Quadruple" (in Dutch) (Antwerp : Omega, 1983) 128 pp.

DIRECTORY CODE NUMBER : 22

Name of Institution : North Atlantic Assembly

Address : 3, place du Petit Sablon
          1000 BRUSSELS

Telephone : (2) 513-28-65

Founding Date : July 1955   Founding Place : Paris

Type of Organization : International

Objectives : Fostering greater understanding of Alliance issues among NATO parliamentarians; providing a link between the intergovernmental structure of NATO and the Alliance parliamentarians.

Secretary-General : Philippe Deshormes

Total Staff : 30

Number of researchers on security and defense issues : 5

Projects in Progress : Title
                              Name(s) of Researcher(s)

---

1. East-West economic relations.
   F. Klein

2. Free Flow of information and people.
   G. Parmentier

3. Successor generation.
   G. Parmentier

4. Defense cooperation.
   J. Seabright

5. Conventional defense.
   J. Seabright

6. The Southern region.
   J. Dittberner

7. Out-of-area challenges to Alliance security.
   J. Dittberner

8. Ballistic missile defense.
   D. Hobbs

9. East-West technology transfer.
   D. Hobbs

10. Nuclear weapons in Europe.
    J. Dittberner/J. Seabright

Regular Periodicals : Title	Founding Date	Issues Annually
1. North Atlantic Assembly News		5
2. Bulletin : Report on Developments relative to the Humanitarian Provisions of the Final Act of the Conference on Security and Cooperation in Europe	May 1976	4

Other Publications (since January 1983)

1. The Economics of Atlantic Security.
2. East-West Economic Relations.
3. General Report of the Committee on Education, Cultural Affairs and Information.
4. Interim Report of the Sub-committee on the Free Flow of Information and People.
5. Interim Report of the Sub-committee on the Successor Generation.
6. Alliance Security.
7. The Implications of Technology for the Battlefield.
8. Manpower Issues for NATO.
9. Interim Report of the Sub-committee on Conventional Defence.
10. Interim Report of the Sub-committee on Defence Cooperation.
11. Alliance Political Developments.
12. Interim Report of the Sub-committee on the Southern Region.
13. Interim Report of the Scientific and Technical Committee on Ballistic Missile Defence and East-West Technology Transfer.

DIRECTORY CODE NUMBER : 23

Name of Institution : Royal Institute for International Relations

Address : Kroonlaan 88
1050 BRUSSELS

Telephone : (2) 648-20-00

Founding Date : 1947   Founding Place : Brussels

Type of Organization : National Private Non-Profit

Objectives : Study of international relations, international economy and international law, especially from Belgian, Luxembourg, and European viewpoints.

Director : Prof. E. Coppieters

Regular Periodicals : Title	Founding Date	Issues Annually
1. Studia Diplomatica	1948	6
2. Internationale Spectator (in Dutch)	1961	12

Collaboration with Foreign Study Centers

The Institute publishes Internationale Spectator in collaboration with the Netherlands Institute for International Relations (Clingendael).

Library services provided for outside researchers : yes

Comments : Each year, the Institute organizes a series of lectures about international relations, including security and defense issues. It also plans to stimulate workshops about (1) sources of international distrust; (2) generational, regional, social, or philosophical influences on peace and security thinking; (3) the economic and social aspects of the weapons industry in Belgium and abroad.

DIRECTORY CODE NUMBER : 24

Name of Institution : Université de Paix

Address : Boulevard du Nord, 4
5000 NAMUR

Telephone : (81) 22-61-02

Founding Date : 1960   Founding Place : Huy

Objectives : To pursue the previous work of Dominique Pire with respect to contributing through dialogue to the establishment and maintenance of peace.

Director : Luc Heymans

Total Staff : 18

Projects in Progress : Title	Name(s) of Researcher(s)
1. Peace education.	Pierre Colet
2. Security and defense.	Mirelle Jacquet
3. Non-violence.	Jean-Jacques Lecocq

Regular Periodicals : Title	Founding Date	Issues Annually
U.P. Information	1980	4

DENMARK

DENMARK

In May 1984, the Center-Right government led by Poul Schlüter found itself in the minority after a parliamentary debate on motions favoring the creation of a Nordic nuclear-free-zone and cancelling Danish payments for the NATO Pershing-cruise deployment. While the government did not fall, the debate did underscore the critical importance of security and defense questions in the Danish political context.

In January 1981, largely as a response to this growing concern, the government of the day established the Danish Commission on Security and Disarmament Affairs. The Commission, an independent body charged with evaluating national security policy and promoting ideas for disarmament and detente, is basically a revised version of the Danish Disarmament Commission which had been in existence for almost twenty years. The new Commission consists of civil servants, military officers, academics, journalists, and--most noteworthy--representatives of all nine political parties. It publishes an annual survey entitled Security and Disarmament (in Danish) and sponsors relevant research, with emphasis on the Euromissile crisis and proposals for a nuclear-free-zone.

Two other independent organizations are important centers for analysis of Danish security issues. The Danish Institute of International Studies supports and occasionally initiates research mainly through the universities, while the Foreign Policy Society publishes the quarterly journal, Fremtiden (The Future), as well as a pamphlet series on foreign and defense questions. The director of the Institute of International Studies, Niels J. Haagerup, undertook the 1982 study of security issues for the European Parliament. Haagerup also founded the Danish strategic study group which is affiliated with the Foreign Policy Society. This study group, which is about twenty years old, has recently done work on Nordic defense problems and on crisis management.

Research at Danish universities (Copenhagen, Aarhus, and Odense) has concentrated on East-West conflict analysis and on regional/national studies. Faculty members from these three universities also serve as members of the Commission on Security and Disarmament Affairs.

DIRECTORY CODE NUMBER : 25

Name of Institution : Danish Commission on Security and Disarmament Affairs

Address : Rådhusstraede 1
1466 COPENHAGEN K

Telephone : (1) 15-72-22

Founding Date : Jan. 1981   Founding Place : Copenhagen

Type of Organization : National Public (but officially independent of Government)

Objectives : (1) evaluate security policy of Denmark in a broad political and economic context;
(2) consider possibilities for Denmark to present proposals bearing on international efforts to promote detente and disarmament;
(3) stimulate research and dissemination of information concerning security and disarmament policy;
(4) initiate relevant analyses at the request of the Government or the Commission itself.

Chairman : Ambassador Kjeld Mortensen

Director : Svend Aage Christensen

Total Staff : 8

Projects in Progress : Title

Western policy alternatives toward the Soviet Union and Eastern Europe (Commission Report).

Regular Periodicals : Title	Founding Date	Issues Annually
Security and Disarmament : Annual Report (in Danish)	1982	1

Other Publications (since January 1983)
(all in Danish)

1. Bertel Heurlin (Ed.), <u>Nuclear Weapons Policy in the Nordic Countries</u>, 1983.

2. <u>Missiles in Europe : Views and Documentation</u>, 1983.

3. <u>The New Nuclear Missiles in Europe</u> (with preface by Anders Boserup and Michael H. Clemmesen), 1983.

4. <u>United Nations on Disarmament</u> (with preface by Anders Boserup), 1983.

5. <u>Defence Technology in the 1980s</u> (prepared by the Danish Defence Command), 1983.

6. Julian Perry Robinson, <u>Biological and Chemical Warfare</u>, 1983.

7. Wilhelm Agrell, <u>A Third Point-of-View on Defence Matters</u>, 1983.

8. Hans-Henrik Holm and Nikolaj Peterson (Eds.), <u>The Battle of the Missiles : the Dual Track Decision and Security in Europe</u>, 1983.

<u>Comments</u> : All nine Danish political parties are represented in the Commission which supports research and information activities, but does not undertake any independent research.

DIRECTORY CODE NUMBER : 26

<u>Name of Institution</u> : Danish Institute of International Studies

<u>Address</u> : Bremerholm 6
　　　　　　1069 COPENHAGEN K

<u>Telephone</u> : (1) 15-87-13

<u>Objectives</u> : Supports and occasionally initiates research mainly in university institutes; holds seminars and publishes relevant books.

<u>Director</u> : Niels J. Haagerup

Regular Periodicals : Title	Founding date	Issues Annually
Danish Foreign Policy (in Danish)		1

Other Publications (since January 1983)

1. Book (in Danish) on European Parliament.
2. Monograph (in Danish) on reinforcement aspect of Danish security policy.

DIRECTORY CODE NUMBER : 27

Name of Institution : Danish Peace Research Association

Address : Stenslegergrieg 18
         Allerup
         5672 BROLEY

Founding Date : 1977   Founding Place : Copenhagen

Type of Organization : National Private Non-Profit

Objectives : To have a forum to stimulate peace research in Denmark as an interdisciplinary area open for the growing peace movement (does not undertake research directly).

Director : M. Naur

DIRECTORY CODE NUMBER : 28

Name of Institution : Foreign Policy Society

Address : Amaliegade 40 A
          1256 COPENHAGEN K

Telephone : (1) 14-88-86
            (1) 14-85-20

Founding Date : Oct. 1946   Founding Place : Copenhagen

Type of Organization : National Private Non-Profit

Objectives : To advance the interest and understanding of international affairs in Denmark.

Director : Johan Wilhjelm

Total Staff : 5

Projects in Progress : Title
                                    Name(s) of Researcher(s)

Bibliography on Danish security problems 1945-1983.

                    Anna-Lise Nevald

Regular Periodicals : Title   Founding Date   Issues Annually

Fremtiden   4

Library services provided for outside researchers : yes

Comments : The Danish Strategic Study Group (directed by Niels J.
           Haagerup) is associated with the Foreign Policy Society.
           The Study Group has recently published books on Denmark
           in NATO, on the Baltic, and on crisis management (the
           latter in both Danish and English).

DIRECTORY CODE NUMBER : 29

Name of Institution : Institute of East-West Research

Address : Centre for International Studies
          University Centre of South Jutland
          Glentevej 7
          6705 ESBJERG

Telephone : (5) 14-00-11

Founding Date : 1981   Founding Place : Esbjerg

Type of Organization : National Public University

Objectives : To undertake comparative East-West studies and to
             examine them in their proper international framework.

Director : Andreas Jorgensen

Projects in Progress : Title
                                    Name(s) of Researcher(s)

1. Political Structure in the Soviet Union. The Interplay Between
   Economy and Politics in a Planned Society.
                              Ole Norgaard

2. Problems of integration of Soviet Muslims in modern society.
                              Ewa Chylinski

3. Determinants of the U.S. policy toward peripheral societies.
                              Morten Ougaard

DIRECTORY CODE NUMBER : 30

Name of Institution : Institute of Political Science

Address : University of Aarhus
          Universitetsparken
          8000 Aarhus C

Telephone : (6) 13-01-11

Founding Date : 1959   Founding Place : Aarhus

Type of Organization : National Public University

Director : Erik Damgaard

Projects in Progress : Title
                       Name(s) of Researcher(s)

1. Foreign policy of the Soviet Union.
                       Erling Bjøl

2. Economic-political conflict between the U.S. and Western Europe.
                       Jan Top Christensen

3. Security policies of the Nordic countries.
                       Ib Faurby

4. European nuclear weapons problems.
                       Ib Faurby

5. Danish security policy.
                       Ib Faurby/Nikolaj Petersen

6. Falklands Conflict.
                       Ib Faurby

7. Denmark's membership in NATO.
                       Nikolaj Petersen

8. Decision-making process in defense policy.
                       Nikolaj Petersen

9. Mass media coverage of the Falkland war.
                       Karen Siune

10. Great powers and Austria after World War II.
                       Peter Sørensen

Regular Periodicals : Title	Founding Date	Issues Annually
Politica	1968	4

DIRECTORY CODE NUMBER : 31

Name of Institution : Institute of Political Studies

Address : University of Copenhagen
Rosenborggade 15
1130 COPENHAGEN K

Telephone : (1) 11-26-26

Founding Date : 1971   Founding Date : Copenhagen

Type of Organization : National Public University

Objectives : Teaching and research in political science, political economy, political sociology and political anthropology.

Director : Peter Dencik

Total Staff : 25

Number of researchers on security and defense issues : 7

Projects in Progress : Title	Name(s) of researcher(s)

1. Economics and security politics.
   Ib Damgaard Petersen

2. Correlation between military and diplomatic means in the foreign policy of the superpowers.
   Ib Damgaard Petersen
   Henrik Holtermann

3. Driving forces of armament in the East-West conflict formation.
   Henning Duus

4. Research into alternative models of defense.
   Mogens Godballe

5. Reciprocal conception of the superpowers and their conception of the international system.
   Bertel Heurlin

6. Economic dimension of security politics.
   Ole Karup Pedersen

7. Defensive foreign politics : a study of adaption in security politics and foreign politics.
   Hans Mouritzen

8. Elements of economy and security in Sweden's politics in regard to the EEC.
   Tove Lise Schou

Regular Periodicals : Title	Founding date	Issues Annually
Copenhagen Political Studies Abstracts	1978	1

Other Publications (since January 1983)

1. Wilhelm Christmas-Møller, The Security Policy of Western Europe : Should It Be Revised ? (in Danish), 1983.

2. Kirsten Berker Hansen et al (Eds.), The Soviet Union and Eastern Europe : Foreign and Security Policy (a bibliography in Danish) Slavonic Institute, 1983.

Library services provided for outside researchers : yes

DIRECTORY CODE NUMBER : 32

Name of Institution : Institute of Social Science

Address : University of Odense
          Campusvej 55
          5230 ODENSE M

Telephone : (9) 15-86-00

Type of Organization : National Public University

Projects in Progress : Title
                       Name(s) of Researcher(s)

1. Law of the Sea and international security.
                       Finn Laursen

2. Danish foreign policy.
                       Erik Beukel

3. Soviet Union and the Nordic countries from 1956 to the present.
                       Bent Jensen

DIRECTORY CODE NUMBER : 33

Name of Institution : Working Group for Peace and Conflict Research

Address : University of Copenhagen
          Fiolstraede 22
          1171 COPENHAGEN K

Type of Organization : National Public University

Objectives : To coordinate the different programs on peace and conflict research at the university.

Secretary : Eva Teilmann

Projects in Progress : Title	Name(s) of Researcher(s)

1. Alternative European defense and security policy.
   Anders Boserup

2. Energy policy and security policy in the Soviet Union.
   Niels Erik Rosenfeldt

3. Psychology of peace and pedagogy of peace work.
   Bo Jacobsen

4. Status of peace and conflict research.
   Ole Karup Pedersen

5. Basic features of Soviet foreign and security policy.
   Niels Erik Rosenfeldt

6. Conflict and peace research within the framework of modern futures studies.
   J. Witt-Hansen

FINLAND

FINLAND

Finnish security policy is governed by a strict adherence to the principle of neutrality, as stipulated by the Treaty of Paris in 1947 and the agreement on Friendship, Cooperation, and Mutual Assistance (FCMA) with the USSR in 1948. The FCMA treaty requires Finland to repel any attack on the Soviet Union through its own territory. This agreement has not constrained the Finns from developing close ties with their Scandinavian neighbors (through the Nordic Council) and with Western Europe (through links with the European Free Trade Association and the European Community). Finland has also pursued an active peace policy which culminated in its hosting the Conference on Security and Cooperation in Europe.

This commitment to peace is reinforced by Finnish research efforts. The Tampere Peace Research Institute (TAPRI) studies a variety of topics, including the role of sports in international relations, arms and language, and global water politics, and publishes the quarterly <u>Current Research on Peace and Violence</u>. Peace and conflict studies also predominate in Finnish university projects. As in other Nordic countries, there exists considerable interest in a regional nuclear-free-zone. The "flagship" research organization, the Finnish Institute of International Affairs, maintains a serious preoccupation with disarmament studies. The Institute sponsored an international conference on nuclear weapons and Northern Europe and published the proceedings in 1983. It has also collaborated with the Institute of World Economy and International Relations (Moscow) on a survey of Finnish-Soviet economic relations.

Finland has a territorial defense system to protect its sovereignty and fulfill its FCMA treaty obligations to the Soviet Union. In this respect, the Institute for Military Science provides security- and defense-related research to the Finnish defense forces and also pursues work in military history and sociology. In addition, there are national defense courses for the political, business, and academic elites.

Peace and neutrality continue to be the by-words for security studies in Finland. The prevailing Finnish foreign and defense policy, as formulated by the former Finnish President Urho Kekkonen (1956-1982), benefits from a wide popular and elite consensus. The new President, Mauno Koivisto, has pledged himself to continuity of his predecessor's work.

DIRECTORY CODE NUMBER : 34

Name of Institution : Department of Political Science

Address : Abo Academy
          20500 ABO 50

Telephone : (921) 33-51-33

Projects in Progress : Title
                                    Name(s) of Researcher(s)

1. The Palestine issue and the United Nations in 1947.
                                    Per-Erik Holmström
2. Finnish responses to international conflicts.
                                    Göran Djupsund
3. Nordic stability in security policy - perspectives from inside and outside.
                                    Steve Lindberg

DIRECTORY CODE NUMBER : 35

Name of Institution : Department of Political Science

Address : University of Helsinki
          Alexandersgatan 7
          00100 HELSINKI 10

Telephone : (0) 1912529

Founding Date : 1945   Founding Place : Helsinki

Type of Organization : National Public University

Objectives : Teaching and research.

Director : Prof. Martti Noponen

Projects in Progress : Title	Name(s) of Researcher(s)

1. Foreign Policy of the U.S. with emphasis on crisis management and military strategies.
   Raimo Väyrynen

2. Changes in structure of the international system since World War II (via world system analysis).
   Raimo Väyrynen

DIRECTORY CODE NUMBER : 36

Name of Institution : Department of Political Science

Address : University of Turku
Kasarminkatu 6/24
20500 TURKU 50

Founding Date : 1961   Founding Place : Turku

Type of Organization : National Public University

Objectives : Teaching and research.

Director : Prof. Jaakko Nousiainen

Total Staff : 6

Number of researchers on security and defense issues : 1

Projects in Progress : title	Name(s) of Researcher(s)

1. Western European security options.
   Esko Antola/Tapani Vaahtoranta

2. Future of the non-proliferation regime.
   Esko Antola/Olli Lempiäinen

3. Finnish foreign and security policy in historical perspective.

Publications (since January 1983)

Olli Lempiäinen, Heli Pelkonen and Tapani Vaahtoranta, Pieceworks in Disarmament (in Finnish), Department of Political Science Studies in Politics, N°43, 1983 (131 pp.).

DIRECTORY CODE NUMBER : 37

Name of Institution : Finnish Institute of International Affairs

Address : Dagmarinkatu 8 C 40
00100 HELSINKI 10

Telephone : (0) 441188

Founding Date : 1960   Founding Place : Helsinki

Type of Organization : National Private Non-Profit

Objectives : To contribute to the expert discussion on foreign policy and international relations through publications and seminars; to undertake research and maintain international contacts; to coordinate with research community, political and government officials.

Director : Kari Möttölä

Total Staff : 6

Number of researchers on security and defense issues : 1

Projects in Progress : title
                                    Name(s) of Researcher(s)

1. The European Disarmament Conference : substance, effects and role.
                                    Kari Möttölä

2. The non-proliferation regime and its dynamics.
   Kari Möttölä
3. The Nordic nuclear-weapon-free zone.

Regular Periodicals : Title	Founding Date	Issues Annually
1. Ulkopolitiikka (Foreign Policy)	1961	4
2. Yearbook of Finnish Foreign Policy	1973	1

Other Publications (since January 1983)

1. Bibliography of Finnish Security Policy. List of books and articles published before 1981 (in Finnish) 1983.

2. Kari Möttölä (Ed.), Nuclear Weapons and Northern Europe - Problems and Prospects of Arms Control, 1983.

3. Kari Möttölä, O.N. Bykov and I.S. Korolev (Eds.), Finnish-Soviet Economic Relations, 1983.

Collaboration with Foreign Study Centers

Institute of World Economy and International Relations (USSR) on Finnish-Soviet economic relations project.

Library services provided for outside researchers : yes

DIRECTORY CODE NUMBER : 38

Name of Institution : Finnish Peace Research Association

Address : c/o TAPRI
PO Box 447
33101 TAMPERE 10

Founding Date : 1971   Founding Place : Tampere

Type of Organization : National Private

Objectives : Mainly public education.

Director : Dr. Esko Antola

Regular Periodicals : Title	Founding date	Issues Annually
Ranhaan Tutkien	1971	4-5

Other Publications (since January 1983)

Tuomo Melasuo (Ed.), Liberation and Development (Vol. VII in Monograph Series "Peace Research Today"), 1983.

DIRECTORY CODE NUMBER : 39

Name of Institution : Institute for Military Science

Address : Maurinkatu 1
00170 HELSINKI 17

Telephone : (0) 176681

Founding Date : 1925   Founding Place : Helsinki

Type of Organization : National Public

Objectives : Security- and defense-related research as part of
             Finnish defense force requirements (originally research
             on military history before reorganization in 1971).

Director : Col. Matti Lappalainen

Regular Periodicals : Title	Founding date	Issues Annually
Journal of Military History		1

Other Publications (since January 1983)

Occasional studies on military history, strategic questions and
military sociology.

DIRECTORY CODE NUMBER : 40

Name of Institution : Tampere Peace Research Institute (TAPRI)

Address : Hämeenk 13
          PO Box 447
          33101 TAMPERE 10

Telephone : (31) 32535

Founding Date : 1970   Founding Place : Tampere

Type of Organization : National Public (under Ministry of Education)

Objectives : It was considered necessary that Finland as a country pursuing an active peace policy should have an institute specialized in peace and conflict research. The Institute publishes the results of its research and encourages national and international cooperation.

Director : Dr. Tapio Varis

Total Staff : 14

Number of researchers on security and defense issues : 4

Projects in Progress : Title
                                    Name(s) of Researcher(s)

1. Sports in international relations.
   Tapio Varis and Aki Hietanen

2. Neutrality in the theory of international relations.
   Pertti Joenniemi

3. Peace research as cultural research : arms and language.
   Pertti Joenniemi

4. Europe in the structure of international relations.
   Pertti Joenniemi

5. Finland's disarmament policy.
   Unto Vesa

6. Mass media, public opinion, and disarmament.
   Tapio Varis

7. African conflicts.
   Jyrki Käkönen

Regular Periodicals : Title	Founding Date	Issues Annually
1. Current Research on Peace and Violence	1971	4
2. Reports and occasional papers		

Other Publications (since January 1983)

1. Jakob Berger and Unto Vesa (Eds.), Peace Research in Finnish and Soviet Scientific Literature, 1983.

2. Heikki Hellman, Tarja Seppä and Tapio Varis, Disarmament and Mass Communication (in Finnish), 1983.

Comments : TAPRI sponsored an international workshop on peace and security processes in Europe in September 1984.

DIRECTORY CODE NUMBER : 41

Name of Institution : Tampere (Univ.), Institute of Political Science

Address : Lapintie 4
33101 TAMPERE

Telephone : (31) 156111

Founding Date : 1960

Director : Osmo Apunen

FRANCE

FRANCE

Until quite recently, the development of French security and defense research had been inhibited by the general acceptance of the Gaullist defense consensus, specifically the belief in France's independent nuclear doctrine and foreign policy and, consequently, distrust vis-à-vis the superpowers and arms control. In the late 1970's, however, President Valery Giscard d'Estaing attempted to instill greater doctrinal flexibility by building up conventional forces and expanding cooperation with NATO. As a result, the security debate grew more lively and extensive, and research centers began sprouting up throughout France. A new generation of specialists emerged primarily from academic backgrounds and inevitaly operated out of "think tanks", universities, or political party institutions. Still, much of the debate was carried on by individual experts (largely retired military officers), independent of any organizational structure.

The arrival in power of a Left government in 1981 accentuated this controversy. François Mitterrand has committed himself to a sweeping modernization of French nuclear forces, while, at the same time, strengthening ties to NATO through the creation of an airborne "Force d'Action Rapide" and through closer defense consultations and arms collaboration with Bonn. The French President has firmly supported the Pershing-cruise deployment decision, and this identification with Alliance policy has brought the whole question of France's nuclear autonomy under public scrutiny. Today, there is tremendous interest among the educated French in France's future security options and in East-West relations in general. The French have always been NATO revisionists, and the growing uncertainty among Europeans over American nuclear guarantees seemed to justify their past beliefs and actions. Moreover, the French intellectual elite has lately developed a highly critical attitude toward the Soviet system and the Soviet military build-up. The absence of a broad-based peace movement is further evidence of heightened suspicions about Soviet (and French Communist) intentions.

While the debate over defense issues has opened up, this development should not be exaggerated. The Fifth Republic instituted a highly centralized, presidential system of controls over security and defense policy, and the democratization process is less pronounced than in other Western European countries. The absence of strong, balancing parliamentary power bases also limits the channels of access to the policymaking apparatus. But the growing number of independent and university-based research centers is one healthy sign that French institutions are becoming more responsive to outside analysis and public opinion.

The best-known private research organization is the Institut Français des Relations Internationales (IFRI), established in 1979 to provide France with a forum similar to the Council on Foreign Relations in New York. The new institute was the result of the fusion of the Centre d'Etudes de Politique Etrangère, which had published Politique étrangère since 1936, with the Groupe d'Etudes et de Recherches sur les Problèmes Internationaux, founded by Raymond Aron. Much of the impetus behind this move came from the Foreign Minister Jean François-Ponçet, and the head of the the Ministry's policy planning staff, Thierry de Montbrial, was appointed IFRI's director. The IFRI research program operates on an independent, pluralistic philosophy, with individual specialists representing different schools of thought. One team of researchers, led by Pierre Lellouche, is engaged in a major, multi-year study of European security problems and prospects for European defense collaboration. IFRI staff members are also called upon to represent the French perspective at international conferences, and IFRI itself sponsors a high-level seminar program featuring numerous foreign dignitaries.

Much of the defense-related and strategic research in France is sponsored by the Fondation pour les Etudes de Défense Nationale (FEDN). The Foundation itself does no research, but encourages the dissemination of knowledge and new ideas through its publications, study groups, and financial support. The research results are normally communicated through its quarterly journal, Stratégique, or its special monograph series, Cahiers "Les Sept Epées". In addition, the FEDN supports three semi-autonomous research centers, two dealing with military history and also the Institut Français de Polémologie. The latter organization was founded by Gaston Bouthoul in 1945 to study the sociology of war and conflict and came under the FEDN in 1982. It publishes the quarterly Etudes polémologiques with a special annual report on world violence.

French universities are also becoming quite active in the security and defense research field. The largest university-level institute is the Centre d'Etudes et de Recherches Internationales (CERI) which concentrates on long-term trends at three levels : the analysis of international relations; the comparative study of national political systems; and the study of the internal political and social realities of the principal states. A large part of the research is grouped around area studies : its Soviet experts, for example, are running the study group on Soviet strategies at the FEDN. The CERI staff includes Pierre Hassner, Hélène Carrère d'Encausse, Alfred Grosser, and Guy Hermet.

In 1983, the Institut National Supérieur d'Etudes de Défense et de Désarmement (INSED) was created at the University of Paris through the merger of the Centre d'Etudes Politiques de Défense (CEPODE) and the Centre d'Etudes et de Recherches sur le Désarmement (CEREDE). Two other research groups, the Institut de Politique Internationale et Européenne (IPIE) and the Centre d'Etudes et de Recherches sur les Stratégies et les Conflits (CERSC), are associated with branches of the University of Paris.

A number of highly productive institutions are located in French provincial universities. Two of these, the Centre d'Etudes de Défense et Sécurité Internationale (CEDSI) at Grenoble and the Centre Lyonnais d'Etudes de Sécurité Internationale et de Défense (CLESID) at Lyon, collaborate on an annual compendium, Arès, and co-sponsor a special diploma program. The Centre d'Etudes et de Recherches sur l'Armée (CERSA) at Toulouse and the Centre d'Histoire Militaire et d'Etudes de Défense Nationale at Montpellier specialize in the study of military institutions, civil-military relations, and military history.

There does not appear to be significant private financing or sponsorship of research organizations in France. The few private groups that exist tend to be small or highly political, like the Institut International de Géopolitique whose warnings about the Soviet menace reflect the views of its founder, Marie-France Garaud. There are also relatively few peace research centers compared with other European countries; one noteworthy exception is the Centre Interdisciplinaire de Recherches sur la Paix et d'Etudes Stratégiques (CIRPES). Among international private organizations, the Atlantic Institute for International Affairs stands out for its security studies program, focusing on problems of the Western alliance.

The centralization of French decisionmaking, the historical consensus on national defense policy, and the absence of private interest (and funding) have all exerted a restraining influence on security and defense research in France. The financial dependency of research institutions, in particular, militates against an elite-challenging attitude; even IFRI, though formally independent, depends on the government for 65 percent of its budget. Yet the high level of public interest in security and defense issues should encourage an expansion of the scope of French research efforts in the near future.

DIRECTORY CODE NUMBER : 42

Name of Institution : Assembly of the Western European Union

Address : 43, avenue du Président Wilson
75116 PARIS

Telephone : (1) 723-54-32

Founding Date : Oct. 1954   Founding Place : Paris

Type of Organization : International Public

Objectives : Adopt and transmit to the Council of Ministers and member governments recommendations and resolutions on foreign affairs and defense matters.

Director : Georges Moulias

Total Staff : 28

Number of researchers on security and defense issues : 4

Publications (since January 1983)

Draft Recommendations :

1. Klaas de Vries (Rapporteur), "Control of Armaments and Disarmament", May 1984.

2. Armand de Decker (Rapporteur), "Thirty Years of the Modified Brussels Treaty", May 1984.

3. Sir Dudley Smith (Rapporteur), "State of European Security", May 1984.

4. John Wilkinson (Rapporteur), "Military Use of Space", May 1984.

5. Adolf Spies von Bullesheim (Rapporteur), "AWACS and NIMROD Aircraft", May 1984.

Library services provided for outside researchers : yes

Comments : The Assembly consists of parliamentarians from the seven WEU countries and meets twice a year in plenary session in Paris. The WEU Council and Secretariat are officially located in London.

DIRECTORY CODE NUMBER : 43

Name of Institution : Association pour la Coordination des Etudes et Recherches de Défense et de Stratégie (ACEDES)

Address : 26, avenue de la Marseillaise
67000 STRASBOURG

Founding Date : 1981   Founding Place : Strasbourg

Type of Organization : National Private Non-Profit

Objectives : Organization of university students and others interested in defense studies for research, conferences, visits, and publications.

Director : Prof. Pierre Koenig

DIRECTORY CODE NUMBER : 44

Name of institution : Association pour les Recherches et les Etudes de Défense (ARED)

Address : B.P. 316-16
75767 PARIS CEDEX 16

Founding Date : 1979   Founding Place : Paris

Objectives : To encourage reflection on the optimal strategy and tactics for France and to expand French military thought (while taking into account research in other countries).

Director : Daniel Perochon

Regular Periodicals : Title	Founding Date	Issues Annually
1. Stratégie et Défense	1979	4

Comments : The A.R.E.D. was founded by former students in the diploma program for advanced studies in defense policy.

DIRECTORY CODE NUMBER : 45

Name of Institution : Atlantic Institute for International Affairs

Address : 120, rue de Longchamp
          75116 PARIS

Telephone : (1) 727-24-36

Founding Date : 1961   Founding Place : Brussels

Type of Organization : International Private Non-Profit

Objectives : To provide analysis, promote discussion and make recommendations relating to problems of advanced industrial countries (including international security studies program).

Director : Richard Vine

Total Staff : 17

Number of researchers on security and defense issues : 2

Projects in Progress : Title
                       Name(s) of Researcher(s)

1. Public opinion and Atlantic defense.
   Gregory Flynn/Hans Rattinger/Renate Fritsch-Bournazel/Ivor Crcwc/Ragnar Waldahl/Sergio Rossi/Philip Everts/William Schneider

2. Soviet military doctrine and Western Security policy.
   Peter Vigor/Raymond Garthoff/Falk Bomsdorff/Peter Strattman/Barry Blechman/Laurence Martin/Gregory Flynn

3. Overlooked Allies : NATO's Northern Periphery.
   Martin Heisler/Luc Reychler/Jan Siccama/Arne Brundtland/Josef Joffe/Johan Holst/Gregory Flynn

4. Soviet-East European relations as a Western policy problem.
   René Herrmann/Philip Windsor/James Brown/Heinrich Vogel/Stephen Larrabee/Christoph Royen

Regular Periodicals : Title	Founding Date	Issues Annually
1. Atlantic Papers	1969	4
2. Special Reports	1983	occasional

Collaboration with Foreign Study Centers

"Overlooked Allies" project :

1. Dutch Institute for International Relations (Clingendael).

2. Center for Strategic Studies, University of Leuven, Belgium.

3. Danish Institute for International Studies.

4. Norwegian Institute for International Affairs.

Library services provided for outside researchers : yes

Comments : The Institute's international security studies program explores "the key aspects of the emerging global security situation from the perspective of advanced industrial nations, particularly those of the North Atlantic Alliance." Research in the program is grouped under four subject headings : (1) Atlantic Alliance studies;
(2) East-West relations;
(3) Western security and the Third World;
(4) the Pacific basin.

DIRECTORY CODE NUMBER : 46

Name of Institution : Centre d'Etudes de Défense et de Sécurité
                      Internationale (CEDSI)

Address : Faculté de Droit de Grenoble
          Domaine Universitaire de Saint-Martin-d'Hères, 47X
          38040 GRENOBLR CEDEX

Telephone : (76) 54-81-78   x. 286 and 304

Founding Date : 1977   Founding Place : Grenoble

Type of Organization : National Public University

Objectives : (1) Research in the fields of international security,
                 disarmament and defense on an interdisciplinary
                 basis;
             (2) Formation of students through diploma and doctoral
                 courses.

Director : Prof. J.F. Guilhaudis

Total Staff : 17

Number of researchers on security and defense issues : 14

Projects in Progress : Title
                               Name(s) of Researcher(s)

1. Studies on pacifism.
                          J.F. Guilhaudis/J. Fontanel/
                          D. Colard

2. France and disarmament.
                          J.F. Guilhaudis

3. A denuclearized zone in the Middle East.
                          K. Ouhichi

4. Collection of primary documentation on European security, French
   security and disarmament.
                          J.F. Guilhaudis/M. Paul/
                          C. Schneider

5. French security studies.
                          Collective

Regular Periodicals : Title	Founding Date	Issues Annually
1. Arès : Défense et Sécurité	1978	1
2. Cahiers du CEDSI	1982	2
3. Défense et sécurité dans le Journal Officiel français	1983	1
4. Documents intéressant la sécurité de l'Europe	1983	1
5. Défense et sécurité : chronologie	1983	1
6. Notes de recherches du CEDSI	1983	occasional

Other Publications (since January 1983)

1. The Crisis of Disarmament (in French). Supplement N°1 to the Arès yearbook, 1983, 171 pp.

2. J. F. Guilhaudis, J. Fontanel and D. Colard, In-Search of the "Peace Movement" in France (in French). Supplement N°2 to the Arès yearbook, 1983, ca. 300 pp. (Cahier du CEDSI, N°4).

3. B. Jacquier, The United States and Nicaragua (in French), 1983, Cahier du CEDSI, N°2.

4. J. Fontanel. The Economics of Arms (in French) (Paris : Maspéro, 1983).

Collaboration with Foreign Study Centers

United Nations and UNIDIR on disarmament and development studies.

Library services provided for outside researchers : yes

Comments : The Arès yearbook is a collaborative project of the CEDSI
and the CLESID at the Université de Lyon-III. The two
centers also offer a special diploma degree in international security and defense.

DIRECTORY CODE NUMBER : 47

Name of Institution : Centre d'Etudes de Défense Nationale

Address : 1, place Joffre
75700 PARIS

Regular Periodicals : Title	Founding Date	Issues Annually
Défense nationale		4

DIRECTORY CODE NUMBER : 48

Name of Institution : Centre d'Etudes et de Documentation sur l'URSS, la Chine et l'Europe de l'Est (CEDUCEE)

Address : La Documentation Française
29-31, quai Voltaire
75340 PARIS CEDEX 07

Telephone : (1) 261-50-10

Founding Date : 1967   Founding Place : Paris

Type of Organization : National Public

Objectives : To bring together economic documentation on countries with planned economies and to publish the journal, Le Courrier des Pays de l'Est.

Director : Françoise Barry

Total Staff : 18

Number of researchers on security and defense issues : 0

Regular Periodicals : Title	Founding Date	Issues Annually
Le Courrier des Pays de l'Est		12

DIRECTORY CODE NUMBER : 49

Name of Institution : Centre d'Etudes et de Recherches Internationales (CERI)

Address : Fondation Nationale des Sciences Politiques
27, rue Saint-Guillaume
75341 PARIS CEDEX 07

Founding Date : 1952   Founding Place : Paris

Type of Organization : National Public

Objectives : Analysis of international political phenomena and foreign political systems.

Director : Prof. Guy Hermet

Projects in Progress : Title
                            Name(s) of Researcher(s)

1. International System.
                            Pierre Hassner et al

2. Comparative analysis of political systems.

3. International economic relations.

4. European integration.

5. Area studies : Latin America, Southeast Asia, China-Far East, United States, Western Europe, India-Southern Asia, Arab World, USSR-Eastern Europe.

6. Soviet strategy.

Pierre Hassner et al

Regular Periodicals : Title	Founding Date	Issues Annually
Maghreb-Machrek		6

Comments : The CERI depends on the Fondation Nationale des Sciences Politiques for its budget and is also associated with the Centre National de Recherches Scientifiques. Most of its staff teaches at the Institut d'Etudes Politiques in Paris.

DIRECTORY CODE NUMBER : 50

Name of institution : Centre d'Etudes et de Recherches sur l'Armée (CERSA)

Address : Université de Toulouse-I
2ter, rue des Puits Creusés
31000 TOULOUSE CEDEX

Telephone : (61) 21-69-38

Founding Date : Nov. 1974   Founding Place : Toulouse

Type of Organization : National Public University

Objectives : (1) Comparative research on military institutions as an element of a global social system;
(2) Creation of an international documentation service on armed forces and problems of defense;
(3) Study of the culture of the military environment.

Director : Prof. Lucien Mandeville

Total Staff : 14

Number of researchers on security and defense issues : 8

Projects in Progress : Title
                               Name(s) of Researchers

1. Study of the central organization of the defense system in France.
                          Jean-Pierre Marichy

2. Comparative study on elites and the military professional mentality.
                          Lucien Mandeville

3. Spanish defense policy.
                          J.M. Comas/J.F. Daguzan/
                          B. Labatut/L. Mandeville

4. Military system and defense policy in Southern Europe (Greece, Italy, Portugal)
                          L. Mandeville/A. Montech/A. Sorbara

5. Maintenance of order in France and in the United Kingdom.
                          J.P. Marichy/M. Edmonds/
                          J.L. Loubet del Bayle/A. Mandeville

6. Comparative study of the recruitment system in France and the United States.
                          L. Mandeville

7. Study of the defense system and the communication system and the military culture.
                          A. Thieblemont/L. Mandeville/
                          J.L. Maurin

Publications (since January 1983)

CERSA typed reports :

1. Jean Pierre Marichy, "Military System and Human Systems" (in French), 1983, 20pp.

2. Jean-Marie Crouzatier, "Pacifism in France" (in French), 1983, 16 pp.

3. Martin Edmonds, "Peace Movements in Contemporary Europe - the British Experience", 1983, 13 pp.

4. Jean-Pierre Marichy, "Pacifism, Neutralism and Public Opinion in the West", (in French), 1983, 10 pp.

5. Wilfried von Bredow, "The Peace Movement in the Federal Republic of Germany", (in French), 1983, 15 pp;

6. José-Maria Comas and Bernard Labutat, "The Superior Organisms of National Defense in France : Comparative Study" (in Spanish), 1983, 13 pp.

7. Jean-François Daguzan, "The Withdrawal of France from the Military Organization of the North Atlantic Treaty", (in French), 1983, 32 pp.

8. José-Maria Comas, "The Army and Power from Franco to Felipe Gonzalez", (in French), 1983, 32 pp.

9. José-Maria Comas, "The Structures of Direction of the Spanish Armed Forces : Power over the Army, Power in the Army", (in French), 1983, 32 pp.

10. Jean-François Daguzan, "The Evolution of the Economic and Financial Resources of the spanish Military system", (in French), 1983, 46 pp.

11. Alain Sorbara, "The Action Française and the Army", (in French), 1983, 12 pp.

12. Auguste Rivet, "Jaurès and the Army : Experience and Ideology" (in French), 1983, 9 pp.

13. Lucien Mandeville, "the Army under the Third Republic, relating to the work of Douglas Porch : the March to the Marne (1870-1914)" (in French), 1983, 5 pp.

14. Anne Mandeville, "Approach to the Debate on the Third Force with Respect to Present British Problems on Maintaining Order" (in French), 1983, 29 pp.

15. Jean-Marie Crouzatier, "French Pacifisms : New Tendencies" (in French), 1983, 16 pp.

16. Bernard Labatut and Jean-Pierre Marichy, "Military Programming and Evolution of the Defense Policy of France" (in French), 1983, 26 pp.

17. Anne Mandeville, "The British Army in Northern Ireland : Contribution to a Theory on the Maintenance of Order" (in French), Publication CERSA/CERP, Series Défense et Sécurité, N°1, 1983, 264 pp.

Collaboration with Foreign Study Centers

1. Instituto de Cuestiones Internacionales (Madrid, Spain) on foreign and defense policies of Spain and France.

2. Instituto Espanol de Estudios Estrategicos du CESEDEN (Madrid) on military institutions and policies in Spain and France in the 1980s.

3. Study group on the Army and Society, University of Lancaster (UK) on defense and security policies of France and the U.K.

<u>Library services provided for outside researchers</u> : yes

DIRECTORY CODE NUMBER : 51

<u>Name of Institution</u> : Centre d'Etudes et de Recherches sur la Défense et la Sécurité. Institut du Droit de la Paix et du Développement (IDPD)

<u>Address</u> : 34, avenue Robert Schuman
06200 NICE

<u>Directors</u> : Prof. Jacques Basso
Prof. Maurice Torrelli

DIRECTORY CODE NUMBER : 52

<u>Name of Institution</u> : Centre d'Etudes et de Recherches sur les Stratégies et les Conflits (CERSC)

<u>Address</u> : Université de Paris-Sorbonne
1, rue Victor-Cousin
75230 PARIS CEDEX 05

<u>Telephone</u> : (1) 329-12-13

<u>Founding Date</u> : 1972   <u>Founding Place</u> : Paris

<u>Type of Organization</u> : National Public University

Objectives : Studies of strategies and conflicts in the different types of human behavior.

Director : Jean-Paul Charnay

Total Staff : 15

Number of researchers on security and defense issues : 12

Projects in Progress : Title
                        Name(s) of Researcher(s)

1. Non-violence and culture.
2. Arab strategic doctrines.
3. Russian and Soviet strategic doctrines.
4. Lazare Carnot and the Revolutionary Strategy.
5. Deterrence and culture.

Publications (since January 1983)

Marshal Sokolovsky, <u>Military Strategy</u> (translation into French) (Paris : Ed. de l'Herne, 1983).

Library services provided for outside researchers : yes

DIRECTORY CODE NUMBER : 53

Name of Institution : Centre d'Etudes Prospectives et d'Informations Internationales

Address : 9, rue Georges Pitard.
75015 PARIS

Telephone : (1) 842-68-00

Founding Date : 1978   Founding Place : Paris

Type of Organization : National Public

Objectives : Structural analysis of the world economy by models, data bases, and sectoral and regional studies.

Director : Yves Berthelot

Total Staff : 55

Number of researchers on security and defense issues : 0

Projects in Progress : Title
                              Name(s) of Researcher(s)

1. Study of dominant economies.
                              J. Pisani-Ferry

2. Economy of the Socialist countries.
                              Gerard Wild

Comments : The Center is part of the Prime Minister's office.

DIRECTORY CODE NUMBER : 54

Name of Institution : Centre de Formation aux Réalités Internationales (CEFRI)

Address : 30, rue Cabanis
75014 PARIS

Telephone : (1) 336-04-41

Founding Date : 1973   Founding Place : Paris

Type of organization : National Private Non-Profit

Objectives : Preparation of professional employees for overseas service.

President : Jean-Pierre Bouyssonnie

Comments : The Center runs a series of training programs including one on East-West strategic tensions and the role of France.

DIRECTORY CODE NUMBER : 55

Name of Institution : Centre d'Histoire Militaire et d'Etudes de Défense Nationale

Address : Université Paul Valéry Montpellier
B.P. 5043
34032 MONTPELLIER CEDEX

Telephone : (7) 639110   x. 415

Founding Date : 1968   Founding Place : Montpellier

Type of Organization : International Public University

Objectives : To develop the study of defense and military history and to disseminate the results.

Director : André Martel

Projects in Progress : Title
                      Name(s) of Researcher(s)

---

1. Officers-scientists in France.
   Anne Blanchard

2. Non-commissioned officers in the French Army.
   Pierre Carles

3. Conscription Army and Professional Army.
   Prof. J. R. Maurin

4. Problems of defense in the Mediterranean.
   Prof. André Martel

5. Comparative study of the development of aeronautics and space vehicles in Atlantic Alliance countries.
                                    Claude Carlier

6. Parliament and defense.
                              J. C. Jauffret

Regular Periodicals : Title	Founding Date	Issues Annually
Cahiers de Montpellier : Forces Armées et Politiques de Défense	1980	2

Other Publications (since January 1983)

Claude Carlier, The French Aeronautical Industry 1945-1975 (in French) (Paris : Editions Lavauzelle, 1983) ca. 700 pp.

Collaboration with Foreign Study Centers

Kent State University (USA)
Southampton University (UK)
University of Genoa (Italy)

Library services provided for outside researchers : yes

Comments : The University offers a special diploma in military history and defense studies. Research at the Center focuses on the study of the armed forces as the symbol and instrument of national will and follows four basic axes : politics and institutions; armies and societies; economics and supply; and war and operations.

DIRECTORY CODE NUMBER : 56

<u>Name of Institution</u> : Centre de Recherches sur la Défense et la
                        Sécurité

<u>Address</u> : 50, avenue Bosquet
          75007 PARIS

<u>Telephone</u> : (1) 705-12-35

<u>Founding Date</u> : 1976   <u>Founding Place</u> : Paris

<u>Type of Organization</u> : National Private Non-Profit

<u>Objectives</u> : Study and research on the strategic, economic and
             military problems of Europe.

<u>Director</u> : Jean-Paul Pigasse

Projects in Progress : Title
                              Name(s) of Researcher(s)

---

1. Theory of alliances in the nuclear era.
                              Jean-Paul Pigasse

2. The Atom : turning point of the century.
                              Jean-Paul Pigasse

Regular Periodicals : Title	Founding Date	Issues Annually
<u>Défense et Sécurité</u>	1976	30

Other Publications (since January 1983)

Jean-Paul Pigasse, <u>The Shield of Europe</u> (in French) (Paris : Ed. Seghers, 1983).

DIRECTORY CODE NUMBER : 57

Name of Institution : Centre de Sociologie de la Défense Nationale

Address : Hôtel National des Invalides
         75007 PARIS

Telephone : (1) 260-39-60   x. 3857

Founding Date : 1969   Founding Place : Paris

Type of Organization : National Public University

Director : H.J.P. Thomas

Total Staff : 13

Number of researchers on security and defense issues : 6

Projects in Progress : Title
                      Name(s) of Researcher(s)

1. Elite selection in the French Army officer corps (plus comparative dimension).
   H.J.P. Thomas/T. Bencheikh/B. Boëne

2. Wife and family in Army NCO's career strategies.
   C. Laharanne

3. The second (civilian) careers of military personnel.
   C. Laharanne

4. History of military sociology in the United States : a study in the cultural, situational, intellectual, and institutional factors that shaped it.
   B. Boëne

5. Recruitment and patterns of performance of career NCO's in the French Army.
   A. Latapie/H.J.P. Thomas

Other Publications (since January 1983)

1. B. Boëne and P. Saint Macary, "With Respect to a Book by Michel Martin" (in French), Révue de Défense Nationale, Feb. 1983.

2. B. Boëne, "American Decisions in the Field of Defense : How Sociologists Contribute to This" (in French), Revue Française de Sociologie, Vol. XXIV, N° 2 (April 1983).

3. B. Paqueteau, Image of the Army on Television (in French). (Paris : CSDN, 1983) 546 pp.

4. B. Paqueteau, "'La Grande Muette' on the Little Screen : 1962-1981" (in French), Stratégique, Vol. XXI (1984).

5. G. Tan Eng Bok, The Modernization of the Chinese Defense and Its Principal Limitations (in French) (Paris : FEDN Cahiers N° XXX, 1984), 384 pp.

6. C. Laharanne, The French Army NCO's Wife : From Dependence to Interdependence Through Negotiation (Munich : SOWI, forthcoming).

Comments : The Center comes under the Fondation Nationale des Sciences Politiques.

DIRECTORY CODE NUMBER : 58

Name of Institution : Centre Interdisciplinaire de Recherches sur la Paix et d'Etudes Stratégiques (CIRPES)

Address : 71, bld. Raspail
75006 PARIS

Telephone : (1) 221-01-07

Director : Alain Joxe

Regular Periodicals : Title	Founding Date	Issues Annually
1. Paix et Conflits		6
2. Cahiers d'études stratégiques		

Other Publications (since January 1983)

1. The New American War Doctrine and European Security (in French) Cahiers d'Etudes stratégiques N°1, 1983.

DIRECTORY CODE NUMBER : 59

Name of Institution : Centre Lyonnais d'Etudes de Sécurité Internationale et de Défense (CLESID)

Address : Université de Lyon-III
15, quai Claude-Bernard
69224 LYON CEDEX 1

Telephone : (78) 69-24-93

Type of Organization : National Public University

Director : Prof. Pierre Vialle

DIRECTORY CODE NUMBER : 60

Name of Institution : Cercle d'Etudes de Stratégie Totale

Address : 15, rue Petrarque
             75016 PARIS

Telephone : (1) 704-48-72

Founding Date : 1975   **Founding Place** : Paris

Type of Organization : National Private Non-Profit

Objectives : To carry on work of Gen. André Beaufre.

Director : Michel Garder

DIRECTORY CODE NUMBER : 61

Name of Institution : Cercle Renaissance

Address : 15, rue Curnonsky
             75017 PARIS

Telephone : (1) 731-37-24

Founding Date : 1970   **Founding Place** : Paris

Type of Organization : National Private Non-Profit

Objectives : Center of reflection and propositions on defense of liberties and promotion of Western values.

Director : Michel de Rostolan

Regular Periodicals : Title	Founding Date	Issues Annually
Renaissance des Hommes et des Idées	1975	12

Collaboration with Foreign Study Centers

World Anti-Communist League

DIRECTORY CODE NUMBER : 62

Name of Institution : Fondation du Futur

Address : 139, avenue de Villiers
          75017 PARIS

Founding Date : Feb. 1980

Type of Organization : National Private Non-Profit

Objectives : Study and analyze world problems and their consequences in the future.

Director : Jacques Baumel

Regular Periodicals : Title	Founding date	Issues Annually
Cahiers de la Fondation		occasional

Comments : The Foundation primarily organizes conferences on specific topics and future repercussions. Among these topics were "Hot Peace or Cold War ?" and "The Dangers and the Stakes of a Multipolar World."

— 89 —

DIRECTORY CODE NUMBER : 63

Name of Institution : Fondation pour les Etudes de Défense Nationale
(FEDN)

Address : Hôtel National des Invalides
75007 PARIS

Telephone : (1) 705-12-07

Founding Date : July 1972   Founding Place : Paris

Type of Organization : National Private Non-Profit

Objectives : (1) to initiate, encourage and carry out research and studies concerning problems of military doctrine, strategy and defense;
(2) to develop information, by encouraging the publication of old or new writing concerning military thining and also by issuing its own publications;
(3) to contribute to the dissemination of knowledge on defense problems;
(4) to organize meetings or symposia.

Director : Gen. Fricaud-Chagnaud

Projects in Progress : Title

Study groups on USSR, China and Central Europe (principally Germany)

Regular Periodicals : Title	Founding Date	Issues Annually
1. Stratégique	1979	4
2. Cahiers : "Les Sept Epées"		occasional
3. Revue d'Histoire de la Deuxième Guerre Mondiale et des Conflits Contemporains		4

Other Publications (since January 1983)

1. Renata Fritsch-Bournazel, André Brigot and Jim Cloos, <u>The Germans at the Heart of Europe</u> (in French), <u>Cahier</u> N° 28, 1983, 270 pp.

2. Michel Tatu, <u>The Battle of the Euromissiles</u> (in French), <u>Cahier</u> N° 29, 1983.

<u>Comments</u> : The FEDN does no research <u>per se</u>, but rather finances research projects, sponsors study groups, and has its own publications. Three research centers are subsidiaries of the FEDN : the Institut Français de Polemologie (see separate entry); the Institut d'Histoire Militaire Comparée, and the Institut d'Histoire des Conflits Contemporains (which publishes the quarterly <u>Revue d'Histoire de la Deuxième Guerre Mondiale et des Conflits Contemporains</u>). Staff members of the Foundation (like Gen. Lucien Poirier, Director of Studies) pursue their own individual research.

DIRECTORY CODE NUMBER : 64

<u>Name of Institution</u> : Institut d'Etudes Politiques d'Aix-en-Provence

<u>Address</u> : 25, avenue Gaston de Saporta
13625 AIX-EN-PROVENCE CEDEX

<u>Telephone</u> : 21-06-72

<u>Type of Organization</u> : National Public

<u>Director</u> : Prof. Yves Daudet

DIRECTORY CODE NUMBER : 65

Name of Institution : Institut de Politique Internationale et
                      Européenne (IPIE)

Address : Université de Paris-X
          200, avenue de la République (Bât. F)
          92001 NANTERRE CEDEX

Telephone : (1) 725-92-34   x.652

Founding Date : 1978   Founding Place : Nanterre

Type of Organization : National Public University

Objectives : Study of European, national, and transnational political
             forces and of defense issues.

Director : Prof. Hugues Portelli

Total Staff : 15

Number of researchers on security and defense issues : 4

Projects in Progress : Title
                                    Name(s) of Researcher(s)

---

1. Nationalism and war in German theory at the beginning of the
   19th century.
                     S. Picart

2. Security in the Western Mediterranean.
                     Hugues Portelli/P. Buffotot et al

Publications (since January 1983)

---

1. Hugues Portelli (Ed.), The Socialist International (in French)
   (Paris : Ed. Ouvrières, 1983), 189 pp. (Collection Enjeux
   internationaux-proceedings of colloquium in Jan. 1981).

2. Social Democracy and the Defense of Europe (in French) (Sage,
   April 1984) (Proceedings of an ECPR colloquium at Salzburg,
   Austria).

3. P. Buffotot, <u>Directory of University Work on Questions of Defense</u> (Paris : Fondation Nationale pour les Etudes de Défense, to appear in 1984).

<u>Comments</u> : The Institute held a colloquium in May 1984 on Christian Democracy as an international force.

DIRECTORY CODE NUMBER : 66

<u>Name of Institution</u> : Institut d'Histoire des Relations Internationales Contemporaines

<u>Address</u> : 17, rue de la Sorbonne
75005 PARIS

<u>Director</u> : Prof. J. B. Duroselle

Regular Periodicals : Title	Founding date	Issues Annually
<u>Relations internationales</u>		

DIRECTORY CODE NUMBER : 67

<u>Name of Institution</u> : Institut Français de Polémologie

<u>Address</u> : Hôtel National des Invalides
75007 PARIS

<u>Telephone</u> : (1) 555-92-30   x. 33-285

<u>Founding Date</u> : 1945   <u>Founding Place</u> : Paris

<u>Type of Organization</u> : National Private Non-Profit

Objectives : Develop research concerning war, peace, and conflicts in connection with the disciplines of strategy, international relations, and peace research.

Director : Jean Paucot

Total Staff : 15

Number of researchers on security and defense issues : 10

Projects in Progress : Title   Name(s) of Researcher(s)

1. Terrorism : French approaches.
    Didier Bigo/Daniel Hermant

2. Social Dimensions of a Security System : France.
    André Brigot/Jean-Max Noyer/Emmanuel Reynaud/Alain Binet

3. The Caribbean zone : conflicts and strategies.

4. Political violence in the world.
    René Carrere/Alain Binet/Francis Benhaim

5. War and the state in German philosophy at the beginning of the 19th century.
    Serge Picart

Regular Periodicals : title	Founding Date	Issues Annually
1. Etudes polémologiques	1971	4
2. Etudes polémologiques-bulletin	1983	3

Library services provided for outside researchers : yes

Comments : The Institute has been a part of the Fondation pour les Etudes de Défense Nationale since 1982. Previous to that, it was associated with the University of Paris.

DIRECTORY CODE NUMBER : 68

Name of Institution : Institut Français des Relations Internationales
                      (IFRI)

Address : 6, rue Ferrus
          75683 PARIS CEDEX 14

Telephone : (1) 580-91-08

Founding Date : 1979   Founding Place : Paris

Type of Organization : National Private Non-Profit

Objectives : (1) undertake research whose results will lead to
                 publications on important aspects of international
                 relations;
             (2) encourage debate on international questions in
                 France;
             (3) participate in international meetings, representing
                 French perspective.

Director : Prof. Thierry de Montbrial

Total Staff : 40

Number of researchers on security and defense issues : 6

Projects in Progress : Title
                              Name(s) of Researcher(s)

1. European security in the 1980s (and perspectives on European
   defense).
                              Pierre Lellouche/Yves Boyer/Nicole
                              Gnesotto/Brigitte Vassort-Rousset

2. Military aspects of security and perspectives of disarmament.
                              Jean Klein

3. European unification.
                              Philippe Moreau Defarges et al

4. Strategic problems of the Persian Gulf.
                              Bassma Kodmani et al

Regular Periodicals : Title	Founding Date	Issues Annually
1. Politique étrangère	1936	4
2. Rapport annuel mondial sur le système économique et les stratégies (RAMSES)	1981	1
3. Lettre d'information		12

Other Publications (since January 1983)

1. The European Community : Decline or Renewal ?, April 1983, 120 pp. (in collaboration with Italian, German, British and Dutch institutes).

2. Pierre Lellouche (Ed.), Pacificism and Deterrence : the Pacifist Protest and the Future of European Security (in French), (Paris : Economica, May 1983), 326 pp.

3. Georges de Ménil, The Economic Summits : National Policies at the Hour of Interdependence (in French), (Paris : Economica, June 1983), 92 pp.

4. Hervé Couteau-Bégarie, Soviet Maritime Power (in French) (Paris : Economica, May 1983), 188 pp.

5. Pierre Mayer, The Metamorphosis : Essay on Multilateralism and Bilateralism (Paris : Economica, Sept. 1983), 110 pp.

Library services provided for outside researchers : yes

Comments : IFRI was formed by a merger of the Centre d'Etudes de Politique Etrangère with the Groupe d'Etudes et de Recherches sur les Problèmes Internationaux.

DIRECTORY CODE NUMBER : 69

Name of Institution : Institut International d'Etudes Diplomatiques

Address : Université de Paris-Sud
54, blvd. Desgranges
92331 SCEAUX

Director : Prof. Charles Zorgbibe

DIRECTORY CODE NUMBER : 70

Name of Institution : Institut International de Géopolitique

Address : 31, quai Anatole-France
75007 PARIS

Telephone : (1) 705-60-35

Founding Date : June 1982   Founding Place : Paris

Type of Organization : International Private Non-Profit

Objectives : To study the general international situation while focusing on East-West relations and their impact on Western security and, if necessary, defense.

Director : Marie-France Garaud

Regular Periodicals : Title	Founding Date	Issues Annually
Géopolitique (in French and English editions)	Jan. 1983	4

Comments : The Institute organized major symposia on "War and Peace" in 1983 and on "The Pacific Basin" in 1984.

DIRECTORY CODE NUMBER : 71

Name of Institution : Institut National Supérieur d'Etudes de Défense et de Désarmement (INSED)

Address : Université de Paris-I
9, rue Malher
75004 PARIS

Telephone : (1) 278-33-22

Founding Date : Jan. 1983   Founding Place : Paris

Type of Organization : National Public University

Objectives : To develop studies and research on questions of defense, disarmament and security.

President : Prof. Jacques Soppelsa

Total Staff : 14

Number of researchers on security and defense issues : 10

Projects in Progress : Title
                       Name(s) of Researcher(s)

1. Study of links between disarmament and development.
2. Strategic dimension of the Islamic revival.
3. Politics of defense and regional security in the Arab-Persian Gulf.
4. Dynamics of regional cooperation and security in Africa.
5. Soviet disarmament policy and confidence-building measures.
6. Evaluation of international force relationships.

Regular Periodicals : Title	Founding Date	Issues Annually
1. La Lettre de l'INSED	1983	12
2. Les Cahiers de l'INSED	1984	4
3. Etudes et recherches	1984	occasional

Comments : The INSED is the result of the merger of the Centre d'Etudes Politiques de Défense (CEPODE), founded by Pierre Dabezies, the Centre d'Etudes et de Recherches sur le Désarmement (CEREDE), founded by Jean-Pierre Cot, and the Centre de Géopolitique. The Institute also trains young researchers, provides information services, sponsors conferences and exchanges with other research centers, and seeks to develop the dialogue and cooperation between universities and the policy-making government organisms.

GERMANY (FEDERAL REPUBLIC)

FEDERAL REPUBLIC OF GERMANY

Nowhere in Europe are security and defense issues more consequential than in the Federal Republic, the keystone of the Western security system but also the logical battlefield for World War III. The fearful reality that West Germany constitutes the front line for NATO in any conflict with the Warsaw Pact was always conceded by the Germans, who also recognized the advantages in American nuclear and conventional guarantees to protect their country. A defense consensus based on total integration within the Atlantic system permitted Bonn to seek political detente with the East, in particular closer relations with the German Democratic Republic. But the breakdown of detente at the superpower level has greatly strained the links achieved by Ostpolitik, and the defense consensus in the Federal Republic has dissolved. The controversies over the neutron bomb deployment and the Pershing-cruise installations have produced a mass peace movement, and uncertainty over American strategic guarantees has incited some Germans to question the fundamental premises of Bonn's security policy. Hence the anxiety expressed in Western capitals over the recrudescence of German nationalist sentiment and the possible evolution toward a policy of "neutralism" with the ultimate goal of reunification.

All these topics are being studied in depth in German research institutions. Two organizations predominate in the field of international relations : the Deutsche Gesellschaft für Auswärtige Politik (DGAP) in Bonn and the Stiftung Wissenschaft und Politik (SWP) in Ebenhausen, near Munich. The DGAP is the representative national research center (or "flagship") which participated in the two collaborative projects on the future of Western security and the European Community. It was founded in 1955 (the year the FRG entered NATO) to study international political issues, to sponsor conferences, seminars and lectures, and to permit an interchange of ideas between researchers and policymakers. The DGAP is politically independent and relies largely on private funds for its operations : "...to safeguard its independence, the Society does not advance opinions of its own on matters of current political importance". Europa Archiv, the twice-monthly journal created in 1945 by Wilhelm Cornides, is the DGAP's best-known publication. Die Internationale Politik is the Society's yearbook, and specialized monographs appear in the series, "Internationale Politik und Wirtschaft" and "Arbeitspapiere zur Internationalen Politik". The DGAP's Research Institute on International Politics and Security divides up into three working themes : 1) Western internal relations, European integration, security policy; 2) East-West relations, East Germany and the German problem; and 3) international economics, new technologies, transnational relations, North-South questions, and regional studies outside Europe. As part of its work on security issues, the DGAP held an international conference in May 1983 on "Confidence-Building Measures" and "co-sponsored another interational conference with the Aspen Institute on "Western Security Policy and Arms Control" in Berlin (June 1983).

With a total staff of 120 and a budget of approximately DM 8 million per annum, the SWP is much larger than the DGAP and pursues a much wider spectrum of research interests. Founded in 1962 on the model of the RAND Corporation, the SWP receives an annual appropriation from the Bundestag, but remains legally independent as a foundation under Bavarian state law. Its location near Munich "enables the Institute to pursue its tasks free from the immediate involvement in day-to-day activities of policy-makers". The emphasis is on long-range, multidisciplinary thinking, and many of the SWP's research reports are disseminated to the Bundestag and its committees, the Chancellery, and the ministries (i.e., policy planning staffs). Some of these papers have been published in the "Internationale Politik und Sicherheit" series. The four primary working areas of the SWP Research Institute are : 1) Western Europe and North America, Soviet Union and Eastern European countries, and East-West relations; 2) national security policy focusing on conceptual issues of defense and arms control; 3) international economic problems, both in an East-West and North-South context; and 4) Third World developments (Asia, Middle East, Africa, and Latin America) with special emphasis on their impact on international relations. The documentation section has a highly advanced computerized bibliographic system on international affairs and area studies.

German universities also make important contributions both to strategic studies and to peace research. At the Free University of Berlin, Prof. Helga Haftendorn is directing a major study on security, detente, and arms control in Transatlantic relations. The Research Institute for Political Science and European Questions at Cologne has strong links to the DGAP (through Profs. Karl Kaiser and Hans-Peter Schwarz). At Hamburg, the Institute for Peace Research and Security Policy (IFSH), now headed by Egon Bahr, attempts to synthesize peace and strategic studies and has just launched a new quarterly journal, S + F : Vierteljahresschrift für Sicherheit und Frieden. The Christian-Albrechts University at Kiel runs an international summer program on security problems and is another important source of strategic research. Dr. Hans Günter Brauch at Stuttgart has published widely on the risks of chemical warfare, space weapons, and related disarmament issues. Other university centers include the Working Group on Peace Research at Tübingen, the Institute for Political Science at Saarbrücken, and the Working Group for Conflict and Peace Research at Heidelberg.

The most influential German peace research organization is the independent Hessische Stiftung Friedens- und Konfliktforschung (HSFK), supported financially by the Land of Hesse and the City of Frankfurt. The HSFK not only studies the nature and causes of conflict, but also, according to its Constitution, "attempts to develop creative concepts for social change and the resolution of conflicts, in which decreasing violence, increasing social justice, and personal freedom in the international system and in individual societies can be interrelated". Research is focused on the dynamics of the East-West arms race, the Western European stake in the East-West competition, the superpower confrontation in the Third World, and psychological analyses of aggression and violence. Study results are communicated through the quarterly Friedensanalysen and the "HSFK Forschungsberichte" monograph series. Another noteworthy institution engaged in peace research is the Forschungstätte der Evangelischen Studiengemeinschaft, sponsored by Protestant churches. Among topics studied here are alternative military strategies, Third World military regimes, and nuclear proliferation. The highly political nature of much German peace research has made it quite controversial, and the major funding source, the Deutsche Gesellschaft für Friedens- und Konfliktforschung (DGFK), largely underwritten by the Federal Government, has terminated its activities at the end of 1983. The Max Planck Institut für Sozialwissenschaften has also cut back considerably on its peace research program.

A Federally-funded center in Cologne, the Bundesinstitut für Ostwissenschaftliche und internationale Studien (BIOSt), does detailed analyses of the Soviet and East European systems, and the Deputy Director, Dr. Gerhard Wettig, is working on the Soviet campaign against the Euromissile deployment. The Deutsche Orient-Institut, another area studies center, undertakes important research projects on security implications of Middle East political developments. The military academies of the <u>Bundeswehr</u> are purely educational institutions and have no scientific research programs. One army-supported center, the Sozialwissenschaftlichen Instituts der Bundeswehr (SOWI), does work in questions of sociology and the military profession.

Four German political parties have set up special foundations, with government support, for political education, cooperative ventures in foreign countries, and some research. The Social Science Research Institute of the CDU Konrad-Adenauer Stiftung has a number of projects on the future of NATO, and the SPD-sponsored Friedrich-Ebert Stiftung has been looking into alternative conventional strategies for the West. The FDP-run Friedrich-Naumann Stiftung and the CSU's Hanns-Seidel Stiftung are less active in security studies.

It should also be noted that major international conferences on security questions are sponsored regularly by the independent Deutsche Strategie Forum and the defense journal, <u>Europäische Wehrkunde</u>.

Despite the growing interest in security and defense research, the impact of these institutions on the policymaking process is limited. Part of the problem derives from the constraints of West Germany's geopolitical situation and its almost total strategic dependence on the United States. Moreover, the disasters of modern German history have evoked popular suspicions about military-related research, and much of the security debate suffers from simple reductionism and an inability to face political realities. This mental attitude apparently carries over to the ministries. As Dr. Gebhard Schweigler, an SWP analyst, has written, "...German bureaucrats, perhaps more than elsewhere, do not feel a need to be enlightened by outside advice (just as potential outside advisors have traditionally not felt compelled to gear their analyses to the specific needs of policymakers). The easy flow from positions of outside advisor to inside policymaker--a necessary precondition for meaningful scientific or scholarly advice--is almost totally absent in the West German political system". ("Strategic Studies in the Federal Republic of Germany", in <u>Trend in Strategic Studies</u> (Turin : Centro Studi Manlio Brosio, 1982) pp. 28-29).

DIRECTORY CODE NUMBER : 72

Name of Institution : Arbeitsgemeinschaft für Friedensforschung und
Europäische Sicherheitspolitik

Address : Institut für Politikwissenschaft
Universität Stuttgart
Keplerstrasse 17, K II, Stock 8A,
7000 STUTTGART 1

Telephone : (711) 2073-835

Founding Date : 1983   Founding Place : Stuttgart

Type of Organization : National Public University

Objectives : To pursue research on atomic and chemical weapons,
militarization of space, and European security matters.

Director : Dr. Hans Günter Brauch

Projects in Progress : Title
                       Name(s) of Researcher(s)

---

1. Militarization of space.
                       Hans Günter Brauch

2. Chemical weapons and warfare.
                       Hans Günter Brauch

3. Alternative conventional defense postures for West Germany in
the NATO context.
                       Hans Günter Brauch

4. Nuclear weapons and nuclear strategy.
                       Hans Günter Brauch

5. Europeanization of European defense.
                       Hans Günter Brauch

Publications (since January 1983)

1. Hans Günter Brauch and Duncan L. Clarke (Eds.), <u>Decisionmaking for Arms Limitation in the 1980s : Assessments and Prospects</u> (Cambridge, MA : Ballinger, 1983).

2. Hans Günter Brauch, <u>The Missiles Are Coming : From the NATO Double-Decision to the Deployment</u> (in German), (Köln : Bund-Verlag, 1983) 360 pp.

3. Hans Günter Brauch, <u>Perspectives on a European Peace Order : Can the European Parliament Play a Role in the Self-Realization of a European Peace Order ?</u> (in German), (Berlin : Berlin Verlag, 1983) 96 pp.

4. Hans Günter Brauch, <u>Nuclear Weapons and Arms Control</u> (in German), (Opladen : Westdeutscher Verlag, 1984).

5. Hans Günter Brauch and Rolf-Dieter Müller (Eds.), <u>Chemical War Conduct-Chemical Disarmament</u> (Berlin : Berlin Verlag, 1984) ca. 400 pp.

6. Hans Günter Brauch (Ed.), <u>Security Policy, All Things Considered</u> (in German), (Stuttgart : Bleicher-Verlag, 1984)

7. Hans Günter Brauch, <u>Space Weapons</u> (in German) (Berlin : Dietz-Verlag, 1984).

Collaboration with Foreign Study Centers

Advisor to <u>The Arms Control Reporter</u>, published by the Institute for Defense and Disarmament Studies (USA).

<u>Comments</u> : Dr. Brauch is Editor of the book series, <u>Rüstungskontroll Aktuell</u>, published by Haag and Herchen in Frankfurt.

DIRECTORY CODE NUMBER : 73

Name of Institution : Arbeitsgemeinschaft für Konflikt- und Friedensforschung

Address : Institut für Politische Wissenschaft
Universität Heidelberg
Marstallstrasse 6
6900 HEIDELBERG

DIRECTORY CODE NUMBER : 74

Name of Institution : Arbeitsgruppe Friedensforschung

Address : Institut für Politikwissenschaft
Universität Tübingen
Brunnenstrasse 30
7400 TUBINGEN 1

Telephone : (7071) 294957

Founding Date : 1968   Founding Place : Tübingen

Type of Organization : National Public University

Objectives : To deal with questions related to arms control and disarmament; alternative security; administrative organization of disarmament-units in developing countries; problems of the Third World; technology transfer.

Director : Prof. Volker Rittberger

Total Staff : 7

Number of researchers on security and defense issues : 3

Projects in Progress : Title
                       Name(s) of Researcher(s)

1. Possibilities and problems of an alternative security policy : European security and the concept of a nuclear-weapon-free zone.
   Volker Rittberger
   W. Kralewski
   T. Nielebock

2. Possibilities and restrictive conditions of international policy-making and administration : the case of OPANAL (Organismo para la Proscripción de las Armas Nucleares en la América Latina).
                              H. Mirek

3. Development and testing of a curriculum on peace and conflict research : global conflicts and peace.
                              W. Schwegler-Rohmeis
                              M. Mendler

Publications (since January 1983)

<u>Freedom from Nuclear Weapons and European Security : Possibilities and Problems of an Alternative Security Policy</u> (in German), (Tübingen, 1983).

Comments : Prof. Rittberger has also published <u>Mechanisms and Institutions for Disarmament</u> (Geneva : UNIDIR Research Paper N°1, 1982).

DIRECTORY CODE NUMBER : 75

<u>Name of Institution</u> : Berghof Stiftung für Konfliktforschung

<u>Address</u> : Wilhelmstrasse 6
             8000 MUNCHEN 40

<u>Founding Date</u> : 1971

<u>Objectives</u> : To support peace research and education.

DIRECTORY CODE NUMBER : 76

Name of Institution : Berliner Projektverbund der Berghofstiftung
                      für Konfliktforschung

Address : Winklerstrasse 4a
          1000 BERLIN 33

Telephone : (30) 49-30-89

Founding Date : 1973

Type of Organization : National Private Non-Profit

DIRECTORY CODE NUMBER : 77

Name of Institution : Bundesinstitut für ostwissenschaftliche und
                      internationale Studien (BIOSt)

Address : Lindenbornstrasse 22
          5000   KOLN 30

Telephone : (221) 52-20-01

Founding Date : April 1961   Founding Place : Köln

Type of Organization : National Public

Objectives : (1) research on political, social, economic and
                 ideological developments in the USSR and Eastern
                 Europe;
             (2) research on the impact of Soviet policy on the
                 policy of other countries;
             (3) survey of developments in Communist parties of
                 other countries;
             (4) research on historical and philosophical basis of
                 Marxism-Leninism and its variants.

Director : Dr. Heinrich Vogel

Total Staff : 81

Number of researchers on security and defense issues : 2

Projects in Progress : Title	Name(s) of Researcher(s)
Security, diplomacy and propaganda in Soviet foreign policy : the case of the Euromissile controversy. Gerhard Wettig	

Regular Periodicals : Title	Founding Date	Issues Annually
Berichte des Bundesinstituts	1967	about 40

Other Publications (since January 1983)

Gerhard Wettig :
----

1. "A Newer, Better Way to Peace ?" (in German), Osteuropa, 1/1983, pp. 28-38.

2. "The Soviet INF-Data Critically Reviewed", Aussenpolitik, 1/1983, pp. 30-42.

3. "Andropov's Solution for an INF Agreement", (in German), Europäische Wehrkunde, 2/1983, pp. 50-55.

4. "An Alternative Security Policy ? The Recommendations of the Palme Commission", (in German), Europäische Wehrkunde, 2/1983, pp. 97-105.

5. "Soviet Westpolitik at the Transition to Andropov", Aussenpolitik, 2/1983, pp. 122-134.

6. "The Garthoff-Pipes Debate on Soviet Strategic Doctrine : A European Perspective", Strategic Review, XI : 2 (Spring 1983), pp. 68-78.

7. "The Security Policy Discussion Today" (in German), Aus Politik und Zeitgeschichte, Beilage zur Wochenzeitung "Das Parlament", 3 Sept. 1983, pp. 19-35.

8. "The CSCE Follow-up Conference in Madrid", in BIOSt, The Soviet Union 1980/81 (NY : Holmes & Meier, 1983) pp. 240-249.

9. "Central Arguments in the Security Policy Debate", (in German) in Security as Challenge. Information and Arguments (in German) Publication series of the Bundeszentrale für politische Bildung, Vol. 202, 1983, pp. 149-159.

10. "The Role of West Germany in Soviet Policies Towards Western Europe", in Herbert J. Ellison (Ed.), Soviet Policies Towards Western Europe (Seattle : Univ. of Washington Press, 1983).

11. "The Role of Intimidation in Soviet Westpolitik", Aussenpolitik, 1/1984.

Library services provided for outside researchers : yes

DIRECTORY CODE NUMBER : 78

Name of Institution : Deutsch-Franzosisches Institut

Address : Asperger Strasse 34/38
         7140   LUDWIGSBURG

Telephone : (7141) 24849

Founding Date : 1948

Type of organization : National Private Non-Profit

Objectives : To encourage cooperation and understanding with France.

Director : Dr. Robert Picht

Total Staff : 25

DIRECTORY CODE NUMBER : 79

Name of Institution : Deutsche Atlantische Gesellschaft

Address : Thomas-Mann-Strasse 62
5300 BONN 1

Telephone : (228) 63-14-38

Founding Date : March 1956   Founding Place : Bonn

Type of Organization : National Private Non-Profit

Objectives : Public relations for NATO

Director : Reglind Vogt

Total Staff : 4

DIRECTORY CODE NUMBER : 80

Name of Institution : Deutsche Friedensgesellschaft-Vereinigte
Kriegsdienstgegner (DFG-VK)

Address : Rellinghauserstrasse 214
43 ESSEN 1

Telephone : (201) 25806

Founding Date : 1892   Founding Place : Berlin

Type of Organization : National Private Non-Profit

Objectives : To study disarmament, detente, conscientious objection, peace education.

Directors : Klaus Mannhardt, Gerd Greune

Total Staff : 20

Number of researchers on security and defense issues : 5

Projects in Progress : Title	Name(s) of Researcher(s)

1. Nuclear-weapon-free zones at the community level.
   Tobias Thomas

2. United Nations and disarmament.
   Gerd Greune

3. Environmental destruction, war, and militarism.
   Klaus Mannhardt

4. Conscientious objection as a fundamental human right.
   Gerd Greune

5. Media, education, schoolbooks : their role in peace education.
   Renate Kerbst
   Gregor Witt

6. Non-violent actions, peace camps and disarmament.
   Christian Schmidt

7. History of peace work - the IPB.
   Guido Grünewald

Regular Periodicals : Title	Founding Date	Issues Annually
1. Zivilcourage, antimili-taristische Zeitschriften	1974	6
2. Friedenspolitischer Informationsdienst	1980	10
3. 413 Info Dienst	1984	10
4. Informationsdienst Atomwaffenfreie Zonen	1982	12

Other Publications (since January 1983)

1. <u>Air Land Battle 2000</u> (in German), 1984.
2. <u>Militarization of Education</u> (in German), 1984.

Collaboration with Foreign Study Centers

European office for Conscientious Objectors (Brussels).

<u>Library services provided for outside researchers</u> : yes

<u>Comments</u> : DFG-VK is the German branch of War Resisters' International.

DIRECTORY CODE NUMBER : 81

<u>Name of Institution</u> : Deutsches Strategie-Forum

<u>Address</u> : Südstrasse 125
5300 BONN 2

<u>Telephone</u> : (228) 31-17-12

<u>Founding Date</u> : Feb. 1983   <u>Founding Place</u> : Bonn

<u>Type of Organization</u> : National Private Non-Profit

<u>Objectives</u> : To further the study of security and freedom in the FRG within the framework of a democratic order.

President : Dr. Rolf Friedemann Pauls

Publications (since January 1983)

1. "The Nuclear Balance in Europe" (in German), <u>Pro Pace</u>,
   July 1983, 45 pp. (translation of a study by United States
   Strategic Institute).

2. "Controversy over Peace : Reflections and Opinions on the NATO
   Double-Decision" (in German), <u>Pro Pace</u>, Oct. 1983, 39 pp.
   (conference proceedings).

3. "Safeguarding Freedom" (in German), <u>Pro Pace</u>, 1984, 44pp.
   (conference proceedings).

4. Albert Wohlstetter, "Statesmen, Bishops, and other Strategists
   on the Bombing Attacks of the Innocents" (in German), <u>Pro Pace</u>,
   1984, 30 pp. (translation of <u>Commentary</u> article).

5. Phillip A. Karber, "The Strategy : In Defense of Forward Defense"
   (in German), <u>Pro Pace</u>, 1984, 23 pp. (translation of <u>Armed Forces
   Journal International</u> article).

Comments : The Forum sponsored international conferences on
"Improving NATO's Forward Defense" in March 1984 and on
"Air Superiority and the Operational Maneuver in Soviet
War Planning" in June 1984 (both held in Bonn).

DIRECTORY CODE NUMBER : 82

Name of Institution : Deutsches Orient-Institute

Address : Mittelweg 150
          2000 HAMBURG 13

Telephone : (40) 44-14-81

Founding Date : 1960   Founding Place : Hamburg

Type of Organization : National Public

Objectives : Interdisciplinary research, information and docu-
             mentation on the Near and Middle East.

Director : Dr. Udo Steinbach

Total Staff : 25

Number of researchers on security and defense issues : 7

Projects in Progress : Title
                                 Name(s) of Researcher(s)

1. Egypt in transition.
   Thomas Koszinowski

2. Regional aspects of Egyptian security policy : the "Nile Valley Union" project.
   Thomas Koszinowski

3. State crisis in Sudan.
   D. Khalid

4. Libya's African policy : concepts and strategies.
   Hanspeter Mattes

5. Relations between Libya and the U.S.
   Hanspeter Mattes

6. The re-democratization of Turkey : internal and foreign policy perspectives.
   Udo Steinbach

7. Economic development in Turkey.
   Haluk Açikalin

8. Decisionmaking in Turkey.
   Ahmed Evin

9. Revolution in Iran and Afghanistan : a comparative study.
   Jan-Heeren Grevemeyer

10. Role of minorities in the Middle East.
    Udo Steinbach

Regular Periodicals : Title	Founding Date	Issues Annually
1. Orient	1959	4
2. Schriftenreihe des Deutschen Orientinstituts	1966	occasional
3. Mitteilungen des Deutschen Orientinstituts	1972	occasional

Other Publications (since January 1983)

1. Michael Wolffsohn, Politics in Israel (in German), (Opladen : Leske Verlag, 1983) 767 pp.

2. Thomas Koszinowski (Ed.), Saudi Arabia : Oil Power and a Developing Country (in German), 1983, 365 pp.

Collaboration with Foreign Study Centers

1. Istituto Affari Internazionali, Rome
2. Federal Trust, London
3. Center for Strategic Studies, Cairo
4. Foreign Policy Institute, Ankara

Library services provided for outside researchers : yes

Comments : The Institute's research program for 1984 concentrates on
Turkey and North Africa. Among other themes, Institute
researchers examine the concern of countries in the Near
and Middle East for a more independent position within
international politics and also the status of European-
Arab relations. The Middle East Documentation Center
(attached to the Institute) provides information support.

DIRECTORY CODE NUMBER : 83

Name of Institution : Fachbereich Politische Wissenschaft

Address : Universität Konstanz
          Postfach 733
          775 KONSTANZ

Telephone : (7531) 88-23-01

DIRECTORY CODE NUMBER : 84

Name of Institution : Forschungsinstitut der Deutschen Gesellschaft
                      für Auswärtige Politik (DGAP)

Address : Adenauerallee 131
          5300 BONN 1

Telephone : (228) 217021

Founding Date : March 1955   Founding Place : Frankfurt

Type of Organization : National Private Non-Profit

Objectives : To discuss the problems of international (especially
European) politics, security, and economics; to promote
research on these problems; and to stimulate and extend
understanding of international facts and problems by
means of lectures, study groups, and publications.

Director : Prof. Karl Kaiser

Total Staff : 39

Number of researchers on security and defense issues : 12

Projects in Progress : Title   Name(s) of Researcher(s)

1. The USA and the United Nations.
   Beate Lindemann

2. American foreign policy in transition : relations with the Near East and Africa.
   Christian Hacke

3. Military strategies and confidence-building measures.
   Harald Rüddenklau

4. Factors of continuity and change in the conception of French foreign policy.
   Ernst Weisenfeld

5. Evolution of German-French relations.
   Karl Kaiser
   Ingo Kolboom

6. International aspects of German politics.
   Eberhard Schulz
   Peter Danylow

7. Documents on the Berlin question.
   Hans-Heinrich Mahnke

8. East-West economic relations as an Alliance problem.
   Claudia Wörmann

9. The Near East and the East-West Conflict.
   Karl Kaiser
   Eberhard Schulz
   Helmut Hubel
   Peter Hünseler

10. Petroleum and economic security of the Federal Republic.
    Ulrich Strempel

11. Space and international politics.
    Stephan von Welck

Regular Periodicals : Title	Founding Date	Issues Annually
1. Europa-Archiv	1946	24
2. Die Internationale Politik	1955	1

Other Publications (since January 1983)

1. Friedbert Pflüger, The Human Rights Policy of the USA : American Foreign Policy between Idealism and Realism 1972-1982 (in German), (Munich : Oldenbourg Verlag, 1983) N°48 of "International Politics and Economics" series, 405 pp.

2. Helmut Hubel, The USA in the Near East Conflict (in German), (Bonn : Europa Union Verlag, 1983) N°23 of "Working Papers on International Politics", 96 pp.

3. Angela E. Stent, Technology Transfer to the Soviet Union. A Challenge for the Cohesiveness of the Western Alliance (Bonn : Europa Union Verlag, 1983) N°24 of "Working Papers on International Politics", 135 pp.

4. Franke Heard-Bey, The Arab Gulf States in the Sign of the Islamic Revolution, (in German), (Bonn : Europa Union Verlag, 1983) N°25 of "Working Papers on International Politics", 239 pp.

5. George de Menil and Anthony Solomon, World Economic Summits (in German), (Bonn : Europa Union Verlag, 1983) N°26 of "Working Papers on International Politics", 130 pp.

6. Parliamentary Cooperation in the Alliance : The Future of the North Atlantic Assembly (in German), (Bonn : Europa Union Verlag, 1983) N°27 of "Working Papers on International Politics", 42 pp.

7. Karl Kaiser (Ed.), Confidence-Building Measures : Proceedings of an International Symposium 24-27 May 1983 at Bonn (Bonn : Europa Union Verlag, 1983) N°28 of "Working Papers on International Politics" series, 237 pp.

8. Ulf Marwege, <u>New Orientations in the Western Trade of the DDR</u> (in German), (Bonn : Europa Union Verlag, 1983) N°30 of "Working Papers on International Politics" series, 122 pp.

Collaboration with Foreign Study Centers

1. German collaborator for "the European Community in the 1980s" project (published as <u>The European Community : Progress or Decline ?</u>) (1983).

2. Trilateral Commission (NY) for study, <u>East-West Trade at a Crossroads</u> (1983).

<u>Library services provided for outside researchers</u> : yes

<u>Comments</u> : The DGAP arose from the reorganization of the Institut für Europäische Politik und Wirtschaft in Frankfurt and moved to Bonn in 1960. In addition to its research work, the Society sponsors special study groups of experts in
(1) international security, disarmament, and arms control;
(2) East-West relations;
(3) world economic cooperation.

DIRECTORY CODE NUMBER : 85

<u>Name of Institution</u> : Forschungsinstitut für Internationale Politik und Sicherheit

<u>Address</u> : Stiftung Wissenschaft und Politik (SWP)
Haus Eggenberg
8026 EBENHAUSEN/ISARTAL

<u>Telephone</u> : (8178) 701

<u>Founding Date</u> : 1962

<u>Type of Organization</u> : National Private Non-Profit

Objectives : Interdisciplinary research in international affairs with special emphasis on issues of national security and arms control.

Director : Prof. Klaus Ritter

Total Staff : 120

Number of researchers on security and defense issues : 12

Projects in Progress : Title
                                Name(s) of Researcher(s)

A. Political Developments in East-West Relations with Respect to Europe

1. Development of US-USSR relations (confrontation vs. cooperation).

2. Foreign policy consensus-building in the USA.

3. German-American relations in the evolution of the Atlantic partnership.

4. Conceptual problems of Western policy in relation to the global strategy and internal development of the Soviet Union and its allies.

5. European unification problems.

6. Possibilities of further development of Western european unity (and its relation to the U.S.).

7. Adaptation problems and necessities for reform of the EC.

8. Turkey as a support of the Western security system.

9. Questions of NATO policy with respect to security menaces in the Third World.

10. Soviet leadership after Brezhnev.

11. Political development in Eastern Europe (including GDR).

12. Goals and strategies of Soviet Western European policy.

13. Soviet military power and the Western response.

14. Soviet policy toward the Third World.

B. International Security in East-West Relations

   1. Tendencies in strategic thinking in the U.S.
   2. U.S. strategic missile potential and possibilities of missile defense.
   3. Military utilization of space technology.
   4. Strengthening NATO conventional defense capacities.
   5. Problems of Western relations with respect to Warsaw Pact "out-of-area" operations.
   6. Evaluation of alternative structural models for the army (and effect on NATO), especially relating to demographic trends.
   7. Improvements for close air support and battlefield interdiction.
   8. Enlargement of command and control systems.
   9. Chemical weapons in the military doctrine and planning of the Warsaw Pact.
   10. Necessities for the total defense of the FRG.
   11. Security policy cooperation between France and the FRG.
   12. Maritime strategy of NATO.
   13. Problems of military force comparisons in Europe.
   14. Conceptual beginnings for new orientations of Western arms control policy.
   15. Limitation and reduction of conventional offensive capacities in Europe.
   16. Limitation of intercontinental strategic and regional nuclear weapons potential as well as other means of mass extermination (i.e. chemical weapons) and verification possibilities.
   17. Nuclear-weapon-free zones in Europe as an element in arms control.
   18. UN, arms control, and law of the sea.

C. Economic Problems of International Policy

1. Solution of economic conflicts between U.S., Western Europe and Japan.

2. Economic problems of Alliance military security in the 1980s.

3. Stabilization of international finance system.

4. Global economic adjustment process in commercial and financial relations.

5. Economic South-South relations as development strategy.

6. Foreign economic policy of the U.S. (and West-West and East-West relations).

7. Development of East-West economic relations.

8. East-West financial relations (and international debt situation).

9. Western participation in Soviet economic projects (esp. energy area).

10. East-South cooperation.

11. Economic significance and organization of weapons sectors in the USSR.

D. The Third World

1. European-US relations and the Middle East.
   Reinhardt Rummel

2. Soviet Union and the non-aligned movement after Afghanistan.
   Christoph Royen

3. Law of the Sea : consequences for international law.
   Renate Platzöder

4. Major powers' arms transfers to the Gulf region.

5. USSR's arms transfers to the Third World.
   Joachim Krause

6. Economic relations between industrial, developing and oil-exporting countries.
   Veronika Düttner
   Achim von Heynitz

7. Soviet economic aid to Third World Comecon countries.
   Werner Deitel

8. South Asia : conflicts and cooperation.
   Dieter Braun

9. Recent shifts in China's foreign policy.
   Joachim Glaubitz

10. China and the Eastern European nations.

11. Lebanon and Western security.
    Rainer Büren

12. Islamic countries' foreign policies and domestic conditions : overview.
    Rainer Büren

13. Egypt : domestic political forces and foreign policy.
    Gudrun Krämer

14. Iran : political determinants and Iranian-Iraqi conflict.

15. Persian Gulf Cooperation Council.

16. Africa's socialist-oriented countries and the West.
    Winrich Kühne

17. Regional integration in southern Africa.
    Bernhard Weimer

18. Argentine foreign policy.
    Wolf Grabendorff

19. Brazil : ambivalence of political and economic orientation.
    Manfred Wöhlcke

Regular Periodicals : Title	Founding Date	Issues Annually
1. "Internationale Politik und Sicherheit" monograph series	1978	occasional
2. "Aktuelle Materialien zur internationalen Politik" series		occasional

Other Publications (since January 1983)

1. Hannes Adomeit, <u>Soviet Power in International Crises and Conflicts</u> (in German), (Baden-Baden : Nomos Verlagsgesellschaft, 1983) Vol. 11 of the "Internationale Politik und Sicherheit" series, 496 pp.

2. Winrich Kühne, <u>The Policy of the Soviet Union in Africa</u> (in German), (Baden-Baden : Nomos Verlagsgesellschaft, 1983) Vol. 10 of the "Internationale Politik und Sicherheit" series.

3. Dieter Braun, <u>The Indian Ocean - Region of Conflict or 'Zone of Peace'</u> ? (London : C.Hurst, 1983).

4. Uwe Nerlich (Ed.), <u>Soviet Power and Western Negotiating Policies</u>
   Vol. 1 : <u>The Soviet Asset : Military Power in the Competition over Europe</u>.
   Vol. 2 : <u>The Western Panacea Constraining Soviet Power Through Negotiation</u> (Cambridge, MA : Ballinger, 1983).

5. Uwe Nerlich (Ed.), <u>The Containment of Soviet Power</u> (in German) (Baden-Baden, Nomos Verlagsgesellschaft, 1983), vol. 14 of the "Internationale Politik und Sicherheit" series, 500 pp.

6. Uwe Nerlich, <u>The Precarious Peace : European Security over Four Decades</u> (in German, in preparation).

7. Joachim Krause, <u>Soviet Military Assistance Policy Towards Developing Countries</u> (in German, in preparation).

8. Wolf Grabendorff and Riordan Roett (Eds.), <u>Latin America-Western Europe-United States : An Atlantic Triangle ?</u> (in German, in preparation).

9. Jürg von Kalckreuth, <u>Civil Defense in the Concept of Total Defense</u> (in German, in preparation).

10. Joachim Glaubitz, <u>Japan and the Soviet Union : Confrontation and Beginnings of Cooperation since the Start of the 1970s</u> (in German, in preparation).

11. Friedmann Müller et al, <u>Economic Sanctions in East-West Relations</u> (in German), (Baden-Baden, Nomos Verlagsgesellschaft, 1983), Vol. I of the "Aktuelle Materialien zur Internationalen Politik", Series, 233 pp.

12. Bernhard Weimer, <u>Mozambique's Foreign Policy 1975-1982</u> (in German), (Baden-Baden, Nomos Verlagsgesellschaft, 1983), Vol. II of the "Aktuelle Materialen zur Internationalen Politik" series, 213 pp.

13. Manfred Wöhlcke, <u>Brazil 1983 : Ambivalence of its Political and Economic Orientation</u> (in German), (Baden-Baden, Nomos Verlagsgesellschaft, 1983), Vol. III of the "Aktuelle Materialen zur Internationalen Politik" series, 123 pp.

14. Hanns-Dieter Jacobsen, <u>East-West Economic Relations as a German-American Problem</u> (in German, in preparation).

15. Falk Bomsdorf, <u>Aspects of Security Policy in Northern Europe</u> (in German, in preparation).

Collaboration with Foreign Study Centers

RAND Corporation (USA)

<u>Comments</u> : SWP is governed by a 17-member <u>Stiftungsrat</u> and is financed through an annual appropriation in the Federal budget (with supplementary grants from national and foreign foundations). The research program is divided into four broad areas : East-West relations, national security policy, international economic problems, and Third World developments (projects listed above).

DIRECTORY CODE NUMBER : 86

<u>Name of Institution</u> : Forschungsinstitut für Politische Wissenschaft und Europäische Fragen

<u>Address</u> : Universität Köln
Gottfried-Keller-Strasse 6
5000 KOLN 41

<u>Telephone</u> : (221) 470-2855
470-2851

<u>Founding Date</u> : 1960   <u>Founding Place</u> : Köln

Type of Organization : National Public University

Objectives : Teaching and research in political science.

Directors : Prof. Hans-Peter Schwarz, Prof. Ulrich Matz

Total Staff : 10

Number of researchers on security and defense issues : 5

Projects in Progress : Title
                              Name(s) of Researcher(s)

---

1. Political control by means of general elections as a problem of legitimation.
                           Peter Kielmansegg/Ulrich Matz

2. Realistic and utopian models of peace : value bases and institutional hypotheses about peace.
                           Ulrich Matz

3. International comparative analysis of environmental protection.
                           Ulrich Matz

4. German-French relations.
                           Karl Kaiser

5. European-American relations.
                           Karl Kaiser

6. Development of strategy.
                           Karl Kaiser

7. Political science analysis of US development policy under the Reagan Administration.
                           Karl Kaiser/Bernhard May

Publications (since January 1983)

---

1. Ulrich Matz, Force and Legitimacy (in German), (Opladen, 1983).

2. Hans-Peter Schwarz, The Adenauer Era : Period of Change, 1957-1963 (in German), (Stuttgart, 1983).

3. Hans-Peter Schwarz, "International Politics from a Global and Particularist Viewpoint" (in German), Europa-Archiv, N°15, 1983.

4. Ulrich Krafft, Belgium in the Structure of East-West Relations (in German), (Köln : 1983).

5. Ulrich Krafft, "NATO, the Eastern Mediterranean, and Greek Interests" (in German), Beiträge zur Konfliktforschung, 13,1983.

6. Henning von Löwis, Namibia in the East-West Conflict (in German), (Köln : Verlag Wissenschaft und Politik, 1983).

7. Henning von Löwis, "Bibliography on Conflict Research, 1982-83" (in German), Beiträge zur Konfliktforschung, 13, 1983.

8. Bernhard May, "A Program of Revitalization for the European Community" (in German), Europa-Archiv, N°6 (1983).

9. Manfred Spieker, "The Defense of Peace against Pacifism" (in German), in Klaus Hornung (Ed.), Peace without Utopia (in German), (Krefeld, 1983).

10. Manfred Spieker, "Is Defense A Sin ? The Problem of the Safeguarding of Peace in Catholic Social Teaching" (in German), Die politische Meinung, N°208 (May-June 1983).

11. Karl Kaiser, "An Ostpolitik for the West : Discrepancies and Convergences in Conflict" (in German) in Daniel Frei (Ed.), Free World : Balance Sheet and Perspective (Zurich, 1983).

12. Karl Kaiser, "FRG : a Challenge to the Consensus" (in French), in Pierre Lellouche (Ed.), Pacifism and Deterrence (in French), (Paris : IFRI, 1983).

13. Karl Kaiser, No-First-Use and Conventional Defence (Rome : NATO Defense College, April 1983).

14. Karl Kaiser, "Partners in Troubled Times", Scala, July 1983.

15. Karl Kaiser, "No-First-Use of Nuclear Weapons : A False Step in the Right Direction" (in German), in Peace and Security as Challenge (Bonn, 1983) Schriftenreihe der Bundeszentrale für politische Bildung, N°202.

16. Karl Kaiser, "Security as a New EC Responsibility . Generals in the Rue de la Loi, Brussels" (in German), EG-Magazin, Nov. 1983.

17. Karl Kaiser, "The Future of NATO Strategy : Looking Toward the year 2000", Naval War College Review, Nov.-Dec. 1983.

Library services provided for outside researchers : yes

DIRECTORY CODE NUMBER : 87

Name of Institution : Forschungsstätte der Evangelischen Studiengemeinschaft (FEST)

Address : Schmeilweg 5
6900 HEIDELBERG

Telephone : (6221) 14061

Founding Date : 1957   Founding Place : Heidelberg

Type of Organization : National Private Non-Profit

Objectives : Coordination between German Protestant churches and
scientific researchers and institutions.

Total Staff : 11

Number of researchers on security and defense issues : 3

Projects in Progress : Title
Name(s) of Researcher(s)

1. Military strategy and international security : follow-up of the Heidelberg peace memorandum (1983).
F. Solms

2. Alternatives in Western military thinking and common European security.
S. Tiedtke

3. Military regimes and international security in Third World countries.
Bernhard Moltmann

4. Third World energy needs and nuclear proliferation.
C. Eisenbart
K. Stahl
U. Ratsch

Publications (since January 1983)

Heidelberg Peace Memorandum (in German), (Hamburg : Rowohl Taschenbuch, 1983).

Library services provided for outside researchers : yes

Comments : FEST has done studies of the political and social situation of the Bundeswehr, the arms race and technological innovation, peace and war in the history of socialism and of the Church.

DIRECTORY CODE NUMBER : 88

Name of Institution : Friedrich-Ebert Stiftung (Forschungsinstitut)

Address : Godesberger Allee 149
5300 BONN 2

Telephone : (228) 88-36-53

Founding Date : April 1925

Type of Organization : National Private Political-Party-Affiliated

Objectives : (1) socio-political education in the FRG and abroad;
(2) policy-oriented research for political decision-makers in the FRG and abroad;
(3) financial aid to German and foreign students;
(4) international cooperation, in coordination with the German Social Democratic Party (SPD).

Director : Dr. Günter Grunwald

Publications (since January 1983)

1. Eckhard Lübkemeier, "Problems, Prerequisites, and Prospects of Conventionalizing NATO's Strategy", July 1983, 88 pp.

2. Wilhelm Bruns, "European Disarmament Conference - an Agent of Hope in East-West Relations" (in German), Autumn 1983, 19 pp.

3. Eckhard Lübkemeier, "Pershing II : On the Weapon for an American First-Strike Capacity ?" (in German), July 1983, 9 pp.

4. Wilhelm Bruns, "Toward the First European Disarmament Conference in the Framework of the CSCE" (in German), Oct.-Dec. 1983, 14 pp.

5. Wilhelm Bruns and Christian Krause, <u>Reflections on a European Peace Order</u> July 1983, 31 pp.

<u>Library services provided for outside researchers</u> : yes

<u>Comments</u> : The Foundation's study group on security and disarmament was established in 1978. In June 1983, the Foundation sponsored the fourth European-American conference on problems of international security.

DIRECTORY CODE NUMBER : 89

<u>Name of Institution</u> : Friedrich-Naumann-Stiftung

<u>Address</u> : Baunscheidtstrasse 15
5300 BONN 1

<u>Telephone</u> : (228) 54 70

<u>Founding Date</u> : May 1958

<u>Type of organization</u> : National Private Political-Party-Affiliated

<u>Objectives</u> : Education and research, in association with the Free Democratic Party.

<u>Director</u> : Dr. Fritz Fliszar

<u>Total Staff</u> : 11

Comments : The Foundation sponsors numerous conferences and seminars, and supports an active program in Third World countries.

DIRECTORY CODE NUMBER : 90

Name of Institution : Führungsakademie der Bundeswehr

Address : Manteuffelstrasse 20
Clausewitz-Kaserne
2000 HAMBURG 55

Telephone : (40) 86-59-41

Type of Organization : National Public

Objectives : Education of Army officers.

Director : Brig. Gen. Hermann Teske

DIRECTORY CODE NUMBER : 91

Name of Institution : Hanns-Seidel-Stiftung

Address : Lazarettstrasse 19
8000 MUNCHEN

Telephone : (89)-1258-1

Founding Date : Oct. 1967   Founding Place : München

Type of Organization : National Private Political-Party-Affiliated

Objectives : Political education and cooperation, in association with the Christian Social Union.

Director : Wolfgang Maurus

Total Staff : 8

Regular Periodicals : Title	Founding Date	Issues Annually
Politischen Studien	1949	

Comments : The Foundation's Institut für Politische Zusammenarbeit runs a program on global cooperation for peace.

DIRECTORY CODE NUMBER : 92

Name of Institution : Haus Rissen : Internationales Institut für Politik und Wirtschaft

Address : Rissener Landstrasse 193
2000　HAMBURG 56

Telephone : (40) 81-80-21

Founding Date : 1954　　　　　Founding Place : Hamburg

Type of Organization : International Private Non-Profit

Objectives : Information and orientation of key people from administration, politics and defense on international affairs.

Directors : Dr. Hans-Viktor Schierwater, Uwe Möller

Total Staff : 7

Number of researchers on security and defense issues : 2

Projects in Progress : Title
　　　　　　　　　　　　Name(s) of Researcher(s)

Europe after 2000 (project of German association of the Club of Rome).
　　　　　　　　Uwe Möller
　　　　　　　　Peter Robejsek

Regular Periodicals : Title	Founding Date	Issues Annually
Rissener Rundbrief		12

DIRECTORY CODE NUMBER : 93

Name of Institution : Hessische Stiftung Friedens- und Konfliktforschung (HSFK)

Address : Leimenrode 29
6000 FRANKFURT 1

Telephone : (611) 55-01-91

Founding Date : 1970

Type of Organization : National Public

Objectives : To examine the causes of conflict, their manifestations, and the possibility of their resolution or management; and to develop creative concepts for social change and the resolution of conflicts.

Director : Prof. Lothar Brock

Total Staff : 36

Number of researchers on security and defense issues : 23

Projects in Progress : Title	Name(s) of Researcher(s)

1. Causes of the arms race.
2. Development of nuclear and conventional military potential : problem of military force comparisons.
3. Theory and practice of arms control.

                              Gert Krell
                              Thomas Risse-Kappen
                              Hans-Joachim Schmidt

4. Domestic conditioning factors of American foreign policy.
5. Foreign commerce policy of the USA.
6. Energy policy of the USA.
7. Arms and arms control policy of the USA.

                              Ernst-Otto Czempiel
                              Bernd W. Kubbig
                              Harald Müller
                              Reinhard Rode

8. Problems of security and cooperation in Europe.
9. Confidence-building measures.
10. Economic cooperation (W. Germany).
11. Exchange of people and views (Germany).
12. Consequences of the East-West conflict and detente to the Third World.

                              Lothar Brock
                              Mathias Jopp
                              Berthold Meyer
                              Norbert Ropers
                              Peter Schlotter

13. Domestic conditioning factors of Soviet foreign policy.
14. Arms and arms control policy of the Soviet Union.
15. Eurocommunism and the CPSU : effect on East-West relations.
16. Foreign and development policy of the GDR.

                              Egbert Jahn
                              Bruno Schoch
                              Achim Spanger
                              Stephan Tiedtke

17. Security needs and transformation of the East-West conflict in social groups.
18. War games, game conduct, and aggressivity.
19. Foundations for a peace education curriculum.

                              Hans Nicklas
                              Christian Büttner
                              Anne Ostermann
                              Ute Volmerg

20. Preventing war and securing peace in Central Europe.

                              Gert Krell
                              Hans-Joachim Schmidt
                              Thomas Risse-Kappen

21. The US and detente in the East-West conflict : economic, military, and political interests in US foreign policy towards the USSR and Eastern Europe.
   Ernst-Otto Czempiel
   Bernd Kubbig
   Harald Müller
   Reinhard Rode

22. Detente and the CSCE framework.
   Lothar Brock
   Mathias Jopp
   Berthold Meyer
   Norbert Ropers
   Peter Schlotter

23. Soviet reactions to the debate about military strategy in NATO.
24. Soviet and GDR Military Aid to the Third World and its effect on East-West relations and development.
   Egbert Jahn
   Bruno Schoch
   Achim Spanger
   Stephan Tiedtke

Regular Periodicals : Title	Founding Date	Issues Annually
1. Friedensanalysen	1975	4
2. Mitteilungen		1

Other Publications (since January 1983)

1. Mathias Jopp, Military and Society in the Federal Republic of Germany (in German), (Frankfurt : Campus-Verlag, 1983).

2. Hans-Joachim Schmidt, The Conventional Arms Competition in Europe (in German), (Frankfurt : HSFK-Forschungsberichte, 1983) 102 pp.

3. Gert Krell, On the Problematic of Nuclear Options (in German), (Frankfurt : HSFK - Forschungsberichte, 1983) 60 pp.

4. Gert Krell, Thomas Risse-Kappen, and Hans-Joachim Schmidt, The Challenge of Nuclear Arms : Views on the Pastoral Letter of the US Bishops' Conference (in German), (Frankfurt : HSFK-Forschungsberichte, 1983) 77 pp.

5. Reinhard Rode et al. The New Protectionism (in German), (Bonn : Verlag Neue Gesellschaft, 1983).

Collaboration with Foreign Study Centers

1. Collaborator with IISS (London) on project "Future of Strategic Deterrence".

2. Collaborator with Centre for European Policy Studies (Brussels) on project "New Approaches to Non-Proliferation".

3. Collaborator with Brookings Institution (Washington) on project concerning future of "flexible response".

4. Cooperation with Peace Studies Program, Cornell Univ. (Ithaca, NY).

Library services provided for outside researchers : yes

Comments : HSFK studies are divided into five research units :
(1) International Arms Race and Arms Control (Project Nos. 1-3, 20);
(2) the United States (Project Nos. 4-7, 21);
(3) Federal Republic of Germany (Project Nos. 8-12, 22);
(4) the Socialist countries (Project Nos. 13-16, 23-24);
(5) Political Psychology and Peace Education (Project Nos. 17-19).

DIRECTORY CODE NUMBER : 94

Name of Institution : Institut für Friedensforschung und Sicherheitspolitik (IFSH)

Address : Universität Hamburg
Falkenstein 1
2000 HAMBURG 55

Telephone : (40) 86-90-54

Founding Date : 1971   Founding Place : Hamburg

Type of Organization : National Public University

Objectives : To teach and conduct research on peace and international
security issues.

Director : Egon Bahr

Total Staff : 21

Number of researchers on security and defense issues : 9

Projects in Progress : Title
                              Name(s) of Researcher(s)

1. Cooperative arms control and the policy of detente.
                              Wolf Graf von Baudissin

2. Crisis of East-West relations.
                              Andreas Pott

3. East-West economic relations and detente policy.
                              Herbert Wulf

4. Alternative security policies.
                              Dieter S. Lutz
                              Erwin Muller

5. Legal questions of security and military policy.
                              Dieter S. Lutz

6. Military force comparisons at the conventional and nuclear
   levels.
                              Franz Borkenhagen

7. Arms exports.   Michael Brzoska

8. Arms and underdevelopment.   Herbert Wulf

Regular Periodicals : Title	Founding Date	Issues Annually
1. S + F : Vierteljahres-schrift für Sicherheit und Frieden	1983	4
2. IFSH-Forschungsberichte	1977	occasional
3. IFSH-Diskussionbei-trage	1977	occasional

Other Publications (since January 1983)

1. Wolf Graf von Baudissin (Ed.), From Distrust to Confidence. Concepts, Experiences and Dimensions of Confidence Building Measures (Baden Baden : NOMOS Verlagsgesellschaft, 1983) 121 pp.

2. Volker Böge and Peter Wilke, "New Paths for Peace Policy ? Inventory of Alternative Security Conceptions" (in German), Sozialwissenschaftliche Informationen für Unterricht und Studium, 1/1983, pp. 18-28.

3. Michael Brzoska, "Reconversion from Arms to Civil Production" (in German) Osterreichische Zeitschrift für Politikwissen-schaft, 2/1983, pp. 167-184.

4. Michael Brzoska, "Third World Arms Control", Bulletin of Peace Proposals, 2/1983, pp. 165-173.

5. Michael Brzoska, "Arms Production in the FRG", in N. Ball and M. Leitenberg (Eds.), The Structure of Defense Industries (London : 1983) pp. 111-139.

6. Michael Brzoska, "The Military Dimension of Foreign Debts", Journal of Peace Research, 3/1983, pp. 271-277.

7. Dieter S. Lutz, "Security Policy Alternatives for the FRG ? Legal Questions on the Sovereignty of the Federal Republic" (in German), Frankfurter Hefte, 2/1983, pp. 15-23.

8. Dieter S. Lutz, "A Counterforce/Countervalue Scenario - or How Much Destructive Capability Is Enough ?" Journal of Peace Research, Vol. 20, N°1/1983, pp. 1-10.

9. Dieter S. Lutz, "World war in Spite of Ourselves ? The Controversy over the Euromissiles" (in French), (Paris : 1983).

10. Andreas Pott, "Detente and Security Policy in the 1980s" (in German) in Institut für Internationale Politik und Wirtschaft der DDR (Ed.), Security Policy - Security Partnership (in German) (Berlin : 1983) pp. 34-47.

11. Peter Wilke, "Peace Movement and Politics : the Example of the Concept of the Nuclear-Free zone" (in German) in Hanne Birchenbach (Ed.) Peace Research, Churches and Church-related Peace Movements (in German), (Frankfurt : Arbeitsgemeinschaft für Friedens- und Konfliktforschung, 1983) pp. 139-151.

12. Herbert Wulf, "Developing Countries", in N. Ball and M. Leitenberg (Eds.), The Structure of the Defense Industry (London : 1983) pp. 310-343.

13. Herbert Wulf (Ed.), Rearmament and Underdevelopment : from the Reports of the United Nations (in German), (Reinbek : 1983).

14. Herbert Wulf, "More Arms - Fewer Working Places", in Rolf Seeliger (Ed.) Reduction of Jobs and Rearmament (in German), (München : 1983), pp. 36-44.

15. Volker Böge, Turkey - Corner-stone of the Western Alliance (in German), (Baden Baden : NOMOS Verlagsgesellschaft, 1983).

16. Dieter S. Lutz (Ed.), Neither Military Knowledge Nor Peace Education ? (in German), (Baden Baden : NOMOS Verlagsgesellschaft, 1983).

17. Dieter S. Lutz, Towards a Methodology of Force Comparison (Baden Baden : NOMOS Verlagsgesellschaft, 1983).

18. Dieter S. Lutz, Andreas Pott, and Günter Schwartz, Sea Power and Peace Policy (Baden Baden : NOMOS Verlagsgesellschaft, 1983).

Collaboration with Foreign Study Centers

Cooperation with CIRPES (Paris), CSIS (Washington), Institut für Politik und Wirtschaft (IPW) der DDR, International Peace Research Association, Oesterreichisches Institut für Internationale Politik (Laxenburg), Oesterreichisches Institut für Friedensforschung (Stadt Schlaing), Sektion Rechtswissenschaft der Universität von Leipzig (DDR), Stanford University (USA), SIPRI.

Library services provided for outside researchers : yes

Comments : In June 1983, the IFSH held a colloquium on "The Military Strategic Conception of Security Policy : NATO Strategy vs. Alternative Concepts". The proceedings were published in German as Volume 30 of the IFSH-Diskussionsbeiträge. The IFSH also co-sponsored a conference with the IPW (East Berlin), in November 1983, "Confidence-and-security-Building Measures and Disarmament in Europe" (published in German as Vol. 34 of the IFSH-Diskussionsbeiträge in March 1984). Three recent IFSH studies have been translated into English : Dieter S. Lutz, "Towards a New European Peace Order", IFSH-Diskussionsbeiträge, vol. 33, Feb. 1984; Dieter S. Lutz, "The Unintended World War III : On the Danger of War, the various Scenarios, the Chance of Damage Limiting and the Bonus of the First Strike", IFSH-Forschungsberichte, Vol. 29, May 1983; and Herbert Wulf, "The Arms Industry in Developing Countries", IFSH-Forschungsberichte, Vol. 30, Sept. 1983.

DIRECTORY CODE NUMBER : 95

Name of Institution : Institut für Internationale Politik und Regionalstudien

Address : Freie Universität Berlin
Ihnestrasse 22
1000 BERLIN 33

Telephone : (30) 838-55-27

Founding Date : 1948   Founding Place : Berlin

Type of Organization : National Public University

Objectives : Teaching and research.

Director : Helga Haftendorn

Number of researchers on Security and defense issues : 8

Projects in Progress : Title
                      Name(s) of Researcher(s)

---

1. Security, deterrence, and arms control in U.S.-Western European relations (general theme of projects).
   Helga Haftendorn et al

2. Conventional force reduction in Europe.
   Reinhard Mutz

3. Nuclear non-proliferation policies.
   Lothar Wilker

4. Economic dimensions of Western security.
   Claudia Wörmann

5. British nuclear arms as a problem of East-West arms control.
   Karin Eifert

6. Western position at the conference on security and confidence-building measures.
   Ingo Peters

7. Conditions of success for arms control in the Third World (example of ASEAN).
   Susanne Feske

8. Initiation of arms control agreement through unilateral measures.
   Nikolaus Brubach

Publications (since January 1983)

1. Helga Haftendorn, <u>Security and Detente. The Foreign Policy of the Federal Republic of Germany 1955-1982</u> (in German), (Baden Baden : NOMOS Verlagsgesellschaft, 1983).

2. Reinhard Mutz, <u>The Vienna Negotiations on Troop Reduction in Central Europe</u> (in German), (Baden-Baden : Nomos Verlagsgesellschaft, 1983).

Library services provided for outside researchers : yes

Comments : The Institute began as the Deutsche Hochschule für Politik and was later integrated into the Free University of Berlin as the Otto-Suhr-Institute. Doctoral research on Western security, deterrence, and arms control is supported by a three-year Ford Foundation grant.

DIRECTORY CODE NUMBER : 96

Name of Institution : Institut für Internationales Recht

Address : Christian Albrechts Universität
Olshausenstrasse 40/60
2300 KIEL

Telephone : (431) 880-2149
880-2150

Founding Date : 1913   Founding Place : Kiel

Type of Organization : National Public University

Objectives : Teaching, research, organization of colloquia and conferences.

Director : Prof. Jost Delbrück

Total Staff : 41

Number of researchers on security and defense issues : 3

Projects in Progress : Title

1. Publication of peace and disarmament documents - a collection from five centuries.

Publications (since January 1983)

Hans-Joachim Schütz, <u>Military Confidence-Building Measures from the Perspective of International Law</u> (in German), (Kiel : Institut für Internationales Recht, 1984).

<u>Library services provided for outside researchers</u> : yes

DIRECTORY CODE NUMBER : 97

<u>Name of Institution</u> : Institut für Politikwissenschaft

<u>Address</u> : Universität des Saarlandes
6600 SAARBRUCKEN

<u>Telephone</u> : (681) 302-2126

<u>Founding Date</u> : May 1965   <u>Founding Date</u> : Saarbrücken

<u>Type of organization</u> : National Public University

<u>Objectives</u> : Research and teaching in political science, including problems of European and national security as well as special studies of Chinese and East Asian politics.

Director : Prof. Jürgen Domes

Total Staff : 16

Number of researchers on security and defense issues : 3

Projects in Progress : Title
                                    Name(s) of Researcher(s)

1. Confrontation and co-existence : basic trends of international politics and security since World War II.
   Hans Wassmund

2. Germany as a factor in Soviet-American relations during the period of Cold War and detente.
   Hans Wassmund

3. Contemporary problems of Atlantic relations, European security, and national defense in Europe.
   Armand Clesse

4. The armed forces in the politics of the Chinese People's Republic, 1971-1982.
   Eberhard Sandschneider

Publications (since January 1983)

Armand Clesse (Ed.), Pacifism and the Search for a European Security Order (in German), Sept. 1983.

Collaboration with Foreign Study Centers

Institute for Foreign Policy Analysis (Cambridge, MA, USA) on a project, "International security and national defense projections for the People's Republic of China in the 1980s".

DIRECTORY CODE NUMBER : 98

Name of Institution : Institut für Politische Wissenschaft

Address : Christian-Albrechts-Universität
Olshausenstrasse 40
2300 KIEL 1

Telephone : (431) 880-2169

Founding Date : Jan. 1951   Founding Place : Kiel

Type of Organization : National Public University

Objectives : Teaching, researching, organizing of conferences and the international summer course on security.

Director : Prof. Werner Kaltefleiter

Total Staff : 30

Number of researchers on security and defense issues : 4

Projects in Progress : Title
                          Name(s) of Researcher(s)

1. Arms control as an instrument of Soviet foreign policy.
   Schumacher

2. The nuclear threshold.
   H.J. Fesefeldt

3. Nuclear-free zones.
Oldewurtel

4. INF history.
W. Kaltefleiter
Schumacher

5. Franco-American conflict over strategy.
Prasuhn

6. Case study of enhanced radiation weapons.
Matthée

Regular Periodicals : Title	Founding Date	Issues Annually
Conflict, Options, Strategies in a Threatened World	1982	1

Collaboration with Foreign Study Centers

Cooperation with Institute of Foreign Policy Analysis, Cambridge, Mass.

Library services provided for outside researchers : yes

DIRECTORY CODE NUMBER : 99

Name of Institution : Internationales Institut für Vergleichende
Gesellschaftsforschung (IIVG)

Address : Steinplatz 2
1000 BERLIN 12

Telephone : (30) 313-4801

Founding Date : 1976

Objectives : To conduct comparative social research.

Director : Prof. Karl W. Deutsch

Publications (since January 1983)

1. Security Politics in Crisis ? Elite Opinion in Five Countries :
   Preliminary Results (Berlin : IIVG, 1983) 27 pp.

2. Stuart A. Bremer, "Exploring Paths to International Stability
   with the GLOBUS Model", IIVG/dp 83-112, Sept. 1983, 13 pp.

3. Ulrich Widmaier and Michael Peltzer, "Interstate Conflict and
   Force Elements : Data and Hypotheses" (in German),
   IIVG/dp 83-102, 1983, 36 pp.

DIRECTORY CODE NUMBER : 100

Name of Institution : Konrad Adenauer Stiftung

Address : Sozialwissenschaftliches Forschungsinstitut
Rathausallee 12
5205 SANKT AUGUSTIN 1

Telephone : (2241) 246-0

Founding Date : 1970   Founding Place : Sankt Augustin

Type of Organization : National Private Political-Party-Affiliated

Objectives : Research on international and security policy issues in the East-West context and holding of conferences and colloquia on relevant political issues.

Director : Dr. Hans-Joachim Veen

Total Staff : 4 (in International and Security Studies Division)

Number of researchers on security and defense issues : 2

Projects in Progress : Title
                      Name(s) of Researcher(s)

---

1. Political and strategic implications of space defense.
   Wolfgang Schreiber

2. Determinants of Soviet power and their political implications.
   W. Pfeiler

3. Consequences of the unifying of the START and INF negotiations.
   Wolfgang Schreiber

4. Soviet critiques of German, European, and NATO policy.
   W. Pfeiler

5. Nuclear-weapon-free zones in Europe.

6. German, European and NATO political critiques of the USA.

7. Future of the Atlantic Alliance-Security policy options and structural consequences.

Regular Periodicals : Title	Founding Date	Issues Annually
Forschungsberichten		occasional

Collaboration with Foreign Study Centers

1. CSIS (Georgetown Univ., USA) for a scientific conference on "Foreign Policy Relevance of Internal Policy Issues".

2. Institute for Foreign Policy Analysis (Cambridge, MA) for German-American round-table conferences.

Library services provided for outside researchers : yes

Comments : The Foundation has recently published reports on the future of German-American relations, the NATO "double decision", the determinants of Soviet power, neo-conservatism in the U.S. and its consequences for the Atlantic Alliance, and arguments for peace and freedom.

DIRECTORY CODE NUMBER : 101

Name of Institution : Max Planck Institut für Sozialwissenschaften

Address : Arbeitsgruppe Afheldt
Bahnhofstrasse 7
8130 STARNBERG

Telephone : (8151) 89143

Founding Date : 1970   Founding Place : Starnberg

Type of Organization : National Public

Objectives : The Institute, which succeeded the Max Planck-Institut zur Erforschung der Lebensbedingungen der Wissenschaftlich-technischen Welt, is at present undergoing a reorganization.

Director : Prof. Weinert

Total Staff : 4 (in working group)

Number of researchers on security and defense issues : 2

Projects in Progress : Title
                      Name(s) of Researcher(s)

1. Nuclear war as a political means.
                      Horst Afheldt

2. Practice of a defensive security policy (collection of papers to be published by Sponholtz-Verlag, Hannover).
                      Horst Afheldt et al

Publications (since January 1983)

1. Horst Afheldt, <u>Nuclear War - Political Means ?</u> (in German) (Munich : Hanser-Verlag, 1984).

2. Horst Afheldt, <u>Defensive Defense</u> (<u>Defensive Verteidigung</u>) (Reinbek : Rowohlt, 1983).

3. A. von Müller, <u>The Art of Peace</u> (in German), (München : Carl Hanser Verlag, 1984).

Comments : Dr. Afheldt also contributed a paper on "The Unacceptability of a First-Use-Based Policy for the European NATO-Partners", at the International Seminar on Nuclear War, held at Erice, Italy (Center for Scientific Culture) in August 1982.

DIRECTORY CODE NUMBER : 102

<u>Name of Institution</u> : Seminar für Politische Wissenschaft

<u>Address</u> : Universität Bonn
            Am Hofgarten 15
            5300 BONN

Objectives : Study of contemporary history, comparative politics, international relations, peace and conflict.

DIRECTORY CODE NUMBER : 103

Name of Institution : Sozialwissenschaftlichen Instituts der Bundeswehr (SOWI)

Address : Winzererstrasse 52
8000 MUNCHEN 40

Telephone : (89) 129-9021

Founding Date : 1975   Founding Place : München

Type of Organization : National Public

Objectives : Social research on the military and society.

Director : Ekkehard Lippert (acting)

Total Staff : 50

Number of researchers on security and defense issues : 24

Projects in Progress : Title
                              Name(s) of Researcher(s)

Self-understanding and social image of the officer.
          Heinz-Ulrich Kohr
          Hans-Georg Räder
          Matthias Schönborn
          Günther Wachtler
          Ralf Zoll

Publications (since January 1983)

1. Andrä Simon and Fritz F. Zelinka, <u>1958 to 1980 : Political Formation in the Bundeswehr</u> (in German), (München, 1983) N°29 of the "Berichtsreihe des SOWI", 244 pp.

2. Herbert Kruse, <u>Churches and the Military Institution</u> (in German), (München, 1983) N°30 of the "Berichtsreihe des SOWI", 220 pp.

3. Werner Habermeyer, <u>Military Administration - Outline of a Structural Analysis</u> (in German), (München, 1983) N°31 of the "Berichtsreihe des SOWI", 135 pp.

4. Michael Bührer, <u>Officer of the Bundeswehr : Self-Image and "Other-Image"</u> (in German), (München, 1983) N°32 of the "Berichtsreihe des SOWI", 114 pp.

Collaboration with Foreign Study Centers

International University Seminar on Armed Forces and Society, Chicago, USA.

<u>Library services provided for outside researchers</u> : yes

<u>Comments</u> : SOWI's research is divided into four project areas :
  (1) problems of organization, information and communication in the Bundeswehr;
  (2) the military and society;
  (3) theory and practice of education;
  (4) empirical social research, quantitative procedures, data processing.

DIRECTORY CODE NUMBER : 104

Name of Institution : Studiengesellschaft für Friedensforschung, E.V.

Address : Bernhard-Borst-Strasse 3/II
          8000 MUNCHEN 19

Telephone : (89) 15-37-31

Founding Date : 1958

Type of Organization : National Private Non-Profit

Objectives : To engage in peace education and research.

Publications (since January 1983)

Nuclear Weapons and Conscience (in German), 1983

GREECE

GREECE

At present, Greece has no major independent research institution dealing with security and defense issues. Nonetheless, two organizations have recently been created with the intention of filling part of this gap :
   1) The Hellenic Institute for Defense Studies, formed in January 1984, which is a collaboration of independent experts interested in developing a Greek perspective on these problems;
   2) The Hellenic Society of International Law and Relations, established in 1982, which is making a concerted effort to provide a shelter for research and study of current questions of international law and relations.

These two private, non-profit bodies are basically study groups consisting of university-level academics and civil servants. Before their creation, security and defense research was carried out exclusively by individual scholars. These individuals still make important contributions to the Greek debate on these questions : for example, Prof. Theodore A. Couloumbis of the University of Thessaloniki has written <u>U.S., Greece and Turkey : The Troubled Triangle</u> (1983) among other books and has taught at American universities. The study of international relations had, until very late, been submerged in the international law faculties. At the University of Athens, the Department of Political Science has finally succeeded in gaining autonomous status. Another university-level institution, the Pantios School of Political Science, is primarily devoted to teaching public administration and training future civil servants. Faculty members at both these schools play instrumental roles in the two new research groups listed above.

Other sources of security and defense research include the National Defence College and two small "think tanks" attached to the main political parties (PASOK and New Democracy).

DIRECTORY CODE NUMBER : 105

Name of Institution : Foundation for Mediterranean Studies

Address : 2 Lykavittou Street
ATHENS

Director : Lina Bozer

DIRECTORY CODE NUMBER : 106

Name of Institution : Hellenic Institute for Defense Studies

Address : Faculty of Political Science
c/o Prof. Thanos Veremis
University of Athens
19 Omirou Street
ATHENS 135

Telephone : (1) 8131-223

Founding Date : Jan. 1984   Founding Place : Athens

Type of Organization : National Private Non-Profit

Objectives : The study of security and defense issues with special reference to the Mediterranean region.

Directors : Athanasios Platyas, Thanos Veremis, John Roubatis, Paris Kitsos, Yannis Valinakis

Total Staff : 10

Number of researchers on security and defense issues : 10

Projects in Progress : Title

Greek and Turkish security issues.

Library services provided for outside researchers : yes

DIRECTORY CODE NUMBER : 107

Name of Institution : Hellenic Society of International Law and Relations

Address : 6 Kriezotou Street
ATHENS

Telephone : (1) 3632-671

Founding Date : 1982   Founding Place : Athens

Type of Organization : National Private Non-Profit

Objectives : (1) study and research on international law and relations;
(2) elaboration of proposals concerning Greek international relations;
(3) cooperation with national and international bodies on matters of international law and relations.

President : Prof. Christos L. Rozakis

Total Staff : 25

Number of researchers on security and defense issues : 6

Projects in Progress : Title
                      Name(s) of Researcher(s)

1. The Cyprus question : legal and political dimensions.
   C. Economides/C. Varvitsiotou/
   E. Ioannou/G. Tsaltas et al

2. Greek parliament and foreign policy.
   D. Constas/T. Couloumbis/
   C. Rozakis/G. Papadimitriou/
   M. Conallis et al

3. Turkish foreign policy since the end of the Second World War.
   G. Tenerides/T. Veremis/
   P. Uitromilides/C. Bouras et al

Regular Periodicals : Title	Founding Date	Issues Annually
International Law and Politics (in Greek)	Oct. 1984 (to appear)	1

Collaboration with Foreign Study Centers

1. Institut du droit de la paix et du développement, Nice, France.
2. CEDSI, Université de Grenoble, France.
3. Observatoire stratégique méditerranéen.

DIRECTORY CODE NUMBER : 108

Name of Institution : Institute of Public International Law and International Relations

Address : School of Law and Economics
University of Thessaloniki
THESSALONIKI

Director : Prof. Dimitri Constantopoulos

Regular Periodicals : Title	Founding Date	Issues Annually
Hellenic Review of International Relations	1980	2

Other Publications (since January 1983)

1. Theodore A. Couloumbis, *U.S., Greece and Turkey : The Troubled Triangle* (N.Y. : Praeger, 1983).

2. Theodore A. Couloumbis, "The Structures of Greek Foreign Policy" in Richard Clogg (Ed.), *Greece in the 1980s*, (London : Macmillan 1983), pp. 95-122.

3. Theodore A. Couloumbis and Prodromos M. Yannis, "The Stability Quotient of Greece's Post-1974 Democratic Institutions", *Journal of Modern Greek Studies*, Dec. 1983, pp. 359-372.

ICELAND

ICELAND

Iceland is the only country in NATO with no military force of its own. Nonetheless, it plays a major role in North Atlantic strategy with its central geographic position in the Greenland-Iceland-United Kingdom (GIUK) "choke point". The American base at Keflavik attests to Iceland's importance in guarding sea lanes of communication and acting as a bridgehead for NATO reinforcement operations.

The maintenance of the Keflavik base remains the most controversial Icelandic security issue. Since the country has no national military establishment, it has lacked strategic expertise in assessing the repercussions of its security and defense policy. Recognizing this gap, the Icelandic government set up the Commission on Security and International Affairs in 1979. The Commission, consisting of two members from each of the four political parties, conducts a research program on issues of arms control, Icelandic security, and related issues. According to its director, the Commission seeks "to stimulate discussions on national security affairs" by publishing reports which "may be interpreted as reflecting a consensus by the political parties that (the report) constitutes an acceptable basis for a debate on that particular subject". (Gunnar Gunnarsson, "Icelandic Security Policy : Context and Trends", <u>Cooperation and Conflict</u>, XVII, 1982, p. 268).

DIRECTORY CODE NUMBER : 109

Name of Institution : Faculty of Social Sciences

Address : University of Iceland.
REYKJAVIK

Telephone : (1) 24717

Projects in Progress : Title
                        Name(s) of Researcher(s)

Political attitudes and voting in Iceland (with attention to Icelandic membership in NATO, Keflavik base, peace movement, Nordic nuclear-free zone).
                        Olafur Hardarson

DIRECTORY CODE NUMBER : 110

Name of Institution : Icelandic Commission on Security and International Affairs

Address : Laugavegur 170
REYKJAVIK

Telephone : (1) 25612

Founding Date : 1979   Founding Place : Reykjavik

Type of Organization : National Public

Objectives : To conduct research into national and international security affairs and provide information through publications.

Director : Gunnar Gunnarsson

Total Staff : 2

Number of researchers on security and defense issues : 2

Projects in Progress : Title	Name(s) of Researcher(s)

1. Arms control and disarmament
   Gunnar Gunnarsson
2. Soviet military strategy.
   Thordur Oskarsson
3. Bilateral arms control agreements.
   Albert Jónsson
4. Multilateral arms control agreements.
   Thordur Gudmundsson
5. Icelandic security policy.
   Gunnar Gunnarsson
6. Survey of public opinion in Iceland relating to foreign and security policy.
   Olafur Hardarson

Publications (since January 1983)

1. Albert Jónsson, <u>Nuclear Weapons and Nuclear Strategy</u> (in Icelandic, with summary in English), <u>Research Reports</u>, N°4, 1984.

2. Gunnar Gunnarsson, <u>The Atlantic Alliance and the No-First-Use Debate</u> (in Icelandic), <u>Research Papers</u>, N°1, 1984.

<u>Library services provided for outside researchers</u> : yes

IRELAND

IRELAND

Ireland is the one European Community nation that is not a member of NATO and is therefore politically neutral. The critical factor in Ireland's refusal to join NATO in 1949 was the partition of the island and Britain's "occupation" (in Irish eyes) of the six Northern countries. The festering sectarian strife in Northern Ireland has confronted the Dublin government with a fundamental security problem. The Irish have proposed a series of political solutions (most recently through the Forum report), yet nothing concrete has materialized. There is an obvious need for serious research to define long-term policy options and assess the state of public opinion on security and defense issues. Any future plan for European defense cooperation (through the EC) would present Ireland with a number of difficult choices.

Unfortunately, in the words of Prof. Patrick Keatinge of Trinity College, "there simply is no academic research institution which is concerned with European security as such, or even with International Relations in general". Prof. Keatinge is undertaking his own research on the Irish role at the Stockholm conference on European disarmament and on the latest propositions of the Irish Forum regarding the future of Northern Ireland. In addition, the International Relations Committee of the Royal Irish Academy holds some seminars on security issues and funds research in the field. But it does not perform the task of providing long-range thinking to assist government policy.

DIRECTORY CODE NUMBER : 111

Name of Institution : Department of Political Science

Address : Trinity College
          DUBLIN 2

Telephone : (1) 77-29-41

Founding Place : Dublin

Type of Organization : University

Contact : Prof. Patrick Keatinge

Total Staff : 6

Number of researchers on security and defense issues : 1

Projects in Progress : Title
                              Name(s) of Researcher(s)

1. Conference on Disarmament in Europe (CDE) : Irish positions vis-à-vis the EC countries and the neutral and non-aligned countries.
                              Patrick Keatinge

2. The New Irish Forum : the strategic dimension in Anglo-Irish relations.
                              Patrick Keatinge

Publications (since January 1983)

1. Patrick Keatinge, "Ireland : Neutrality inside EPC" in Christopher Hill (Ed.), National Foreign Policies and European Political Cooperation (London : Allen and Unwin, 1983).

2. Patrick Keatinge, A Singular Stance : Irish Neutrality in the 1980s (Dublin : Institute of Public Administration, 1984)

Collaboration with Foreign Study Centers

Participant in European Foreign Policy Study-Group, organized by the Institut für Europaïsche Politik (Bonn) and the Trans-European Policy Studies Association (TEPSA).

Library services provided for outside researchers : yes

DIRECTORY CODE NUMBER : 112

Name of Institution : International Relations Committee of the Royal Irish Academy

Address : 19 Dawson Street
          DUBLIN 2

Director : Patrick Keatinge

Comments : The Committee sponsors some research of international relations and holds discussions of papers on security and disarmament.

ITALY

ITALY

Security and defense research in Italy has developed extensively over the past few years. Military-related studies had fallen into discredit following the collapse of the Fascist regime, and during the late 1940's a defense consensus based on NATO integration prevailed. In the words of one scholar, "Italian military policy seemed to vanish in a sort of permanent delegation of authority, in an identification of aims and interests, and in a too frequently uncritical acceptance of NATO decisions (in which Italy had a voice), even of those which were potentially expensive and not altogether justifiable in terms of operational requirements". (Maurizio Cremasco, "The Issue of Strategic Studies in Italy", in Trend in Strategic Studies (Turin : Centro Studi Manlio Brosio, 1982) p. 38). Furthermore, as in other European countries, both the military and university hierarchies were hostile to policy-oriented research on these issues.

Lately, the defense consensus has come under challenge, and a number of independent, university, and political party-affiliated study centers have been established. The challenge arose partially from the crisis over the Euromissiles, but also from the public recognition that Italy exists in an interdependent world and that the various global forces at work require careful examination. Yet Italian defense policymaking still remains the responsibility of a relatively closed circle of military and ministry experts and is, for the most part, impervious to external analysis.

In Italy, there is no single private research organization that dominates the field of international studies (unlike the case in many European countries). The most prominent institutions are the Istituto Affari Internazionali (IAI), the Instituto per gli Studi di Politica Internazionale (ISPI), the Società Italiana per l'Organizzazione Internazionale (SIOI), and the Istituto per le Relazioni tra l'Italia e i Paesi dell'Africa, America Latina e Medio Oriente (IPALMO). The IAI (founded in 1965) has perhaps the strongest network of international contacts and is most often called upon to represent the Italian point-of-view at conferences abroad. The Institute's security studies program is designed to introduce these subjects into an environment where, according to the IAI Director, "they were unknown by the majority, misunderstood by the Catholic and Socialist pacifist tradition, and studied for professional purposes only by the military". One focus has been on security problems in the Mediterranean and in the Middle East (particularly the Red Sea region). The AIA's quarterly journal has been published in English since 1982, thereby increasing its global audience.

ISPI is much older (having been founded in 1933 by a group of anti-Fascists) and publishes the authoritative weekly Relazioni Internazionali. In addition, it operates advanced postgraduate courses for Italian foreign service officers. The SIOI, also created by opponents of Fascism in 1944, has primary responsibility for training Italian personnel interested in careers in international organizations. In addition, the Society sponsors conferences on defense-related topics, publishes a quarterly review, La Communità Internazionale, and does research on international conflict. For its part, IPALMO is more concerned with Italian relations with the Third World, but also does research work on subjects like the Persian Gulf crisis.

Other centers concentrate entirely on security and defense problems. The most important of these centers, the Istituto Studi e Ricerche Difesa (ISTRID), created in 1979, is dedicated to promoting a constructive dialogue between civilian society and the military world through publications, conferences, debates, and round-table discussions. Its major publication, the fortnightly Informazioni Parlamentari Difesa, attempts to analyze complicated defense issues in terms understandable to parlementarians and to the general public. The director, Sen. Paolo Vittorelli, contributed to the twenty-sixth report of the Trilateral Commission on "trilateral security". In Turin, the Centro Studi Manlio Brosio has published the proceedings of two conferences on problems of strategic studies (in English) and has just launched the quarterly Rivista Italiana di Strategia Globale.

Academics have also demonstrated a growing interest in security questions and have begun to organize themselves in university "think tanks". Among these must be mentioned the Free University of Rome's Centro di Studi Strategici (whose director, Enrico Jacchia, often participates in major international conferences), Genoa's Centro Studi sulla Difesa (which recently co-sponsored a colloquium on NATO's southern flank with Kent State University), Florence's Centro Analizi Relazioni Internazionali, Turin's Centro Studi e Documentazione Internazionale, Milan's Gruppo di Studio su Armi e Disarmo, and Pisa's Centro Interuniversitario di Studi e Ricerche Storico-Militari. Peace research is less highly developed than in Northern European countries; the main centers are the Istituto Italiano Ricerca sulla Pace (IPRI) in Naples and the International School on Disarmament and Arms Control (ISODARCO) in Rome. Two international organizations, the NATO Defense College and the Bologna Center of The Johns Hopkins University, must also be noted in any analysis of security and defense research based in Italy.

Another source of defense thinking is the group of centers affiliated with political parties. The Communist Party's Centro Studi di Politica Internazionale has produced a number of studies critical of the NATO Euromissile decision. The Istituto di Ricerca per il Disarmo, lo Sviluppo e la Pace (IRDISP), associated with the Radical Party, has published analyses of the Italian defense budget and military force structure (translated into English) as well as a special study, What the Russians Know Already and the Italians Must Not Know. The group, Archivo Disarmo, affiliated with the Independent Left, produces a series of information sheets on the Italian "military-industrial complex", nuclear "no-first-use" doctrine in Europe, the defense budget process, and other topics. By contrast, the Christian Democratic and Socialist Parties appear to rely primarily on individual specialists from the larger independent research institutions.

For all its domestic political instability, Italy has had a remarkable degree of continuity in its foreign and defense policies. It remains a solid member of both NATO and the European Community--notwithstanding all the crises that these international structures have faced. But these policies are now--for the first time--coming under close public scrutiny, and the proliferation of research centers (of all denominations) is one indicator of this democratization process. The policymaking elite cannot afford to continue to ignore this valuable source of expertise representing the latest national and international thinking and the diverse currents in public opinion.

DIRECTORY CODE NUMBER : 113

Name of Institution : Archivio Disarmo : Centro Studi e Documentazione sulla Pace e sul Disarmo

Address : Via di Torre Argentina, 18
00186 ROMA

Telephone : (6) 655-447

Founding Date : April 1982   Founding Place : Roma

Type of Organization : National Private Non-Profit

Objectives : Peace research (providing information concerning peace and defense with special emphasis on specifically Italian issues).

Director : Dr. Fabrizio Battistelli

Total Staff : 6

Number of researchers on security and defense issues : 3

Projects in Progress : Title
                       Name(s) of Researcher(s)

1. The economic characteristics of the Italian armaments industry : prospects for reconversion.
   Carlo Presciuttini

2. The peace movement and the information problem in Italy.
   Fabrizio Battistelli

3. Parliament, the Government and military administration : defense policy in Italy.
   Fabrizio Battistelli
   Carlo Presciuttini et al

4. Constitutional aspects of the installation of Euromissiles in Italy.
   Carlo Crocella

5. Legal and sociological aspects of conscientious objection in Italy.
   Maurizio Simoncelli
   Giorgio Giannini

Regular Periodicals : Title   Founding Date   Issues Annually

Archivio Disarmo does not publish a regular periodical. Rather it concentrates on the production of information sheets on a wide range of topics, e.g. conscientious objection in Italy, Italian defense budgets, the Italian military industry, the debate on "first use" in Europe, etc.

Other Publications (since January 1983)

Italian edition of SIPRI, The Arms Race and Arms Control 1982 (Bari : De Donato, 1983); 1984 edition under translation.

Library services provided for outside researchers : yes

Comments : Archivio Disarmo is associated politically with the Independent Left.

DIRECTORY CODE NUMBER : 114

Name of Institution : Associazione Italiana Studi di Politica Estera (AISPE)

Address : Via Monte Zebio, 24
00195 ROMA

Founding Date : 1968   Founding Place : Roma

President : Giuseppe Medici

Regular Periodicals : Title	Founding date	Issues Annually
Affari Esteri		4

DIRECTORY CODE NUMBER : 115

<u>Name of Institution</u> : Bologna Center of the Johns Hopkins University

<u>Address</u> : Via Belmeloro, 11
         40126 BOLOGNA

<u>Telephone</u> : (51)232-185/6/7/8/9

<u>Founding Date</u> : 1955   <u>Founding Place</u> : Bologna

<u>Type of Organization</u> : International Private University

<u>Objectives</u> : To provide advanced professional training, to conduct scholarly research and to provide special educational opportunities to experts already working in appropriate fields.

<u>Director</u> : Dr. Robert G. Gard, Jr.

Regular Periodicals : Title	Founding Date	Issues Annually
Occasional Papers		

Library services provided for outside researchers : yes

Comments : The Center is an integral part of the Johns Hopkins School of Advanced International Studies, and it is the only resident American graduate school of international studies in Europe.

DIRECTORY CODE NUMBER : 116

Name of Institution : Centro Alti Studi Difesa

Address : Ministry of Defense
ROMA

Type of Organization : National Public

Objectives : To provide a defense college for colonels and one-star general officers and high civil servants of the Ministries of Defense, Foreign Affairs, Home Affairs and Finance (with nine-month courses and also workshops on specific topics).

Comments : The Center has published proceedings of its 1982-83 sessions on NATO strategic concepts for the 1990s and on potential consequences of NATO "out-of-area" operations.

DIRECTORY CODE NUMBER : 117

Name of Institution : Centro Analizi Relazioni Internazionali (CARI)

Address : Univ. di Firenze
Via Laura, 60
50121 FIRENZE

Telephone : (55) 28-28-66

Director : Prof. Umberto Gori

DIRECTORY CODE NUMBER : 118

Name of Institution : Centro di Studi Strategici

Address : Libera Università Internazionale di Studi Sociale
Viale Gorizia, 17
00198 ROMA

Telephone : (6) 841-051

Founding Date : 1980   Founding Place : Roma

Type of Organization : National Private University

Objectives : Research on foreign policy and defense.

Director : Prof. Enrico Jacchia

Number of researchers on security and defense issues : 3

Regular Periodicals : Title	Founding Date	Issues Annually
Politica Estera e di Difesa	1981	1

Other Publications (since January 1983)

Chemical Weapons and Arms Control. Views from Europe
(Roma : LUISS, 1983) 72 pp.

DIRECTORY CODE NUMBER : 119

Name of Institution : Centro Internazionale di Cultura Scientifica
"Ettore Majorana"

Address : ERICE (TRAPANI)

Founding Date : 1981

Type of Organization : National Private Non-Profit

Director : Prof. Antonino Zichichi

Publications (since January 1983)

Third International Seminar : Technical Basis for Peace
(in Italian), August 1983.

Comments : The Center has organized two other international seminars on "Global Implications of a Nuclear War" in 1981 and 1982. Participants included Edward Teller, Isidor Rabi, Alfred Kastler, Richard Garwin, Oleg Bykof and Piotr Kapitza.

DIRECTORY CODE NUMBER : 120

Name of Institution : Centro Interuniversitario di Studi e Ricerche
Storico-Militari

Address : Department of Modern History
Univ. di Pisa
Piazza Torricelli 2
PISA

Telephone : 501012

Founding Date : 1981   Founding Place : Pisa

Director : Prof. Filippo Frassati

Projects in Progress : Title

Bibliography of Italian military history over last century.

DIRECTORY CODE NUMBER : 121

Name of Institution : Centro Studi e Documentazione Internazionale (CESDI)

Address : Univ. di Torino
           Via Caboto, 44
           10129 TORINO

Telephone : (11) 581-679

Founding Date : 1980   Founding Place : Torino

Type of Organization : National Public University

Objectives : Research and information on economic, political, strategic and industrial problems.

Director : Prof. Giovanni Bressi

DIRECTORY CODE NUMBER : 122

Name of Institution : Centro Studi Manlio Brosio

Address : Corso Re Umberto, 29 bis
           10128 TORINO

Telephone : (11) 548-597

Founding Date : Feb. 1981   Founding Place : Torino

Type of Organization : National Private Non-Profit

Objectives : To carry on the work of Manlio Brosio (former NATO Secretary-General) and to undertake studies of international relations and economic, social, historical, juridical and military disciplines.

Director : Carlo Carducci

Regular Periodicals : Title	Founding Date	Issues Annually
Rivista Italiana di Strategia Globale	1984	4

Other Publications (since January 1983)

Trend in Strategic Studies : University, Armed Forces and Industry Between Antagonism and Collaboration ("Politica Militare" series, 1983, proceedings of international conference, Dec. 1982).

Library services provided for outside researchers : yes

Comments : The Center also sponsored an international conference on "Contemporary Strategic Studies : Scientific Methods and Implementation" in Dec. 1983. Some of the papers have been published in the first issue of the Rivista Italiana di Strategia Globale.

DIRECTORY CODE NUMBER : 123

Name of Institution : Centro Studi Politica Internazionale (CESPI)

Address : Viale IV Novembre, 114
00187 ROMA

Telephone : (6) 679-3705

Founding Date : 1978

Type of Organization : National Private Party-Affiliated

Objectives : To fill need to create a separate Communist apparatus for policy studies and recommendations.

Director : Romano Ledda

Comments : CESPI was founded by the initiative of the Italian Communist Party. The Center's research program concentrates on disarmament and the European Left, but has also done work on North-South relations, the Law of the Sea, China and post-Maoism, and reciprocal security perceptions between the U.S. and the U.S.S.R.

DIRECTORY CODE NUMBER : 124

Name of Institution : Centro Studi sulla Difesa

Address : Univ. di Genova
Via Balbi 6
16126 GENOVA

Telephone : (10) 29-66-07

Founding Date : Nov. 1980   Founding Place : Genova

Type of organization : National Public University

Objectives : To foster the collaboration between universities and armed forces in studying defense problems.

Director : Prof. Raimondo Luraghi

Total Staff : 4

Number of researchers on security and defense issues : 2

Projects in Progress : Title	Name(s) of Researcher(s)

1. U.S. military policy and the defense of Western Europe.
   Raimondo Luraghi

2. Italian armaments industry.
   M. Nones

Collaboration with Foreign Study Centers

Kent State University - conference on NATO's southern flank at Bellagio, Italy (March 1983).

Library services provided for outside researchers : yes

DIRECTORY CODE NUMBER : 125

Name of Institution : Gruppo di Studio su Armi e Disarmo

Address : Università Cattolica
         Istituto di Economia
         Largo Agostino Gemelli, 1
         20123 MILANO

Telephone : (2) 8856458

Founding Date : 1979   Founding Place : Milano

Type of Organization : National Private University

Director : Prof. Giancarlo Graziola

DIRECTORY CODE NUMBER : 126

Name of Institution : International School on Disarmament and
                      Arms Control (ISODARCO)

Address : c/o Istituto di Fisica
          Univ. di Roma
          Piazzale Aldo Moro 2
          00185 ROMA

Telephone : (6) 497-6350

Founding Date : 1966   Founding Place : Roma

Type of Organization : International Private Non-Profit

Director : Prof. Carlo Schaerf

Comments : ISODARCO runs annual summer courses on arms control
           and disarmament. It is affiliated with the Union degli
           Scienziati per il Disarmo (USPID) which organized an
           international conference on the risks of nuclear war in
           Bologna in June 1983.

DIRECTORY CODE NUMBER : 127

Name of Institution : Istituto Affari Internazionali (IAI)

Address : 88, Viale Mazzini
          00195 ROMA

Telephone : (6) 315-892
            (6) 354-456

Founding Date : 1965   Founding Place : Roma

Type of Organization : National Private Non-Profit

Objectives : The IAI was founded with the purpose of promoting
             knowledge of problems of international politics through
             research and the organization of conferences.

Director : Roberto Aliboni

Total Staff : 12

Number of researchers on security and defense issues : 3

Projects in Progress : Title	Name(s) of Researcher(s)
An Italian intervention force : a case study.	M. Cremasco/L. Caligaris

Regular Periodicals : Title	Founding Date	Issues Annually
1. The International Spectator	1983	4
2. Italia nella Politica Internazionale (yearbook)	1972	1
3. IAI Informa	1969	4

Other Publications (since January 1983)

1. S. Silvestri, "Italian Foreign Policy and the Middle East", Doc. IAI/8/83, 10 pp.

2. Mario Zucconi, "The Politics of Dissension in European-American Relations : New American Perceptions of the Global Balance and the Regional Balance", (in Italian), Doc. IAI/15/83, 18 pp.

3. Gianluca Devoto, "The Evolution of NATO Doctrine : Towards an Abandonment of Flexible Response ?" (in Italian), Doc. IAI/16/83, 27 pp.

4. Marco de Andreis, "The New Military Technology and the Conventional Option", (in Italian), Doc. IAI/20/83, 23 pp.

5. Luigi Caligaris, "Significance and Role of the INF with Particular Reference to the European Theater", (in Italian), Doc. IAI/21/83, 14 pp.

6. G. Bonvicini, "The Proposals for Institutional Organization of European Defense", Doc. IAI/24/83, 17 pp.

Library services provided for outside researchers : yes

Comments : The IAI has just completed research projects on "Development and Stability in the Mediterranean", "Growing Economic Interdependence and the Future of Security in the Mediterranean", and "Red Sea Conflict and Cooperation : Regional Balance and Strategic Implications" (the latter in cooperation with the Centre for Political and Strategic Studies, Al Ahram Foundation of Cairo and the Deutsches Orient Institut of Hamburg).

DIRECTORY CODE NUMBER : 128

Name of Institution : Istituto di Ricerca per il Disarmo, lo Sviluppo e la Pace (IRDISP)

Address : Via Principe Amedeo, 168
00185 ROMA

Telephone : (6) 733-676

Founding Date : 1981   Founding Place : Roma

Type of Organization : National Political Party-Affiliated

Objectives : To study international relations, with special reference to the arms race, and the elaboration of proposals for disarmament and for the conversion of military structures and industry into civilian ones; the study of development in the Third World; the promotion of human rights; and the planning and carrying out of peace education.

Director : Roberto Cicciomessere

Total Staff : 6

Number of researchers on security and defense issues : 5

Projects in Progress : Title	Name(s) of Researcher(s)

1. The Italian military budget : a critical review of defense policy, development of military expenditures from 1970 to 1982, and projection of trends for the foreseeable future.
   Roberto Cicciomessere

2. The forces of the Republic : a revision--in light of the 1983 defense budget--of the analysis of Italian military expenditures.
   Marco de Andreis

3. Italian military budget : computerized analysis from 1980 to 1984.
   Alessandra Labbate
   Maurizio Zucchetti

4. Analysis of Italian military manufacturing industries.
   Maurizio Zucchetti

Publications (since January 1983)

1. Marco de Andreis, <u>The Forces of the Republic</u> (in English and Italian), 1983.

2. William M. Arkin, Richard Fieldhouse and Antonio de Marchi, <u>What the Russians Know Already and the Italians Must Not Know</u> (in English and Italian), 1984.

3. Wassily Leontief and Faye Duchin, <u>Military Spending</u> (in Italian), 1984.

Library services provided for outside researchers : yes

Comments : The IRDISP published a major study of the Italian military budget (in English and Italian) in 1982 (by Roberto Cicciomessere). Cicciomessere and Antonio de Marchi have collaborated on a detailed map of all military forces present on Italian territory (location, organization, number of personnel, number and type of nuclear and conventional armaments).

DIRECTORY CODE NUMBER : 129

Name of Institution : Istituto Italiano di Polemologia e di Ricerche sui Conflitti (ISIP)

Address : Via Arco 1
20121 MILANO

Director : F. Fornari

DIRECTORY CODE NUMBER : 130

Name of Institution : Istituto Italiano Ricerca sulla Pace (IPRI)

Address : Largo S. Gennaro a Materdei, 3/A
NAPOLI

Telephone : (81) 342-259

Founding Date : 1977

Type of Organization : National Private Non-Profit

Objectives : To provide linkage between researchers involved in disarmament research, peace education and development education, and to create research networks related to these topics among Italian universities.

Director : Mario Borrelli

Number of researchers on security and defense issues : 3

Publications (since January 1983)

1. Mario Borrelli, "Italian Peace Research Institute", <u>International Peace Research Newsletter</u>, Vol. XXI, N°1, 1983, pp. 19-24.

2. A. Drago and G. Salio, <u>Science and War-Physics Against Nuclear War</u> (in Italian), (Torino : Ed. Abele, 1983).

3. A. Drago, "Towards a Political Program for a Popular Non-Violent Defense", <u>Gandhi Marg</u>, Jan. 1983, p. 41

4. A. Drago, "The Peace of the People and the Peace of the Powers" (in Italian), <u>Azione Nonviolenta</u>, May 1983.

<u>Library services provided for outside researchers</u> : yes

<u>Comments</u> : IPRI came into being more as an association of researchers interested in the study of social conflicts and methodologies for resolving them than as a teaching institute. It is affiliated with the International Peace Research Association and other peace research organizations.

DIRECTORY CODE NUMBER : 131

<u>Name of Institution</u> : Istituto per gli Studi di Politica Internazionale (ISPI)

<u>Address</u> : Via Clerici 5
          20121 MILANO

<u>Telephone</u> : (2) 87-82-66

<u>Founding Date</u> : 1933   <u>Founding Place</u> : Milano

<u>Type of Organization</u> : National Private Non-Profit

<u>Objectives</u> : To study problems of international politics and disseminate knowledge on these problems.

<u>Director</u> : Dr. Giovanni Lovisetti

<u>Total Staff</u> : 25

<u>Number of researchers on security and defense issues</u> : 5

Regular Periodicals : Title	Founding Date	Issues Annually
<u>Relazioni internazionali</u>	1936	52

Other Publications (since January 1983)

Soviet Military Power (in Italian).

Library services provided for outside researchers : yes

Comments : ISPI also offers training courses for future diplomats (in cooperation with the Foreign Ministry).
It co-sponsored (with the U.S. Information Service) a conference on armaments, disarmament and peace in May 1983.

DIRECTORY CODE NUMBER : 132

Name of Institution : Istituto per le Relazioni tra l'Italia e i Paesi dell' Africa, America Latina e Medio Oriente (IPALMO)

Address : Via del Tritone 62-B
00187 ROMA

Telephone : (6) 679-2734   679-2321
679-2311

Founding Date : 1971   Founding Place : Roma

Type of Organization : National Private Non-Profit

Objectives : To promote in Italy a deeper and more correct knowledge of the political, economic, and cultural problems concerning developing countries; to implement all possible joint initiatives between Italy and these countries.

Director : Giampaolo Calchi Novati

total Staff : 11

umber of researchers on security and defense issues : 0

Projects in Progress : Title

1. Debt problems of developing countries and policies of Italy and Europe.
2. Process of change in Southern Africa.
3. Economic relations between Italy and Algeria.

Regular Periodicals : Title	Founding Date	Issues Annually
Politica Internazionale (with two issues published annually in English)	1971	12

Other Publications (since January 1983)

The Gulf of Crisis : Tensions and Italian Policy in the Arabic Gulf (in Italian).

Library services provided for outside researchers : yes

Comments : IPALMO also arranges exchanges between Italian groups and working-class delegations from the Third World, and undertakes parliamentary lobbying activities on Third World issues.

DIRECTORY CODE NUMBER : 133

Name of Institution : Istituto Studi e Ricerche Difesa (ISTRID)

Address : Via Maria Adelaide 4/6
ROMA

Telephone : (6) 360-06-74
(6) 361-21-88

Founding Date : 1979   Founding Place : Roma

Type of Organization : National Private Non-Profit

Objectives : To study problems of politics, of security and of
defense programming.

President : Sen. Paolo Battino Vittorelli

Projects in Progress : Title

1. The arms race and the reciprocal balance.
2. Military budgets, posture, and strategy of the major nations.
3. Dynamics and dimensions of regional conflicts.
4. Regulation of armed forces.
5. Role of defense industries in political process (in Italy and globally).

Regular Periodicals : Title	Founding Date	Issues Annually
1. Informazioni Parlamentari Difesa	1979	26
2. Annuario		1

Comments : The governing board consists of the heads of the defense
bureaus of all democratic parties. ISTRID's Agenzia Informazioni Parlamentari Difesa is designed to keep the press
and the public informed on the latest defense issues
confronting Italy. The Institute also sponsors a series
of conferences, including one on military strategy (with
the SIOI) in 1983.

DIRECTORY CODE NUMBER : 134

Name of Institution : NATO Defense College

Address : Viale della Civiltà del Lavoro, 38
00144 ROMA

Telephone : (6) 592-3741

Founding Date : 1951   Founding Place : Paris

Type of Organization : International Public

Objectives : To conduct informative courses of study on military,
political, economic, technological, geographical, sociological and psychological factors and problems which
affect or may affect NATO.

Director : Lt. Gen. Uhle-Wettler

Projects in Progress : Title
                                Name(s) of Researcher(s)

---

1. Italian peace movement.
                        Hans E. Radbruch

2. Social change in the Italian military.
                        Hans E. Radbruch

Collaboration with Foreign Study Centers

1. U.S. Army War College on Strategy and its development.
2. University of Edinburgh, Defence Studies Centre on Soviet strategy.

Library services provided for outside researchers : yes

Comments : The College is a NATO institution under the direction of the NATO Military Committee. The course program is designed for military officers and civil servants of the member countries. Plans for a College series of publications are under examination.

DIRECTORY CODE NUMBER : 135

Name of Institution : Società Italiana per l'Organizzazione Internazionale (SIOI)

Address : Palazzetto di Venezia
via di San Marco 3
00186 ROMA

Telephone : (6) 679-3566
(6) 679-3949

Founding Date : 1945

Type of Organization : National Private Non-Profit

Objectives : To promote the development of an international spirit overcoming the particularism inspired by the absolute sovereignty of states.

Director : Prof. Franco Alberto Casadio

Regular Periodicals : Title	Founding Date	Issues Annually
1. La Communità Internazionale	1945	4
2. Documenti	1957	occasional
3. Studi	1949	occasional

Other Publications (since January 1983)

Franco Alberto Casadio, World Conflicts and International Relations 1945-1982 (Padova : Cedam, 1983) 298 pp.

Library services provided for outside researchers : yes

Comments : SIOI sponsors conferences and provides documentation on issues like the peacekeeping role of the U.N. and other international organizations; human rights; European security and disarmament; and European integration. The Society also runs specialized courses for civil servants interested in pursuing international careers.

LUXEMBOURG

LUXEMBOURG

The Treaty of London in 1867 recognized the full independence of Luxembourg and also guaranteed the Grand Duchy's perpetual neutrality. This policy of neutrality was formally abandoned when Luxembourg became a charter member of NATO in 1949. Luxembourg is also an active member of the European Community and the seat of the European Court of Justice and other European organizations.

The private European Institute for Security Matters, founded in 1981, is located in Luxembourg. According to its statutes, the Institute "is a non-party organization committed to the principles of freedom and democracy". The Institute intends to produce policy-oriented research : "As well as influencing public opinion at the European level, these works will also clarify the security objectives of the partner states of NATO and new security structures to be created within the context of the European Community". The founding members (from eight EC countries) include university professors and professionals, retired military officers, and eighteen members of the European Parliament, such as Kai-Uwe von Kassel, Dr. Otto von Habsburg, Pierre Pfimlin, and Belgian Foreign Minister Leo Tindemans.

DIRECTORY CODE NUMBER : 136

Name of Institution : European Institute for Security Matters (EIS)

Address : Schuman Building
Third Floor, 3/92
Plateau Kirchberg
LUXEMBURG

Telephone : 43 00/21 41

Founding Date : Dec. 1981   Founding Place : Luxembourg

Type of Organization : International Private Non-Profit

Objectives : To maintain the freedom of Europe. To this effect, the Institute will produce proposals for objectives and analyses for the policy-making bodies in Europe as decision-making aids in the form of studies, publications, seminars, and books.

Director : Jan Christian Blohm

NETHERLANDS

NETHERLANDS

On June 14th, the Dutch Parliament endorsed--by a 79 to 71 vote--the Government proposal to delay deployment of cruise missiles in the Netherlands until 1988. The final decision, to be made by November 1, 1985, will depend on progress in Soviet-American arms limitation talks (specifically whether or not the USSR insists on deploying more SS-20 missiles in the interim). The vote brought to a conclusion one stage of a fierce debate over Dutch security and defense policy. The Netherlands has an active, well-organized anti-missile movement, backed by church groups and a number of serious research institutions. Public opinion polls show that more than 60 percent of the Dutch people oppose the deployment, though approximately 75 percent approve continued membership in NATO. The Christian Democratic-Liberal coalition, seriously strained by the crisis, put forward the compromise plan to preserve the government and postpone the inevitable choice. The opposition Labor Party rejects the cruise missiles, and the whole question of Dutch security has become a major political issue. The Netherlands is the first NATO country to diverge from the 1979 intermediate nuclear force agreement, and its decision could have a significant impact on its neighbors.

Not surprisingly, much of the security research deals with problems associated with the missile deployment or with disarmament in general. Both the universities and political parties are engaged in peace research projects and education. On the other hand, defenders of the missile plan, like the Stichting Atlantische Commissie, are undertaking public relations campaigns and proposing alternative strategies for the Atlantic Alliance.

The Nederlands Instituut voor Internationale Betrekkingen, the major private research group, arose from the merger of four smaller organizations in January 1983. The reason for this move, sanctioned by the Dutch Government, was to avoid the divisions and overlapping that had plagued research activities in the past. The new Institute (which takes its name from its mansion-headquarters, Clingendael, near The Hague), is fully subsidized by the Ministries of Foreign Affairs, Defense, and Education, yet it remains, by statute, independent; "...its activities and views are in no way dependent on any public or private bodies and...it is not tied to any political party or viewpoint or to any denominational or ideological stream". The research program emphasizes security and foreign policy studies, including projects on European-American relations, the causes of war, the Soviet system, and operations of the United Nations. The Clingendael Institute also inherited the publication of the monthly <u>Internationale Spectator</u> (founded in 1947) and provides a daily review of the international press.

As noted above, Dutch universities play an important role in the security debate. Perhaps the most influential peace research group is the Polemological Institute at Groningen, established in 1961 by Prof.

Bert Röling. The Institute is devoted to the study of war, conflict, and peace, and has a wide network of international contacts, largely through the International Peace Research Association (which Prof. Röling co-founded). A quarterly journal, <u>Transaktie</u>, is published in Dutch, and a series of monographs appears in English. Another university-affiliated center, the Institute for International Studies at Leiden, produced major studies on the influence of domestic factors on Dutch foreign policy and on Dutch arms exports. The Center for Studies on Problems of Science and Society at the Twente Institute of Technology collaborated with SIPRI on a study of uranium enrichment and nuclear weapons proliferation. Located at Tilburg, the John F. Kennedy Institute, under the direction of Prof. F.A.M. Alting von Geusau, is another source of European security research; Prof. Alting von Geusau is also Chairman of the Advisory Committee on Disarmament and International Security and Peace to the Dutch Government. Researchers at the University of Amsterdam are studying the history of Dutch and Belgian entry into NATO, and the Polemological Working Group at the Free University of Amsterdam has begun publishing studies and a yearbook on peace and security. While the Institute of Social Studies at The Hague is principally concerned with development issues, one specialist is examining the question of nuclear weapons and world order. Dr. Leon Wecke, head of the Study Center for Peace Questions at Nijmegen, has a research project on perceptions of "the enemy" and legitimation of armaments.

All the political parties do some security and defense research. the Christian Democratic Party has its own Scientific Institute, where a project on alternative models for security policy is now in progress. the Wiardi Beckman Stichting of the Labor Party is also active in foreign affairs and security research, as is the Liberal Party research bureau, whose director has published an analysis of Dutch foreign policy in English.

A comprehensive study of European security issues will appear later in 1984 under the sponsorship of the European Movement in the Netherlands. The Royal Association for the Practice of Military Science, while not a research organization <u>per se</u>, does publish military-related periodicals like <u>Mars in Cathedra</u> and <u>Militaire Spectator</u>.

The Netherlands thus benefit from a high level of scholarly research in security and defense subjects. Some of this work reaches policymakers through the Ministry of Defense's Advisory Council on Defense Matters and the Ministry of Foreign Affair's Advisory Commission on Disarmament (already mentioned above). Also worth noting is the Foundation for Scientific Research in Politics and Public Administration (NESPOB) which is the primary source of financial support for independent research.

DIRECTORY CODE NUMBER : 137

Name of-Institution : Center for Studies on Problems of Science and Society

Address : Technische Hogeschool Twente
P.B. 217
7500 AE ENSCHEDE

Founding Date : 1975   Founding Place : Enschede

Type of Organization : National Public University

Objectives : Teaching and research in the relation between technology, war and peace.

Director : Dr. W.A. Smit

Total Staff : 11

Number of researchers on security and defense issues : 4

Projects in Progress : Title
                        Name(s) of Researcher(s)

1. Nuclear proliferation and "grey zone" technology.
   W.A. Smit/P. Boskma/B. Elsen

2. European Security : concepts and problems.
   P. Boskma/W.A. Smit/Van den Meer

3. Effects of nuclear war in Europe.
   W.A. Smit et al

4. Disarmament and development.
   P. Boskma et al

5. Dynamics of arms race.
   W.A. Smit/P. Boskma et al

Regular Periodicals : Title	Founding Date	Issues Annually
Boerderijcahier		occasional

Other Publications (since January 1983)

1. A. Krass, P. Boskma, B. Elsen, and W.A. Smit, <u>Uranium Enrichment and Nuclear Weapon Proliferation</u> (London : Taylor & Francis/ SIPRI, 1983).

2. "The Electromagnetic Pulse", (in Dutch), <u>Boerderijcahier</u>, 1983.

Collaboration with Foreign Study Centers

SIPRI on nuclear proliferation project.

<u>Library services provided for outside researchers</u> : yes

DIRECTORY CODE NUMBER : 138

Name of Institution : Europese Beweging in Nederland

Address : Alexanderstraat 2
2514 JL DEN HAAG

Telephone : (70) 63-59-52

Founding Date : 1947   Founding Place : Den Haag

Type of Organization : International Public

Objectives : Platform for discussions on European questions through periodicals, congresses, conferences, pressure groups.

President : G.C. Wallis de Vries

Total Staff : 8

Projects in Progress : Title
                      Name(s) of Researcher(s)

1. Crucial points of European security (to appear in 1984).
   J. Voorhoeve/Berkhof/Penders/
   J. Siccama/H. Vredeling/Jaquet/
   Plaauw/Gosses/Singelsma

Regular Periodicals : Title	Founding Date	Issues Annually
Vieuw Europa	1974	4

Library services provided for outside researchers : yes

Comments : In 1982, the organization published a book on European integration in the Atlantic Alliance and Dutch opinion (from Right to Left) on European defense.

DIRECTORY CODE NUMBER : 139

Name of Institution : Institute of Social Studies

Address : P.O. Box 90733
         2509 LS 'S GRAVENHAGE

Telephone : (70) 57-22-01

Founding Date : 1952   Founding Place : 's Gravenhage

Type of Organization : National Public

Objectives : To contribute to national and international efforts to understand and to solve problems related to the development process.

Director : Prof. L.J. Emmerij

Total Staff : 167

Number of researchers on security and defense issues : 2

Projects in Progress : Title
                      Name(s) of Researcher(s)

1. Nuclear weapons and world order : towards a functional equivalent of the monopoly of violence of the state at the world level.
   G. van Benthem van den Bergh

2. East-West-South relations : the quest for a more realistic international cooperation.

Publications (since January 1983)

1. Karel Jansen (Ed.), <u>Monetarism, Economic Crisis and the Third World</u> ('s Gravenhage : ISS, 1983) 194 pp.

2. Mehmet Nezir Uca, "Workers' Participation and Self-Management in Turkey", <u>ISS Research Report</u>, Vol. 13, 1983, 254 pp.

3. G. van Benthem van den Bergh, "Two Scorpions in a Bottle : the Unintended Benefits of Nuclear Weapons", in William Paige (Ed.), The Future of Politics (London : Francis Pinter, 1983).

4. G. van Benthem van den Bergh, "Dynamics of Armament and State Formation Processes", (in German) in P. Gleichmann et al (Eds.), Materials on Norbert Elias' Theory of Civilization (Frankfurt : Suhrkamp, 1983) Vol. II.

5. G. van Benthem van den Bergh, "Nuclear Weapons and Self-Restraint in International Politics" (Györ, Hungary : International Peace Research Association, 1983).

Library services provided for outside researchers : yes

Comments : The Institute offers M.A., Diploma, and Ph.D. programs in development studies.

DIRECTORY CODE NUMBER : 140

Name of Institution : Instituut voor Internationale Studiën

Address : Rijksuniversiteit Leiden
Postbus 9520
2300 RA LEIDEN

Telephone : (71) 14-96-41

Founding Date : 1970   Founding Place : Leiden

Type of Organization : National Public University

Objectives : Teaching and research in the field of international studies.

Director : P. Everts

Total Staff : 10

Number of researchers on security and defense issues : 4

Projects in Progress : Title
                           Name(s) of Researcher(s)

1. Arms trade policies in the Netherlands.
                           J. Colijn/P. Rusman

2. Armaments processes in the Third World.
                           L.M. van der Mers

3. Public opinion on nuclear weapons and its influence on foreign
   policy making.
                           P. Everts

Publications (since January 1983)

1. P. Everts, <u>Public Opinion, the Churches and Foreign Policy :
   Studies of Domestic Factors in the Making of Dutch Foreign
   Policy</u> (Leiden : Institute for International Studies, 1983)
   414 pp.

2. D. Colijn and L.M. van der Mers (Eds.), <u>Netherlands Arms Exports</u>
   (in Dutch) (Den Haag : Nederlands Instituut voor Internationale
   Betrekkingen, 1983) 150 pp.

<u>Library services provided for outside researchers</u> : yes

DIRECTORY CODE NUMBER : 141

<u>Name of Institution</u> : John F. Kennedy Institute, Center for International Studies

<u>Address</u> : Hogeschoollaan 225
             5037 GC TILBURG

<u>Telephone</u> (13) 66-91-11   x. 2435

Founding Date : 1967   Founding Place : Tilburg

Type of Organization : National Private University

Objectives : An interdisciplinary organization to promote research, education, publications, exchange, and dialogue concerning major contemporary international problems.

Director : Prof. F.A.M. Alting von Geusau

Total Staff : 6

Number of researchers on security and defense issues : 2

Projects in Progress : Title   Name(s) of Researcher(s)

---

1. Christendom and policy (nuclear weapons).
    F.A.M. Alting von Geusau

2. Security of Western Europe.
    F.A.M. Alting von Geusau

3. East-West relations (NATO/Warsaw Pact).
    L. Bartalits

4. Relations between Israel and Arab states.
    L. Bartalits

5. Relations between China and the rest of the world.
    L. Bartalits

Collaboration with Foreign Study Centers

International Institute for Strategic Studies and European Institute on Security Matters in connection with book, <u>The Security of Western Europe : a Handbook</u>, to be published by Sherwood Press, London.

Library services provided for outside researchers : yes

Comments : Publications in 1982 included F.A.M. Alting von Geusau (Ed.), <u>Allies in a Turbulent World : Challenges to U.S. and Western European Cooperation</u> (Lexington, MA : Lexington Books, 1982), 192 pp., and F.A.M. Alting von Geusau and Jacques Pelkmans (Eds.), <u>National Economic Security : Perceptions, Threats and Policies</u> (J.F. Kennedy Institute, 1982).

DIRECTORY CODE NUMBER : 142

Name of Institution : Koninklijke Vereniging ter Beoefening van de Krijgswetenschap

Address : Frederikkazerne geb. 110
v.d. Burchlaan 31
Postbus 90701
2509 LS 's GRAVENHAGE

Telephone : (70) 73-24-33

Founding Date : 1865   Founding Place : 's Gravenhage

Type of organization : National Public

Objectives : To promote the discipline of military science in general.

President : Col. H.A. Couzy

Regular Periodicals : Title	Founding Date	Issues Annually
1. Militaire Spectator	1832	12
2. Mars in Cathedra	1969	4

DIRECTORY CODE NUMBER : 143

Name of Institution : Nederlands Instituut voor Internationale
                      Betrekkingen (Clingendael)

Address : P.O. Box 93080
          2509 AB 's GRAVENHAGE

Telephone : (70) 24-53-84

Founding Date : Jan. 1983   Founding Place : Den Haag

Type of Organization : National Private Non-Profit

Objectives : Research and educational activities to broaden and
             deepen understanding and opinion formation in the field
             of international affairs.

Director : H.J. Neuman

Total Staff : 40

Number of researchers on security and defense issues : 4

Projects in Progress : Title
                              Name(s) of Researcher(s)

1. Netherlands policy vis-à-vis the Palestinians.
            Marianne van Leeuwen

2. Quantitative research into the causes of war (1816-1980).
            Jan G. Siccama/Henk Houweling

3. Historical patterns in the relationship between the USA and
   Western Europe (1816-1980).
            Jan G. Siccama/Henk Houweling

4. Stability characteristics of European security after 1945.
            Jan G. Siccama

5. Functioning of the United Nations.
            Dick A. Leurdijk

6. South Africa in her military, economic, and political environment.
            Hans van der Meulen

7. Criteria in Dutch foreign and security policy.
            Sam Rozemond

8. The Soviet Union and its alliances and rivalries.
   H. Hendrikse

9. Human rights.
   C.J. Visser

Regular Periodicals : Title	Founding Date	Issues Annually
Internationale Spectator	1947	12

Other Publications (since January 1983)

1. Hans van der Meulen, "Western Pressure and the Apartheid Regime" (in Dutch), Clingendael-Cahier, 1983.

2. Dick A. Leurdijk, "Pérez de Cuéllar on the Hitch in UN Machinery" (in Dutch), Clingendael-Cahier, 1983.

Library services provided for outside researchers : yes

Comments : The Institute was formed from the merger of the Netherlands Association for International Affairs (NGIZ), the Course on International Relations (LBB), the Netherlands United Nations Association (VVN), the Netherlands Institute for Research on Peace and Security (NIVV), and the Defence Studies Centre (DSC). It is fully subsidized by the Ministries of Foreign Affairs, Defense, and Education and Science.

DIRECTORY CODE NUMBER : 144

Name of Institution : Polemologisch Instituut

Address : Rijksuniversiteit te Groningen
　　　　　 Heresingel 13
　　　　　 9711 ER GRONINGEN

Telephone : (50) 11-55-85

Founding Date : 1961　　　　　Founding Place : Groningen

Type of Organization : National Public University

Objectives : Study of the causes of war and peace, the preconditions for peace, alternative forms of conflict management, and structural violence.

Director : Prof. H.W. Tromp

Total Staff : 24

Number of researchers on security and defense issues : 12

Projects in Progress : Title
　　　　　　　　　　　　Name(s) of Researcher(s)

1. Cold War and its origins.
　　　　　　　　　　Fenna van den Burg
　　　　　　　　　　Herman de Lange
　　　　　　　　　　Jaap Nobel

2. Armaments processes and disarmament strategies.
　　　　　　　　　　Gerard Aupers et al

3. Economic aspects of armaments and war.
　　　　　　　　　　Theo van den Hoogen et al

4. Data on war, conflict, peace : theories of war causation.
　　　　　　　　　　Hans van der Dennen et al

5. Peace education.
　　　　　　　　　　Chris Bartelds et al

Regular Periodicals : Title	Founding Date	Issues Annually
Transaktie	1971	4

Collaboration with Foreign Study Centers

Corporate member of International Peace Research Association

Library services provided for outside researchers : yes

Comments : The Institute offers both undergraduate and graduate courses in peace research.

DIRECTORY CODE NUMBER : 145

Name of Institution : Stichting Atlantische Commissie

Address : Alexanderstraat 2
2514 JL DEN HAAG

Telephone : (70) 63-94-95

Founding Date : 1952   Founding Place : Den Haag

Type of Organization : National Private Non-Profit

Objectives : Study of peace and security within the Atlantic framework and dissemination of information on these matters to the Dutch public.

Director : R.D. Praaning

Total Staff : 5

Projects in Progress : Title

1. Peace and security education (to be published in 1984).
2. Lexicon on Politico-Military-Strategic terms (in Dutch).

Regular Periodicals : Title	Founding Date	Issues Annually
1. Atlantisch Perspektief	1979	6
2. Atlantisch Nieuws	1979	12
3. Atlantische Studies	1979	1-2
4. Atlantische Studiebrieven	1976	2-3

Other Publications (since January 1983)

1. A Transatlantic Dialogue (Atlantische Studie 6), 1983, 71 pp.
2. Less Dependence on Nuclear Weapons ? (in Dutch) (Atlantische Studie 5), 1983, 63 pp.

Library services provided for outside researchers : yes

DIRECTORY CODE NUMBER : 146

Name of Institution : Studiecentrum voor Vredesvraagstukken

Address : Katholieke Universiteit Nijmegen
          Bijleveldsingel 70/72
          6524 AE NIJMEGEN

Telephone : (80) 51-56-87
            (80) 51-56-97

Founding Date : 1965   Founding Place : Nijmegen

Type of Organization : National Public University

Objectives : Teaching and research on problems of war and peace.

Director : Dr. L. Wecke

Total Staff : 15

Number of researchers on security and defense issues : 10

Projects in Progress : Title
                              Name(s) of Researcher(s)

1. Integration of peace and development education in secondary schools.
                              Clemens Wijlens
                              Chris Rövekamp

2. Arms dynamics in the Soviet Union.
                              Herman Fontein

3. The anti-cruise missile demonstration.
                              Ton Bertrand
                              Ben Schennink
                              Leon Wecke

4. Arms production and employment in the Netherlands.
                              Jan Prins
                              Marcel Meys

5. Enemy perception.
                              Leon Wecke

6. Netherlands and the Atlantic Alliance.
                              Gerard Metselaar

Regular Periodicals : Title	Founding Date	Issues Annually
1. Cahiers van het Studie-centrum voor Vredesvraag-stukken	1972	4
2. Dosschriften	1976	occasional

Other Publications (since January 1983)

1. Herman Fontein, Ben Hoogenboom, and Gerard Metselaar, "Flexible Response : the Adjusted Answer and the Dutch Response" (in Dutch), Cahiers, N°26, May 1983, 200 pp.

2. John Karskens, Ben Schennink, and Wim Westerveld, "Pupils Become Wiser : Effects of a Peace Education Project on the Attitude of Pupils in Secondary Schools", (in Dutch), Cahiers, N°27, Aug. 1983, 123 pp.

3. Leon Wecke, Legitimation of Armament and Enemy Perception (Nijmegen : SVV, 1983).

Library services provided for outside researchers : yes

DIRECTORY CODE NUMBER : 147

Name of Institution : Transnational Institute

Address : Paulus Potterstraat 20
1071 DA AMSTERDAM

Telephone : (20) 72-66-08

Type of Organization : International Private Non-Profit

DIRECTORY CODE NUMBER : 148

Name of Institution : Vakgroep Internationale Betrekkingen en
                      Volkenrecht

Address : Univ. of Amsterdam
          FSW-a
          Herengracht 508-510
          1017 CB AMSTERDAM

Telephone : (20) 525-2169

Founding Date : 1974   Founding Place : Amsterdam

Type of Organization : National Public University

Objectives : Teaching and research in the fields of international
             relations and international law.

Director : G. Junne

Total Staff : 21

Number of researchers on security and defense issues : 5

Projects in Progress : Title
                                    Name(s) of Researcher(s)

Belgium, the Netherlands, and the North Atlantic Treaty, 1945-
1949 : a comparative study.
                       C. Wiebes
                       B. Zeeman

Publications (since January 1983)

1. C. Wiebes and B. Zeeman, 'A Star Is Born' : Formation of a
   Military Alliance in the Atlantic Region 1945-1948 (in Dutch)
   (Amsterdam : March 1983) (Mededelingen 31).

2. C. Wiebes and B. Zeeman, "The Pentagon Negotiations March 1948 :
   The Launching of the North Atlantic Treaty", International
   Affairs Vol. 59, N°3 (summer 1983).

Library services provided for outside researchers : yes

DIRECTORY CODE NUMBER : 149

Name of Institution : Wetenschappelijk Instituut voor het CDA

Address : Dr. Kuyperstraat 5
2514 BA DEN HAAG

Telephone : (70) 92-40-21

Founding Date : 1980

Type of Organization : National Private Party-Affiliated

Objectives : To develop ideas for policy within the Christian Democratic Party.

Director : Dr. A.M. Oostlander

Total Staff : 10

Number of researchers on security and defense issues : 1

Projects in Progress : Title	Name(s) of Researcher(s)
Alternative models for security policy : an evaluation.	Theo Brinkel A.M. Oostlander

Regular Periodicals : Title	Founding Date	Issues Annually
Christen Democratische Verkenningen	1981	11

DIRECTORY CODE NUMBER : 150

Name of Institution : Wiardi Beckman Stichting

Address : Nicolaas Witsenkade 30
           1017 ZT AMSTERDAM

Telephone : (20) 26-24-24

Founding Date : 1946   Founding Place : Amsterdam

Type of Organization : National Private Political-Party-Affiliated

Objectives : Research and documentation for the Labor Party (PvdA).

Director : J. van den Berg

DIRECTORY CODE NUMBER : 151

Name of Institution : Werkgroep Polemologie

Address : Vrije Universiteit Amsterdam
           Postbus 7161
           1007 MC AMSTERDAM

Telephone : (20) 71-85-43

Founding Date : 1973   Founding Place : Amsterdam

Type of Organization : National Public University

Objectives : Teaching, research, and organization of conferences,
             debates, and colloquia.

Director : J.B. Oostenbrink

total Staff : 4

Number of researchers on security and defense issues : 2

Projects in Progress : Title
                       Name(s) of Researcher(s)

1. Naval industries and armaments cooperation in NATO-Europe.
   Sami Faltas

2. Nuclear weapons and ethics.
   Koos van der Bruggen

3. Defense without provocation.
   Frank Barnaby
   Egbert Boeker

4. Western European military security.
   J.B. Oostenbrink

Regular Periodicals : Title	Founding Date	Issues Annually
1. VU Studies over Vrede en Veiligheid	1983	3
2. Jaarboek over Vrede en Veiligheid	1984	1

Other Publications (since January 1983)

1. Dick Benschop, Peace Movement and Politics : Origin and Meaning of the November 21st Demonstration (in Dutch) (Amsterdam : VU-Boekhandel, 1983).

2. Siebe Riedstra, Nine Churches in the Front Lines : Peace Discussions in the Churches 1980-1982 (in Dutch), (Amsterdam : VU-Boekhandel, 1983).

3. Egbert Boeker, Modern Weapons : The Functioning of Weapon Systems and Their Military Meaning (Amsterdam : VU-Boekhandel, 1983).

Library services provided for outside researchers : yes

NORWAY

NORWAY

Two independent (though largely government-financed) institutions provide most of the security and defense research in Norway. The International Peace Research Institute (PRIO) and the Norwegian Institute of International Affairs (NUPI) are generally representative of two differing approaches to questions of conflict and conflict resolution. Researchers at the two organizations have, however, been cooperating on a study of the future of the UN peacekeeping operations and the role of the UN Secretary-General in the peaceful settlement of international disputes.

PRIO was founded in 1959 as part of the Institute for Social Research and became an autonomous body in 1966. The Institute is essentially self-governing (through a staff decision-making process), but it still depends on Norwegian government sources for 80 percent of its budget. PRIO researchers come from a number of countries and academic disciplines, though the main working (and publishing) language is English. Its research projects stress both theory and application : "The Institute encourages pluralism, openness and public debate, within a research tradition that is very much aware of social injustice, of conflicts and their resolution, and of mankind's capacity for self-destruction". The Journal of Peace Research and the Bulletin of Peace Proposals are both quarterly periodicals produced by the PRIO (in English). PRIO also publishes four series of special studies primarily concerning questions of disarmament.

As the pre-eminent national research organization, NUPI tends to study international problems from a specifically Norwegian or Nordic perspective. The Institute was established by Act of Parliament in 1959 and began operations in 1960. Although it relies on public funds for 80 percent of its budget, NUPI remains "independent, politically neutral and professionally free" in its research and information programs. Its director, Johan Jorgen Holst, has published widely on questions of European security and the strategic balance on the continent. The Institute's quarterly journal, Internasjonal Politikk, also publishes two special issues each year on specific topics like the Conference on Security and Cooperation in Europe, international economic problems, and the consequences of Norwegian oil production. In addition, NUPI publishes the Norsk Utenrikspolitisk Arbok (Norwegian Foreign Policy Yearbook) with full documentation and analysis, as well as specialized books and reports on international problems (mostly in English).

As in other Scandinavian countries, the government programs in security and defense studies are extensive, and the work is relatively accessible. The Defense Research Establishment in Lillestrom is the largest such organization. The Research Centre for Defence History, located at the National Defence College, publishes a series of studies in military history and is now focusing on the issues involved in Norway's adhesion to NATO. University researchers in Norway are examining aspects of national foreign policy and collaborating on projects at NUPI and PRIO. It should be added that the Science Policy Council has undertaken an assessment of Norwegian security and peace research and has published its findings (in Norwegian).

One other private organization, the Fridtjof Nansen Foundation, specializes in oceanography and related subjects and has sponsored work on the Law of the Sea Treaty and other issues with security implications.

Though members of NATO, Norwegians (like Danes) prohibit the stationing of foreign troops or military bases in peacetime, and do not permit the deployment of nuclear weapons on their soil. Yet Norway is one of two Alliance countries with boundaries on the Soviet Union; the headquarters of the Soviet Northern Fleet on the Kola Peninsula lie just 200 miles off Norway's northernmost extremity. Disputes over demarcation of the continental shelf and the status of the Svalbard archipelago have strained Soviet-Norwegian relations, as have the large-scale Soviet naval maneuvers and reported intrusions into Norwegian territorial waters. Norway thus has a major stake in the reduction of East-West tensions and the adoption of confidence-building measures at the Stockholm disarmament conference, as well as in proposals for a nuclear-free zone in Scandinavia.

DIRECTORY CODE NUMBER : 152

Name of Institution : The Fridtjof Nansen Foundation at Polhøgda

Address : Fridtjof Nansens vei 17
　　　　　1324 LYSAKER

Telephone : (2) 53-89-12

Founding Date : 1958

Director : Willy Ostreng

Projects in Progress : Title
　　　　　　　　　　　　　Name(s) of Researcher(s)

1. Soviet gas : an analysis of critical factors for the determination of export policies.
　　　　　　　　　Helge Ole Bergesen/Arild Moe

2. International regimes : the dynamics of regime-change and evaluation with respect to regimes' impact on order and justice in relations between states (two empirical studies : international oil politics and politics of the deep sea-bed).
　　　　　　　　　Helge Ole Bergesen

3. New territories : an analysis of the development of areas of the world which are, or until recently have been outside national jurisdiction (i.e. the polar areas and the sea-bed).

4. New ocean regimes - implications for Norway.
　　　　　　　　　Steinar Andresen/Willy Ostreng

DIRECTORY CODE NUMBER : 153

Name of Institution : Institute of Political Science

Address : University of Oslo
　　　　　Box 1097
　　　　　Blindern
　　　　　OSLO 3

Telephone : (2) 46-68-00

Projects in Progress : Title   Name(s) of Researcher(s)

1. Coordination problems in Norwegian foreign policy.
   Maurice A. East/Olav Knudsen/ Svein Efjestad

2. Compilation of Norwegian foreign policy events data file.
   Arild Underdal/Olav Knudsen

Publications (since January 1983)

Helge Hveem et al, Norway and the World (in Norwegian), Gyldendal Publishers, 1983.

DIRECTORY CODE NUMBER : 154

Name of Institution : Institute for Alternative Development Research

Address : PO Box 23
          Vestli
          OSLO 9

Telephone : (2) 10-67-08

Projects in Progress : Title

1. Economic and military dimensions of conflict and cooperation between the U.S. and European NATO in the 1980s.

2. Migration, military technology and "maldevelopment".

Publications (since January 1983)

1. Amalendu Guha, "Concepts and Approaches for a Nuclear Weapon-Free Nordic Zone and Dilemmas of a Nuclear Weapon-Free Balkan Zone", Institute research report.
2. S.B. Mohod, "Problems and Perspectives for Disarmament", Institute research report.
3. Mario E. Carranza, "Dependency Theory and Military Issues : The Role of Authoritarianism in Latin America", Institute research report.
4. Mario E. Carranza, "Military Dependency and Military Assistance in Latin America : Interaction of Military and Civil Programs", Institute research report.

DIRECTORY CODE NUMBER : 155

Name of Institution : Institute for Social Sciences

Address : University of Tromso
          9000 TROMSO

Projects in Progress : Title
                                Name(s) of Researcher(s)

Foreign relations between Great Britain and the Nordic countries 1945-1952.
                        Knut Einar Eriksen

DIRECTORY CODE NUMBER : 156

Name of Institution : International Peace Research Institute (PRIO)

Address : Radhusgt. 4
OSLO 1

Telephone : (2) 11-41-05

Founding Date : 1959   **Founding Place** : Oslo

Type of Organization : International Private Non-Profit

Objectives : To engage in scholarly research concerning the conditions necessary for peaceful relations between nations, groups and individuals.

Director : Tord Hoivik

Total Staff : 35

Number of researchers on security and defense issues : 7

Projects in Progress : Title
                       Name(s) of Researcher(s)

---

1. Military infrastructure, bases and arms control in Norway.
   Nils Petter Gleditsch

2. Women and peace.
   Birgit Brock-Utne

3. Disarmament education.
   Birgit Brock-Utne

4. Arms race, armament dynamics, military research and development, and disarmament.
   Marek Thee

5. Deterrence or war-fighting : the development of the U.S. doctrine for the use of tactical nuclear weapons.
   Per Berg

6. Role of the U.N. Secretary-General in peaceful settlement of disputes in the 1970s.
   Kjell Skjelsbaek

7. Human Rights Project.
   Asbjorn Eide/Torkel Opsahl/
   Jan Helgesen

8. War, armaments, and disarmament.
   Tord Hoivik et al

9. "The defective state" : an analysis of its development, characteristics and political and economic implications with special references to the states of the Mediterranean basin.
   Marianne Heiberg

10. Dominance theory and international development strategies.
    Helge Hveem

11. Norway and the global economy in the post-World War II era.
    Lars Mjoset

12. Survey of Nordic peace movements.
    Nigel Young

Regular Periodicals : Title	Founding Date	Issues Annually
1. Journal of Peace Research	1964	4
2. Bulletin of Peace Proposals	1970	4

Other Publications (since January 1983)

1. Marek Thee, "The establishment of a nuclear weapon-free zone in the Nordic countries : informed, rational and imaginative politics", PRIO Report 1/83, 1983, 12 pp.

2. Ruben Barrios, "The political economy of East-South relations", PRIO Report 2/83, 1983, 28 pp.

3. Asmund Stenseth and Tord Hoivik, "Simulation of nuclear attack", PRIO Report 3/83 (in Norwegian), 1983.

4. Miles D. Wolpin, "Comparative perspectives of militarization. Repression and social welfare", PRIO Report 4/83, 1983, 48 pp.

5. Tord Hoivik, "Peace research and science", PRIO Working Paper 6/83, 1983, 15 pp.

6. Asbjorn Eide, "The system of human rights", **PRIO Paper 1/83**, 1983, 22 pp.

7. Magne Barth, "Military industrial cooperation : the case of Norway and West Germany", **PRIO Paper 2/83**, 1983, 20 pp.

8. Nigel Young, "The contemporary European anti-nuclear movement : experiments in the mobilisation of public power", **PRIO Paper 3/83**, 1983, 25 pp.

9. Miles D. Wolpin, "Military radicalism in the Middle East and Mediterranean", **PRIO Report 6/83**, 1983, 59 pp.

10. Miles D. Wolpin, "Militarization, internal repression and social welfare in the Third World", **PRIO Report 7/83**, 1983, 135 pp.

11. Marek Thee, "Conversion of military-related industries to socially useful purposes", **PRIO Report 8/83**, 1983, 27 pp.

12. Marek Thee, "Conceptual issues related to European security. Arms control and confidence-building measures", **PRIO Report 9/83**, 1983, 28 pp.

13. Miles D. Wolpin, "State terrorism and repression in the Third World : parameters and prospects", **PRIO Report 10/83**, 1983.

14. **Ninth Nordic Peace Research Conference : Proceedings, PRIO Inform 4/83**, 1983, 45 pp.

15. Tord Hoivik, "War, conflict and conflict resolution" (in Norwegian) **PRIO Inform 6/83**, 1983, 34 pp.

16. Kjell Skjelsbaek, "Nuclear disarmament and conventional defense of Western Europe" (in Norwegian), **PRIO Inform 8/83**, 1983, 12 pp.

17. Nigel Young, "War resistance, state and society", **PRIO Paper 4/83**, 1983, 26 pp.

18. Nigel Young, "New strategies for disarmament", **PRIO Paper 5/83**, 1983, 23 pp.

19. Nigel Young, "The contemporary peace education movement", **PRIO Paper 6/83**, 1983, 20 pp.

Collaboration with Foreign Study Centers

1. United Nations University on military policy and disarmament.

2. Nordic peace research institutions on various projects.

DIRECTION CODE NUMBER : 157

Name of Institution : Norwegian Defence Research Establishment

Address : Kjeller
2007 LILLESTRØM

Founding Date : 1946   **Founding Place** : Oslo

Type of Organization : National Public

Objectives : Research and development related to national defense problems.

Director : Finn Lied

Total Staff : 500

DIRECTORY CODE NUMBER : 158

Name of Institution : Norwegian Institute of International Affairs (NUPI)

Address : Bygdoy Alle 3   **Mailing Address** : PO Box 8159-DEP
OSLO 2   0033 OSLO-1

Telephone : (2) 44-58-20

Founding Date : 1959   **Founding Place** : Oslo

Type of Organization : National Public Non-Profit

Objectives : (1) to contribute towards increased understanding of international problems and issues;
(2) to disseminate information on international relations;
(3) to promote studies on the problems of international cooperation and the causes of international conflict.

Director : Johan Jorgen Holst

Total Staff : 40

Number of researchers on security and defense issues : 6

Projects in Progress : Title
Name(s) of Researcher(s)

1. Norwegian foreign policy.
   J.J. Holst et al

2. Consensus problems in Norwegian security policy.
   A.O. Brundtland

3. Arms control and the security order in Europe.
   J.J. Holst/J.K. Skogan

4. Changing naval policies of the superpowers and regional stability in Europe.
   J.J. Holst/J.K. Skogan/
   J. Bornsen

5. The future of the U.N. peacekeeping operations.
   J.J. Holst/M. Heiberg/
   D. Heradstveit/K. Skjellsbaek

6. NATO's First-Use option.
   J.K. Skogan

7. Managing Norwegian foreign policy in the 1980s.
   D. Heradstveit/M. Bonham/M. East

Regular Periodicals : Title	Founding Date	Issues Annually
1. Internasjonal Politikk	1936	6
2. Norsk Utenrikspolitisk Arbok	1972	1
3. Norwegian Foreign Policy Studies	1968	occasional
4. NUPI/NOTAT	1969	occasional
5. NUPI/Rapport	1969	occasional

Other Publications (since January 1983)

1. Johan J. Holst, "Towards a Policy of No First Use of Nuclear Weapons", NUPI/NOTAT N° 259.

2. Johan J. Holst, "A European Perspective on the Concept of a Nuclear Freeze", NUPI/NOTAT N° 260.

3. Johan J. Holst, "Nuclear Weapons and Negotiations : What Is to Be Done ?" (in Norwegian) NUPI/NOTAT N° 261.

4. Martin Saeter, "Europe and the World : European Reorganization as part of Global Restructuring", NUPI/NOTAT N° 262.

5. Johan J. Holst, "Arms control for the 1980s : a European Perspective", NUPI/NOTAT N° 263 C.

6. Johan J. Holst, "Norway's Role in the search for International Peace and Security", NUPI/NOTAT N° 264 B.

7. Johan J. Holst, "Lilliputs and Gulliver : Small States in the Great Power Alliance", NUPI/NOTAT N° 266 B.

8. Johan J. Holst, "The 'Dual Track' Decision Revisited", NUPI/NOTAT N° 267 A.

9. Arne Olav Brundtland, "The Consensus Policy in Norwegian Security Policy" (in Norwegian), NUPI/NOTAT N° 268 C.

10. Johan J. Holst, "Nuclear Weapon-Free Zones in Europe : an Option for the Future", NUPI/NOTAT N° 269 B.

11. Johan J. Holst, "Confidence-Building through Openness about Military Activity", NUPI/NOTAT N° 270 A.

12. Johan J. Holst, "A Nuclear Weapon-Free zone in the Nordic Area : Conditions and Options - A Norwegian View", NUPI/NOTAT N° 271 A.

13. Birger Fredriksen, "A Survey of Norway's External Economic Relations", NUPI/NOTAT N° 272 B.

14. Daniel Heradstveit, The Media War in the Middle East (Oslo : NUPI, 1983) 190 pp.

Comments : NUPI was established as an independent, politically neutral research institution by Act of Parliament in the autumn of 1959. It took over publication of Internasjonal Politikk in 1961.

DIRECTORY CODE NUMBER : 159

Name of Institution : Research Centre for Defence History

Address : National Defence College
Tollbugt. 10
OSLO 1

Telephone : (2) 40-30-30

Founding Date : Aug. 1980   Founding Place : Oslo

Type of Organization : National Public

Objectives : Research on the history of Norwegian defense and national security in the contemporary period.

Director : Olav Riste

Total Staff : 5

Number of researchers on security and defense issues : 3

Projects in Progress : Title
                      Name(s) of Researcher(s)

1. NATO, Norway and the question of Allied Military bases.
   Olav Riste

2. NATO, Norway and the question of military build-up and integration after the outbreak of the Korean War.
   Rolf Jamnes

3. The role of defense in the development of the Norwegian electronics industry since 1957.
   O. Wicken

Regular Periodicals : Title	Founding Date	Issues Annually
FHFS NOTAT	Jan. 1981	6-8

Other Publications (since January 1983)

1. Olav Riste (Ed.), Forsvarsstudier - Defence Studies I (Oslo, 1982).

2. J. Tamnes (Ed.), Forsvarsstudier - Defence Studies II (Oslo, 1983).

3. N. Borchgrevink, The Norwegian Defense through British Glasses, (in Norwegian), 1983.

4. Olav Riste, From Integrity Treaty to Nuclear Weapons : Norway and Great Power "Guarantees", 1905-1983, (in Norwegian), 1983.

5. T.V. Skaret, The Norwegian Church and Nuclear Weapons Debate, 1960-1982, (in Norwegian), 1983.

6. D. Pugh, Guns in the Cupboard, The Home Guard, Milorg and the Politics of Reconstruction, 1945-1946, 1983.

7. J. Sanness, Norwegian Historians and the Cold War, 1984.

8. European and Atlantic Defence 1947-1953 (symposium proceedings to be published by Universitetsforlaget in 1984).

DIRECTORY CODE NUMBER : 160

Name of Institution : Science Policy Council of Norway

Address : Nedre Vollgt. 11
PO Box 8031 DEP
0030 OSLO 1

Telephone : (2) 42-29-25

Publications (since January 1983)

1. Odvar Leine (Ed.), Security and Peace Research 1970-1981 (a bibliography in Norwegian), 1982-1983, 253 pp.

2. Research in Security and Peace (in Norwegian), Nov. 1982, 173 pp.

PORTUGAL

PORTUGAL

Portugal has an important strategic position on the South Atlantic and also strong ties to Brazil and its former African colonies (now the scene of intense East-West rivalry). The American military base at Lajes in the Azores is a critical logistics and communications link in the NATO network, and a renewal of the base lease is currently in the discussion stage. But, ten years after "the revolution of the carnations", the major Portuguese concern is not over security problems, but rather over the country's immense economic difficulties, especially as it pursues negotiations on entry into the European Community.

Two organizations carry out advanced security and defense research in Portugal : the Instituto de Estudos Estratégicos e Internacionais (IEEI) and the Instituto da Defesa Nacional (IDN). The latter is the national military college, but strives to improve civil-military relations by opening many of its activities to civilians from the public and private sectors. The IDN's research interests concentrate on national security issues. The IEEI, an independent, non-partisan organization, was established in 1980 to combat the insularity of postwar Portuguese political thinking. As the Institute reports : "Despite Portugal's geostrategic position, and the existing awareness of its importance, despite the fact that Portugal is one of the founding members of NATO, the discussion of defense and foreign policy issues was virtually non-existent or limited to the military institutions". The first priority has been to promote better understanding of the Spanish neighbor through research, lectures, and seminars; in 1982, the Institute published a dossier on Portugal, Spain, and Transatlantic relations. The IEEI has also been investigating questions of Portuguese security and European integration, the Azores, and public opinion on defense matters.

Another important focus is on the political situation in Africa. The Institute has already published a study of major power interests on the African continent, benefitting from its contacts with Angola, Mozambique, and other former colonies. The study also examined the impact of "the new information order" on Africa, the distinction between nationalist and pro-Soviet Marxists in African liberation movements, and the relationship of the Portuguese Communist Party with these movements.

DIRECTORY CODE NUMBER : 161

Name of Institution : Instituto da Defesa Nacional (IDN)

Address : Calçada das Necessidades 5
          1300 LISBOA

Telephone : (1) 60-30-60
            (1) 60-15-16

Founding Date : 1976   Founding Place : Lisboa

Type of Organization : National Public

Objectives : The top-level educational establishment in the Armed
             Forces for the study and investigation of defense
             matters, specifically : (1) the definition of a common
             doctrine of defense policy; (2) the widening of the
             knowledge of armed forces officers; and (3) reciprocal
             knowledge and understanding among armed forces officers,
             officials of the public administration, and representa-
             tives of the private sector through study of major
             issues.

Director : Pelo Comandante Virgilio de Carvalho

Total Staff : 55

Number of researchers on security and defense issues : 20

Projects in Progress : Title
                       Name(s) of Researcher(s)

---

1. The concepts of national defense and national security.
                       Prof. M. Renaud et al

2. New concepts for the evaluation of the national power of
   Portugal-identification of the vulnerabilities and the
   potentialities of the nation.
                       Brig. Gen. Paula Vicente et al

Regular Periodicals : Title	Founding Date	Issues Annually
Naçao e defesa	1976	4

Comments : The IDN offers a six-month National Defense Course open
to both civil and military participants. The course work
concentrates on the international scenario and international relations and on national power. The Institute
also runs courses for military officers on national
defense, joint and combined forces, policy, strategy,
economics and sociology.

DIRECTORY CODE NAME : 162

Name of Institution : Instituto de Estudos Estratégicos e Internacionais (IEEI)

Address : Quinta de Sao Cristóvao
Largo de Sao Sebastiao
Paço do Lumiar
1600 LISBOA

Telephone : (1) 758-27-05
(1) 758-27-01

Founding Date : Feb. 1980   Founding Place : Lisboa

Type of Organization : National Private Non-Profit

Objectives : To fill the need for an independent organization in
Portugal devoted to research, debate, and information on
international relations and the problems of peace,
security, defense, and development.

Director : Alvaro Vasconcelos

Total Staff : 10

Number of researchers on security and defense issues : 6

Projects in Progress : Title	Name(s) of Researcher(s)

1. Unity and diversity in the Iberian Peninsula.
   A. Vasconcelos/Gen. E. Munilla

2. Portugal and Spain - European Integration : areas for cooperation.
   J.L. Cruz Vilaça
   M.C. Athayde Tavares
   Paula Gouveia et al

3. Public opinion and defense.
   N. Cintra Torres

4. The Azores, the United States and Europe.
   Mario Mesquita

5. Portugal, Europe, and the Atlantic.
   J.B. Comprido

6. Angola and Mozambique : regional security and internal conflicts.
   A. Vasconcelos/Eduardo Cintra Torres/M.B. Resendes et al

7. Portugal and the nuclear issue.
   J. Soares

8. Youth, pacifism, and national defense.
   Eduardo Cintra Torres
   Luis Delgado/H. Mota

Regular Periodicals : Title	Founding Date	Issues Annually
1. African Survey	1983	1
2. Estratégia em Debate	1981	6
3. Estudos Estratégicos	1982	3

Collaboration with Foreign Study Centers

1. Instituto de Economia Aplicada (Universidad Autonoma de Madrid)- Portugal and Spain - European Integration : areas for cooperation.
2. Centre d'Etudes et de Recherches sur l'Armée (Univ. de Toulouse, France) - the Portuguese military system.

Library services provided for outside researchers : yes

Comments : The founding members of the IEEI include representatives from the three major democratic parties (PSD, PS and CDS) as well as journalists, retired military men, and other individuals. In addition to its research, the Institute organizes conferences, lectures, courses, and public opinion polls (especially one on Portuguese attitudes towards NATO and national defense).

SPAIN

SPAIN

The growing controversy over Spain's membership in NATO and proposed entry into the European Community has underscored the need for objective, expert analysis on security and defense questions. The Socialist government is officially committed to a referendum on NATO membership and has "frozen" relations with the Atlantic organization since its arrival in power in December 1982. In early June 1984, a major popular demonstration in Madrid demanded not only NATO withdrawal, but also the closing of all American bases in Spain. The whole issue of the integration of the military establishment within Spain's new democratic institutions is another problem of critical importance.

A major Spanish research center is the Instituto de Cuestiones Cuestiones Internacionales (INCI), founded in 1978. INCI, a private, non-profit organization, models itself after the Council on Foreign Relations and is "dedicated to the study of the problems of peace, war, disarmament, social and economic change and international politics". The Institute's members (numbering about 180) are drawn from the ranks of diplomats, military officers, academics, journalists, and other professionals, and its board of directors includes members of the main political parties. At this time, however, the Socialist government has suspended all subsidies to INCI, which must now rely on its monthly membership dues for day-to-day operations. In terms of research, the Tinker Foundation in the U.S. has recently financed a project on the position of Latin America in the international system. INCI also seeks to promote exchanges of opinion through conferences, seminars, public education activities, and "off-the-record" encounters with national and foreign figures. Some of its series of "Publicaciones INCI" have appeared in English (notably studies on Spanish strategic considerations, Gibraltar, and the Canary Islands).

Under the Franco dictatorship, the official "think tank" was the Instituto de Estudios Politicos which was dissolved in 1977 and merged into the government-operated Centro de Estudios Constitucionales. The center sponsors research in political science and constitutional law and publishes the Revista de Estudios Internacionales, the Revista de Instituciones Europeas, all of which have included some articles on security matters. Another private organization studying international relations (now in its fiftieth year) is the Sociedad de Estudios Internacionales, which also sponsors an advanced diploma program in the field. University researchers at Madrid and Barcelona have been examining aspects of Spain's NATO membership, among other activities.

The military-run Centro de Estudios Superiores de Defensa Nacional (CESEDEN), formed in 1976, has established an institute for strategic studies which is doing research on European security, pacifism, the Mediterranean, and other subjects. CESEDEN offers training courses for staff officers and civilians and publishes two information bulletins. Both CESEDEN and INCI have undertaken cooperative research projects with the Centre d'Etudes et de Recherches sur l'Armée in Toulouse, France.

New participants in the Spanish debate are : (1) the Universidad Complutense (Madrid) which organized a 1983 colloquium on the study of defense issues at the university level; (2) the Instituto de Economia Aplicada (Madrid) where Prof. A. Lorca Corrons is setting up a research unit in collaboration with the Spanish National Science Foundation; and (3) the Centre d'Informacio i Documentacio Internacionals (Barcelona) which works with regional universities and publishes Afers Internacional.

One American observer has contrasted the dearth of serious Spanish research on international questions during Franco's rule with a "scholarly renaissance" that has blossomed since his death (see William T. Salisbury, "International Relations Research in Spain", Orbis, Summer 1981, pp. 429-432). Spanish democratic institutions have provided a major impetus for independent research and public discussion. The polemics over a NATO referendum and the pros and cons of a neutralist policy make the role of research centers all the more essential in maintaining an intelligent level of public debate.

DIRECTORY CODE NUMBER : 163

Name of Institution : Centro de Estudios constitucionales (CESCO)

Address : Plaza de la Marina Espanola, 9
MADRID 13

Founding Date : 1977   Founding Place : Madrid

Type of Organization : National Public

Objectives : Research and documentation in the areas of political science and constitutional law. Occasional activities in the fields of public administration, political sociology and political economics.

Directors : Manuel Aragon
Carlos Alba

Total Staff : 92

Number of researchers on security and defense issues : 0

Regular Periodicals : Title	Founding Date	Issues Annually
1. Revista de Estudios Internacionales	1950	4
2. Revista de Estudios Politicos	1941	6
3. Revista de Instituciones Europeos	1974	3

Library services provided for outside researchers : yes

Comments : CESCO was formed from a merger with the Instituto de Estudios Politicos (founded 1939).

DIRECTORY CODE NUMBER : 164

Name of Institution : Department of International Public Law

Address : Faculty of Law
Universidad Autonoma de Madrid
Cantoblanco
MADRID 34

Telephone : (91) 734-01-00   x. 1421

Founding Date : 1971   Founding Place : Madrid

Type of Organization : National Public University

Objectives : Educational activities : teaching courses, seminars, and conferences.

Director : Prof. Antonio Remiro-Brotons

Total Staff : 6

Number of researchers on security and defense issues : 1

Projects in Progress : Title
                           Name(s) of Researcher(s)

1. The nuclear non-proliferation treaty : a Spanish perspective.
                           Antonio Remiro-Brotons

2. Constitutional aspects of Spanish membership in NATO.
                           Antonio Remiro-Brotons

Publications (since January 1983)

Cesáreo Gutierrez Espada, "The Acceleration of the Arms Race in Space and its Legal Status", (in Spanish) in *Disarmament in International Contemporary Law* (Madrid : Publicaciones Universidad Autonoma, 1983-84).

Library services provided for outside researchers : yes

DIRECTORY CODE NUMBER : 165

Name of Institution : Department of Political Science

Address : Faculty of Law
Universidad Autonoma de Barcelona
Campus Universitario
Bellaterra
BARCELONA

Founding Date : 1977   Founding Place : Barcelona

Type of Organization : National Public University

Objectives : To do research on European security and Spain in NATO.

Director : Jesús M. Rodés

Total Staff : 2

Number of researchers on security and defense issues : 2

Projects in Progress : Title
                              Name(s) of Researcher(s)

---

1. European security : from Helsinki to Madrid.
                              Jesús M. Rodés

2. NATO's southern flank : Spain and its involvement in the Atlantic Alliance.
                              Esther Barbe

Other Publications (since January 1983)

Jesús Rodés and Esther Barbe, *European Security : from Helsinki to Madrid* (forthcoming).

Collaboration with Foreign Study Centers

Research on international security with International Institute for Peace (Vienna).

Library services provided for outside researchers : yes

DIRECTORY CODE NUMBER : 166

Name of Institution : Fundacio "Centre d'Informacio i Documentacio Internacionals a Barcelona" (CIDOB)

Address : Roger de Lluria 125, 1er
08037 BARCELONA

Founding Date : 1973   Founding Place : Barcelona

Type of Organization : National Private Non-Profit

Objectives : Study of international themes with the purpose of connecting our reality with the international reality. Priorities are the Mediterranean, Arab world, and Latin America.

Director : Josep Ribera

Total Staff : 12

Number of researchers on security and defense issues : 3

Projects in Progress : Title

1. Comparative study of Western european defense policy.

2. Contribution of Spain to the security of Europe's southern flank (the Mediterranean).

3. Alternative Systems of defense and security.

Regular Periodicals : Title	Founding Date	Issues Annually
1. Afers Internacional	1983	4
2. Dossier-CIDOB	1983	6
3. Sobre Pau/Paz	1984	6

DIRECTORY CODE NUMBER : 167

Name of Institution : Instituto de Cuestiones Internaciónales (INCI)

Address : Almirante 1
          MADRID 4

Telephone : (1) 222-19-38

Founding Date : June 1978   Founding Place : Madrid

Type of Organization : National Private Non-Profit

Objectives : To study the problems of peace, war, disarmament, social and economic change, and international politics.

Director : Antonio Sanchez-Gijón

Total Staff : 6

Number of researchers on security and defense issues : 3

Projects in Progress : Title
                       Name(s) of Researcher(s)

1. Position of Latin America in the International System.
   Antonio Sanchez-Gijón
   Dr. Juan Ferrando
   Dr. Juan Carlos Gonzalez
   Dr. Enrique Alvarez Conde

Dr. Alejandro Lorca
Dr. Alberto Garcia
Prof. Jose Luis Garcia
Prof. Germán Granda
Prof. Tomás Mestre

2. Politics and power in the South Atlantic.

Regular Periodicals : Title	Founding Date	Issues Annually
Publicaciones INCI		occasional

Other Publications (since January 1983)

1. "Strategy in the Western Mediterranean and the Magreb" (in Spanish).
2. "The European Community : decline or renewal ?" (in Spanish).

Collaboration with Foreign Study Centers

Cooperation with Foreign Policy Analysis Institute, Cambridge, Mass.

Comments : The INCI Board of Directors includes members of the main political parties, academics, lawyers, retired military, government officials and journalists. The project on Latin America is funded by a grant from the Tinker Foundation. The Institute also sponsors a series of conferences, seminars, off-the-record meetings, and public information (outreach) programs.

DIRECTORY CODE NUMBER : 168

Name of Institution : Instituto de Economia Aplicada

Address : Universidad Autonoma de Madrid

Director : A. Lorca Corrons

Projects in Progress : Title

The economic dimension of security and defense.

DIRECTORY CODE NUMBER : 169

Name of Institution : Instituto Espanol de Estudios Estrategicos Centro de Estudios Superiores de Defensa Nacional (CESEDEN)

Address : Paseo de la Castellana 61
          MADRID 1

Telephone : (1) 4417781

Founding Date : 1976   Founding Place : Madrid

Type of organization : National Public

<u>Objectives</u> : Study of security and defense through the disciplines of strategy, sociology, polemology, history and technology.

<u>Director</u> : Adm. Jesus Salgado Alba

<u>Total Staff</u> : 18

<u>Number of researchers on security and defense issues</u> : 8

Projects in Progress : Title

---

1. Security and national defense in Europe.
2. Theories of pacifism.
3. Strategic study of the Strait of Gibraltar.
4. Polemology of the Mediterranean area.
5. Military sociology.
6. Economics and national defense.

Regular Periodicals : Title	Founding Date	Issues Annually
1. <u>Boletin del CESEDEN</u>	1976	12
2. <u>Boletin de Informacion Bibliografica</u>	1980	24

Collaboration with Foreign Study Centers

1. Centre d'études et de recherches sur l'armée (CERSA), University of Toulouse (France).

2. Instituto de Estudos Estrategicos e Internacionais, Lisboa, Portugal.

Library services provided for outside researchers : yes

DIRECTORY CODE NUMBER : 170

Name of Institution : Sociedad de Estudios Internacionales (SEI)

Address : Duque de Medinaceli 4-4°
          MADRID 14

Founding Date : Jan. 1934   Founding Place : Madrid

Type of Organization : National Private Non-Profit

Objectives : (1) Establishment of a fairer world system;
             (2) cooperation between all nations and stability in international relations;
             (3) fulfillment of Spain's international mission and cooperation with Latin American countries;
             (4) research concerning conflicts, war and peace.

Director : Fernando de Salas López

Total Staff : 20

Number of researchers on security and defense issues : 4

Projects in Progress : Title
                                Name(s) of Researcher(s)

Concerning war and peace.
                                Fernando de Salas López

Publications (since January 1983)

1. Fernando de Salas López, <u>The Utopia of Peace and the Terror of War</u> (in Spanish) (Colección ADALID, 1983) 279 pp.

2. <u>Estudios Internacionales-1983</u> (Madrid : Sociedad de Estudios Internacionales, 1984).

<u>Library services provided for outside researchers</u> : yes

<u>Comments</u> : Among other conferences, the SEI sponsored one on "The Security and Defense of Spain in Western Europe" in April 1984. The Society also offers a diploma course in advanced international studies.

DIRECTORY CODE NUMBER : 171

<u>Name of Institution</u> : Universidad Complutense de Madrid

<u>Address</u> : Ciudad Universitaria
          MADRID 3

<u>Telephone</u> : (for Prof. Vinas only) : (1) 266-48-00

<u>Contact</u> : Prof. A. Vinas Martin

SWEDEN

SWEDEN

The Stockholm International Peace Research Institute (SIPRI) dominates the Swedish intellectual scene in the security and defense field. SIPRI's World Armaments and Disarmament yearbook is regarded as authoritative by the European peace movement, and its special studies command global attention. The Institute was founded in 1966 to commemorate Sweden's 150 years of unbroken peace, and Alva Myrdal was elected as its first Chairman of the Governing Board. Although almost entirely financed by grants from the Swedish Parliament, SIPRI still maintains its institutional independence from government direction. It also claims to be impartial in its analysis of peace and security issues, and its staff is recruited from Western, Eastern, and neutral countries. In 1982, however, a SIPRI researcher was expelled from Sweden under suspicion of espionage for the Soviets. The Institute has also come under considerable criticism by Western authorities for an allegedly one-sided approach to arms questions. Nevertheless, SIPRI publications serve as an extremely useful ideological counterpoise to those put out by the IISS and similar organizations.

SIPRI has been in the forefront of research on nuclear proliferation, chemical/biological weapons and environmental warfare, and the international arms trade. The yearbook for 1983 contains sections on nuclear weapons stockpiles, theater nuclear weapons, nuclear explosions, the peace movement, military research, space warfare, and other related topics. Many of these subjects are being examined in greater detail by SIPRI analysts whose findings will eventually be published in monograph form. Recent SIPRI books have studied uranium enrichment and the proliferation threat and nuclear-free zones in Europe. According to the Institute's annual report of activities, "researchers work either individually or on research teams on SIPRI projects : project proposals are considered by the Research Collegium and the Governing Board, and publications are refereed by independent experts outside the Institute. In addition to the researchers recruited for some years, there is a flow of guest researchers who spend a short time at SIPRI, and the Institute also uses consultants who work in their own countries on SIPRI's behalf".

The Swedish Institute of International Affairs is the major national organization dealing in all problems of the international environment. In terms of security questions, research has mostly concentrated on European problems of military security, balances and imbalances, tension and detente, and political and economic integration. Over the past decade, the Institute has moved from a highly theoretical, closely-knit structure for research to a more individualistic, decentralized approach. Particular attention is being paid to economic security problems and to studies of Soviet policy and long-term objectives and their effect on neutral Sweden. One team of researchers will examine the geopolitics of Soviet-rimland relations in a large-scale, multi-year project. The Nordic Cooperation Committee for International Politics, located at the Institute, publishes the quarterly Cooperation and Conflict (in English) and also a very valuable semi-annual description (in English) of international studies in the Nordic countries. The Committee is directed by a board of scholars from all five countries.

Swedish university studies are principally oriented towards peace and conflict research. There are specialized departments at Gothenburg, Lund, and Uppsala, all engaged in cross-disciplinary work on the causes and prevention of war and violence. Researchers in the Political Science Department at the University of Stockholm have been systematically analyzing (over a number of years) the processes of change in the foreign policy of states. Another source of peace research in Sweden is the Peace Forum of the Labour Movement, established by Alva Myrdal.

The Defense Ministry has been relatively open about its policy-oriented research, and the Division for International Relations of the Defense Research Institute (FOA) has published a lengthy series of sophisticated reports on global issues.

Security and defense research in Sweden is thus highly developed and broad-based. The internationalism of Scandinavian "think tanks" is impressive, and their organization could serve as a model for other countries seeking to create a policy-oriented "brain trust". SIPRI and other peace research groups have done much to publicize the multi-dimensional arms race and the deleterious effects on economic and social development. Yet the Soviet submarine incidents and the unresolved debate over a nuclear-free zone have reminded Swedes (and other Scandinavians) that they play a role in the East-West power struggle. Partly for this reason, research organizations like the Institute of International Affairs and the FOA have been focusing on problems of regional security and defense and relations with the Soviet neighbor. Many of the Swedish publications appear in English and thus benefit from a much wider circulation around the globe.

DIRECTORY CODE NUMBER : 172

Name of Institution : Centre for the Study of International Relations

Address : Dobelnsgatan 81
Box 19112
10432 STOCKHOLM 19

DIRECTORY CODE NUMBER : 173

Name of Institution : Department of Peace and Conflict Research

Address : University of Gothenburg
Viktoriagatan 30
41125 GOTHENBURG

Telephone : (31) 63-14-28

Founding Date : 1971   Founding Place : Gothenburg

Type of Organization : National Public University

Objectives : Promote research on international relations which would increase the understanding of causes behind conflicts and war.

Director : Prof. Björn Hettne

Total Staff : 6

Number of researchers on security and defense issues : 2

Projects in Progress : Title   Name(s) of Researcher(s)

1. The role of force in development.
   Björn Hettne/Svante Karlsson/
   Peter Magnusson/Gösta Tompuri/
   Björn Andersson/Jerker Carlsson/
   Thomas Sterner/Eugeneo Rovzar

2. Mobilization project : social and political movements in the Third World.
   Mats Friberg

Collaboration with Foreign Study Centers

Coordinate peace and development research as members of the European Association for Development Research and Institute Training.

Library services provided for outside researchers : yes

DIRECTORY CODE NUMBER : 174

Name of Institution : Department of Peace and Conflict Research

Address : Lund University
          Dag Hammarskjölds väg 2B
          22364 LUND

Telephone : (46) 14-54-60

Founding Date : 1971   Founding Place : Lund

Type of Organization : National Public University

Objectives : To conduct research and analyses on conflicts and violence in a broad sense and to study the conditions of peaceful development on a variety of social levels of local as well as global society.

Director : Jan Oberg

Total Staff : 6

Number of researchers on security and defense issues : 5

Projects in Progress : Title
                              Name(s) of Researcher(s)

1. Conflict in the Horn of Africa.
                              Hakan Wiberg

2. Armaments and arms race.
                              Hakan Wiberg

3. Military research and development in Denmark and Greenland.
   Jan Oberg

4. Military technology and the dynamics of the arms race.
   Wilhelm Agrell

5. New international military order.
   Jan Oberg

6. Trade and war.
   Hakan Wiberg

7. War, militarization, and military-economic relations.
   Kent Lindkvist

8. Ideology, mobilization and conflict.
   Kent Lindkvist

9. Changing character and role of the intelligence function.
   Wilhelm Agrell

10. Alternatives to war and violence.
    Hakan Wiberg

11. Peace and disarmament education.
    Hakan Wiberg

12. Theories of militarism, security and peace.
    Jan Oberg

13. Denmark in the Global Society : security and defense policies.
    Jan Oberg

14. New concepts of common Nordic security.
    Wilhelm Agrell/Jan Andersson/
    Hakan Wiberg/Jan Oberg

15. Low-level conflicts and the civilian flank of national security.
    Wilhelm Agrell

16. Swedish defense doctrine 1945-1977.
    Wilhelm Agrell

17. Technology and conflicts.
    Charles Edquist

Publications (since January 1983)

1. Hakan Wiberg, "Measuring Military Expenditures : Purposes, Methods, Sources", <u>Cooperation and Conflict</u>, 1983 : 3, pp. 161-177.

2. Jan Oberg, "Why Disarmament and Arms Control Negotiations Will Fail - What Can Be Done ?" <u>Bulletin of Peace Proposals</u>, 1983 : 3, pp. 277-282.

3. Wilhelm Agrell, <u>Neutrality at Stake</u> (in Swedish) (Stockholm : 1983) 41 pp.

4. Jan Andersson and Jan Oberg (Eds), <u>Perspectives on Nordic Peace Policies</u> (in Swedish) (Lund, 1983), 103 pp.

5. Hakan Wiberg (Ed.), <u>Conflict and Solidarity in Poland</u> (in Swedish) (Stockholm : Prisma, 1983), 239 pp.

6. Jan Oberg, <u>Developing Security and Securing Development</u> (in Danish) (Copenhagen : Vindrose, 1983) 337 pp.

<u>Library services provided for outside researchers</u> : yes

DIRECTORY CODE NUMBER : 175

<u>Name of Institution</u> : Department of Peace and Conflict Research

<u>Address</u> : Uppsala University
Oestra Agatan 53
PO Box 278
75105 UPPSALA

<u>Telephone</u> : (18) 15-54-00

<u>Founding Date</u> : 1971   <u>Founding Place</u> : Uppsala

<u>Type of Organization</u> : National Public University

<u>Objectives</u> : To provide a milieu for cross-disciplinary research and teaching within the university in the field of peace and conflict research.

<u>Director</u> : Dr. Peter Wallensteen

Total Staff : 12

Number of researchers on security and defense issues : 8

Projects in Progress : title
         Name(s) of Researcher(s)

1. Armed conflicts and durable conflict resolution.
  Peter Wallensteen/Kjell-Ake Nordquist/Ken Wilson/Adele Aranki

2. Soviet research and development and the SS-20 missiles.
  Björn Hagelin

3. Military and civilian research and development.
  Göran Lindgren

4. Studies in research ethics.
  Lars Rydén

5. Mineral supplies and major power intervention in the Third World.
  Mats Hammarström

Publications (since January 1983)

1. Erik Noreen, "The Nordic Balance : a Security Policy Concept in Theory and Practice", 1983, 14 pp.

2. Peter Wallensteen, "Incompatibility, Confrontation and War : Four Models and Three Historical Systems, 1816-1976", 1982, 31 pp.

3. Göran Lindgren, "Why Do States Arm ?" (in Swedish), 1983, 24 pp.

4. Kjell-Ake Nordquist, "Conflicting Peace Proposals : a Theoretical Perspective on the Palestine Conflict", 1983, 90 pp.

Library services provided for outside researchers : yes

Comments : The Department is engaged in general studies on military research and development and on the classification of on-going armed conflicts over the government of territory.

DIRECTORY CODE NUMBER : 176

Name of Institution : Department of Political Science

Address : University of Gothenburg
          Box 5048
          40221 GOTHENBURG

Telephone : (31) 63-10-00

Projects in Progress : Title

Name(s) of Researcher(s)

Tension and detente in Europe : a study of schools of thought and their role in the foreign policy of the Soviet Union, the Federal Republic of Germany, and the German Democratic Republic.

Rutger Lindahl/Lena Jonsson/
Irene Nilsson

DIRECTORY CODE NUMBER : 177

Name of Institution : Department of Political Science

Address : University of Stockholm
          10691 STOCKHOLM

Telephone : (8) 16-20-00

Type of Organization : National Public University

Objectives : University instruction and teaching.

Director : Gunnar Wallin

Total Staff : 22

Number of researchers on security and defense issues : 5

Projects in Progress : Title
                      Name(s) of Researcher(s)

1. Foreign policy change - the conditions under which fundamental
   changes in the foreign policy of states occur.
                      Kjell Goldmann/Jan Hallenberg

2. Democracy and bureaucracy in foreign and domestic policy.
                      Kjell Goldmann

Publications (since January 1983)

1. Kjell Goldmann, "Detente : Evaluation of an Experiment" (in
   Swedish) in Bo Huldt and Erik Holm (Eds.) Peace and Security :
   Debate and Analysis 1982-1983 (in Swedish) (Stockholm :
   Akademilitteratur, 1983).

2. Kjell Goldmann, Detente : Domestic Politics as a Stabilizer of
   Foreign Policy, Center of International Studies, Princeton
   University and Dept. of Political Science, University of
   Stockholm, 1984.

Comments : The Department set up a group for research on peace
           and security policy in autumn 1983. Kjell Goldmann is
           the chairman.

DIRECTORY CODE NUMBER : 178

Name of Institution : Division for International Studies
                     National Defence Research Institute (FOA)

Address : Box 27322
          10254 STOCKHOLM

Telephone : (8) 63-15-00

Founding Date : 1968   Founding Place : Stockholm

Objectives : Research in support of long-range defense planning, carried out both by the Ministry of Defense and by the various military and civil branches of the national defense.

Director : Nils Andrén

Projects in Progress : Title
                               Name(s) of Researcher(s)

1. North-South issues and security implications.

2. Comparative study of Soviet policy behavior in relation to Poland in 1980-1981 and Czechoslovakia in 1968.

                               Ingmar Oldberg

Publications (since January 1983)

1. Hans Sjöberg, "French Security Policy" (in Swedish), FOA Report.

2. Irene Nilsson, "GDR between East and West" (in Swedish), FOA Report.

3. Lena Jonsson, "The Soviet Union and Western Europe" (in Swedish), FOA Report.

4. Mette Skak, "Soviet Policy in East Asia", FOA Report.

5. Nils Andrén, The World and We : a Security Policy Perspective (in Swedish) (Stockholm : Centralförbundet Folkoch Försvar, 1983), 36 pp.

6. Bengt-Göran Bergstrand, "The Defense Expenditures of the Western Countries - statistics, trends, comparisons" (in Swedish), FOA Report, 1983, 243 pp.

7. Björn Hagelin, "Military Production in the Third World" (in Swedish), FOA Report, 1983, 37 pp.

8. Erik Moberg, "The World Economy and the East-West Conflict : Developments in the 1970s" (in Swedish), FOA Report, 1983, 135 pp.

9. Ingmar Oldberg, "A Small Useful Capitalist State - Sweden in Current Soviet Foreign Policy" (in Swedish), FOA Report, 1982, 24 pp.

DIRECTORY CODE NUMBER : 179

Name of Institution : Nordic Cooperation Committee for International Politics

Address : c/o Swedish Institute of International Affairs
Lilla Nygatan 23
11128 STOCKHOLM

Telephone : (8) 23-40-60

Type of Organization : International Public Non-Profit

Objectives : Publications and information on research in the Nordic countries; gives financial support to advanced students and scholars.

Director : Asbjørn Eide

Total Staff : 2

Regular Periodicals : Title	Founding Date	Issues Annually
1. Cooperation and Conflict : Nordic Journal of International Politics		4
2. International Studies in the Nordic Countries		2

Comments : The Committee includes representatives of universities and research institutions from the five Nordic countries.

DIRECTORY CODE NUMBER : 180

Name of Institution : Peace Forum of the Swedish Labour Movement

Address : 10553 STOCKHOLM

Telephone : (8) 22-55-80

Founding Date : 1981   Founding Place : Stockholm

Type of Organization : National Private Non-Profit (affiliated with political party)

Objectives : (1) nuclear weapon disarmament;
             (2) nuclear weapon-free zones;
             (3) trade union activities and conversion;
             (4) peace education;
             (5) confidence-building measures.

Director : Gunnar Lassinantti

Total Staff : 4

Regular Periodicals : Title	Founding Date	Issues Annually
Freds Fakta	1983	8

Other Publications (since January 1983)

1. "Europe, Nuclear Weapons and Unemployment", Hearing Report, 1983 (in Swedish).

2. "Report from an International Trade Union Conference on Conversion", 1984 (to be translated into English).

Comments : The Forum is run by the Trade Union Congress and the Social Democratic Party.

DIRECTORY CODE NUMBER : 181

Name of Institution : Stockholm International Peace Research
Institute (SIPRI)

Address : Bergshamra
17173 SOLNA

Telephone : (8) 55-97-00

Founding Date : 1966   Founding Place : Stockholm

Type of Organization : International Private Non-Profit

Objectives : To conduct scientific research on questions of conflict
and cooperation of importance for international peace
and security - with particular attention to the problems
of disarmament and arms regulation.

Director : Frank Blackaby

Total Staff : 60

Number of researchers on security and defense issues : 30

Projects in Progress : Title

1. Statistical study of world expenditure on military research and development.

2. World arms trade (esp. economic aspects).

3. World-wide foreign military presence.

4. Third World navies.

5. Possible military applications of high-energy beams.

6. Technological advances in conventional weapon technologies.

7. Effects of chemical warfare.

8. Effects of military activity on the environment (esp. long-term effects of herbicides and the unexploded material remnants of war).

9. Nuclear disengagement zones in Europe.

10. Possible confidence-building measures in Europe.

11. Ways in which conflicts outside Europe might spread to Europe.

12. Follow-up to Palme Commission report, <u>Common Security, a Programme for Disarmament</u>.

13. No-First-Use of nuclear weapons.

14. Arms Control measures in outer space.

15. Asian security.

16. Non-nuclear defense of Western Europe.

17. Negotiations concerned with a chemical weapons convention.

18. Arms control dictionary.

19. Measures to reduce the fear of surprise attack.

20. Second-generation confidence and security-building measures.
    Karl Birnbaum/Sverre Lodgaard

21. Development of South Africa's military industry.
    Signe Landgren

Regular Periodicals : Title	Founding Date	Issues Annually
World Armaments and Disarmament, SIPRI Yearbook	1968	1

Other Publications (since January 1983)

1. Allan Krass, Peter Boskma, Boelie Elzen and Wim A. Smit, <u>Uranium Enrichment and Nuclear Weapon Proliferation</u> (London : Taylor and Francis, 1983), ca. 300 pp.

2. Sverre Lodgaard and Marek Thee (Eds.), <u>Nuclear Disengagement in Europe</u> (London : Taylor and Francis, 1983).

3. Frank Blackaby, Josef Goldblat and Sverre Lodgaard (Eds.), No-First-Use (London : Taylor and Francis, 1984).

4. Miroslav Nincic, An Expanding Vortex ? Soviet-American Third World Conflicts and European Security (London : Taylor and Francis, forthcoming 1984).

Comments : SIPRI is a problem-oriented research institute : that is, it starts by considering what the topics of importance are in the area of world armaments and disarmament, and then considers what research approach is appropriate to these problems. It has important data banks on the transfer of major weapons, launches of military satellites and world military expenditure. SIPRI research interests may be grouped under three headings :
(1) military expenditure, military deployment, and the arms trade;
(2) military technology;
(3) arms control and disarmament issues.

DIRECTORY CODE NUMBER : 182

Name of Institution : Swedish Institute of International Affairs

Address : Lilla Nygatan 23
11128 STOCKHOLM

Telephone : (8) 23-40-60

Founding Date : 1938   Founding Place : Stockholm

Type of Organization : National Private Non-Profit

Objectives : Promote research on international developments, with special attention to Swedish foreign and security policies.

Director : Dr. Ake Sparring

Total Staff : 45

Number of researchers on security and defense issues : 8

Projects in Progress : Title	Name(s) of Researcher(s)

1. Confidence-building measures between East and West.
   Karl Birnbaum

2. Neutral states and security in Europe.
   Karl Birnbaum

3. Energy policy and Swedish national security.
   Walter Carlsnaes

4. Economic security policies and Atlantic cooperation.
   Gunnar Sjöstedt

5. Freedom from alliances and freedom of action : Sweden and the USA.
   Bengt Sundelius

6. Foreign intervention in civil wars : a comparative analysis of several case studies.
   Dertil Dunér

7. Future development of the Sino-Soviet conflict.
   Thomas Hart

8. West German military thought in the 1970s and 1980s.
   Julian Lider

9. Correlation of forces : a study of Marxist-Leninist concepts.
   Julian Lider

10. Role of West German defense in the NATO defense structure.
    Bo Huldt

11. European theater nuclear weapons.
    Milton Leitenberg

Regular Periodicals : Title	Founding Date	Issues Annually
1. Internationella Studier		6
2. Världspolitikens dagsfragor		12
3. Fred Och Säkerhat	1983	2

Other Publications (since January 1983)

1. Julian Lider, "Essays on British Military Thought : Military Thought of a Medium Power, 1960s and Afterwards", Institute Research Report, N° 8, 1983.

2. Kristian Gerner, "The Soviet Union and Central Europe : a Study in Precarious Security", Institute Research Report, N° 9, 1983.

3. Bo Huldt and Atis Lejins (Eds.), "Militarism and Militarization", Institute Conference Papers, N° 3, 1983.

Library services provided for outside researchers : yes

Comments : The Institute plans to undertake a research project on Soviet-rimlands relations during 1984-1985. Prof. Karl Birnbaum and Bo Huldt will direct the project.

SWITZERLAND

SWITZERLAND

The basis for the actual Swiss Confederation of twenty-three cantons dates back to August 1291 when three of the cantons agreed to the "Eternal Alliance" for joint protection against foreign rule. The principle of Swiss neutrality developed during the sixteenth century and was reaffirmed by the Treaty of Westphalia in 1648. The neutrality of the country was last violated by the armies of the French Revolution in 1798 and was ultimately recognized as part of international law at the Congress of Vienna in 1815. The Federal Constitution of 1848 (as amended in 1874) gave the central government authority for defense and foreign policy. The Swiss have instituted a system of territorial defense and universal military conscription, in which every Swiss male is liable for duty between the ages of 20 and 50. As a neutral country, Switzerland has regularly hosted summit talks, peace and disarmament negotiations, and international organizations, most notably the League of Nations, established in Geneva in May 1920. Today, Switzerland is the headquarters for the International Red Cross, the Universal Postal Union, the International Labor Office, and numerous other United Nations agencies (including UNIDIR), even though the country itself is not officially a member of the UN.

The most noted Swiss research organization in the security and defense field is the Programme for Strategic and International Security Studies (PSIS) of the Institut Universitaire de Hautes Etudes internationales of Geneva. PSIS operates independently in setting up its own projects, though it depends largely on the Institute for funding and facilities. Research work is concentrated around two main themes, "security in the developing countries and the changing environment of international security in Europe and its implications for neutral states". The nature of conflict and the perception of security in the Third World make up one project pertaining to the first theme; the study will also attempt a structured comparison between the Iran-Iraq war, the Western Sahara dispute, and the civil war in Chad. In terms of the European security theme, PSIS researchers are looking at the role of neutral states like Switzerland in the process of arms control and regional stability. This two-year project is part of a study on Swiss security policy financed by the Swiss National Fund. Another European security project is examining the situation in the Nordic countries. Results of PSIS studies are communicated through its Occasional Papers series.

The foremost national organization devoted to international studies is the Schweizerisches Institut für Auslandforschung, a private, non-profit center located in Zurich. The Institute sponsors a working group on Swiss security issues, headed by Prof. Daniel Frei, who is both Director of the Institute and of the Forschungstelle für Politische Wissenschaft at the University of Zurich. The latter organization is doing a number of studies on subjects like threat perception, arms transfers, and crisis management. In Bern, the private Schweizerische Ost-Institut undertakes critical analyses of the Soviet and Eastern European systems.

The Division of Military Science at the Swiss Federal Institute of Technology (Eidgenössische Technische Hochschule Zürich) is the closest equivalent to a military academy, training the permanent instructors corps of the Swiss army and doing research on Swiss security policy and on East-West strategic considerations. Another subject of particular interest is the critical examination of the doctrine of territorial defense, the basis of Swiss military strategy. The official Central Defense Office in Bern also does research work on comparative defense policy, crisis management, and long-term ecological and economic problems.

The Geneva International Peace Research Institute (GIPRI) is the best-known peace research organization in Switzerland. The former director of GIPRI has recently created the Independent Scientific Research Institute (ISRI), which focuses on technological determinants of disarmament. ISRI collaborates with the Stockholm International Peace Research Institute on projects concerning laser and particle-beam weapons and the nuclear fuel cycle. The Geneva-based Centre d'Etudes Pratiques de la Négociation Internationale holds conferences principally on North-South economic questions, and some of the topics on global interdependence have security implications.

Lastly, the International Civil Defence Organization (ICDO) is devoted to the protection of civilian populations during natural disasters and wartime. ICDO has also been instrumental in introducing the idea of civil defense into international law, especially in the 1949 and 1977 revisions of the Geneva Conventions. The organization also holds a series of world-wide conferences and exhibitions and trains civil defense officers from its member-states.

DIRECTORY CODE NUMBER : 183

Name of Institution : Centre d'Etudes Pratiques de la Négociation
Internationale

Address : 11a, avenue de la Paix
1202 GENEVE

Telephone : (22) 34-89-50

Founding Date : 1980   Founding Place : Genève

Type of Organization : National Private Non-Profit

Objectives : To organize colloquia, conferences and seminars.

Director : J.F. Freymond

Total Staff : 2

Number of researchers on security and defense issues : 1

Comments : The Center has organized conferences on the North-South
dialogue, human rights, and European unification, among
other subjects.

DIRECTORY CODE NUMBER : 184

Name of Institution : Department of Military Science

Address : Swiss Federal Institute of Technology
(Eidgenössische Technische Hochschule Zürich)
8092 ZURICH

Telephone : (1) 256-39-93

Founding Date : 1918   Founding Place : Zürich

Type of Organization : National Public

Objectives : (1) educational activities (teaching courses, seminars,
conferences) for the instruction of the Swiss Army;
(2) research activities for the Swiss Government in the
field of military science.

Director : Alfred Stutz

Total Staff : 10

Number of researchers on security and defense issues : 6

Projects in Progress : Title

1. The Swiss Air Force as a means of the Swiss security policy.
2. The Soviet nuclear targeting policy.
3. Partisans during World War II.
4. The NATO strategy of "flexible response" : causes and consequences.

Other Publications (since January 1983)

Albert A. Stahel, USA-USSR : Nuclear War ? The Arsenals of the Superpowers since 1945 (in German), (Frauenfeld : Verlag Huber, 1983).

Collaboration with Foreign Study Centers

1. Bundeswehrhochschule, München (FRG).
2. U.S. Army War College, Carlisle Barracks, PA (USA).

Comments : The Department (Militarwissenschaftliche Abteilung) is the equivalent of a military war college with courses of instruction for Army Officers.

DIRECTORY CODE NUMBER : 185

Name of Institution : Forschungstelle für Politische Wissenschaft

Address : Universität Zürich
Münstergasse 9
8001 ZURICH

Telephone : (1) 257-11-11
(1) 257-28-41

Founding Date : 1972   Founding Place : Zürich

Type of Organization : National Public University

Objectives : Research and teaching in political science.

Director : Prof. Daniel Frei

Total Staff : 15

Number of researchers on security and defense issues : 4

Projects in Progress : Title
                      Name(s) of Researcher(s)

---

1. Strategic cognition : assumptions regarding the potential adversary (USA and USSR).
   Daniel Frei/Dieter Ruloff

2. Arms transfer dependence.
   Christian Catrina

3. International norms and crisis behavior.
   Heinz Krummenacher

4. A synoptical analysis of selected terms used in the strategic doctrines of the nuclear powers (China, France, Great Britain, USSR, USA).
   Stephan Kux

5. Analysis of arguments against disarmament proposals.
   Bruno Rösli

Regular Periodicals : Title	Founding Date	Issues Annually
Kleine Studien zur Politischer Wissenschaft	1973	occasional

Other Publications (since January 1983)

1. Daniel Frei and Dieter Ruloff, East-West Relations in Europe (Cambridge, Mass. : Gunn & Hain, 1983) 2 vols.

2. Daniel Frei (Ed.), Managing International Crises (Beverly Hills, CA : Sage Publications, 1983).

3. Daniel Frei and Dieter Ruloff, Handbook for Analysis of International Politics : Methods for Practice, Consultation and Research (in German) (Diessenhofen, Switz. : Verlag Ruegger, 1984), 500 pp.

Collaboration with Foreign Study Centers

Cooperation with the United Nations Institute for Disarmament Research (UNIDIR).

Comments : The Research Division has two departments : one concerned with comparative politics (headed by Prof. Ulrich Klöti) and the other devoted to international politics (headed by Prof. Frei).

DIRECTORY CODE NUMBER : 186

Name of Institution : Geneva International Peace Research Institute
(GIPRI)

Address : 41, rue de Zürich
1201 GENEVE

Telephone : (22) 32-14-38

Founding Date : 1980   Founding Place : Genève

Comments : GIPRI has studied topics like energy and security
(especially provisioning of energy to Switzerland);
children and war; and processes of peaceful resolution
of disputes between nations.

DIRECTORY CODE NUMBER : 187

Name of Institution : Independent Scientific Research Institute
(ISRI)

Address : 9, rue Amat
1202 GENEVE

Telephone : (22) 31-33-26
(22) 31-83-26

Founding Date : Sept. 1982   Founding Place : Genève

Type of Organization : International Private Non-Profit

Objectives : To conduct research and provide scientific expertise
on contemporary problems which have significant technological aspects, especially in the areas of disarmament.

Director : Dr. André Gsponer

Total Staff : 5

Number of researchers on security and defense issues : 5

Projects in Progress : Title

1. Technological assessment of the feasibility of laser and particle beam weapons.

2. Efficacy of the neutron-bomb as an anti-tank weapon.

3. Assessment of thermonuclear energy in areas such as energy production, nuclear materials production and nuclear weapons proliferation.

4. Military impact of the social sciences.

5. Military nuclear-fuel cycle.

Publications (since January 1983)

1. André Gsponer, "Technical Feasibility of the Detection of Nuclear Weapons", in SIPRI-Pugwash, Nuclear Disengagement in Europe (London : Taylor & Francis, 1983).

2. S. Geer and A. Gsponer, "Radiation Doses Close to the Shower Axis Calculated for High-Energy Electron Beams in Air", Atomkernenergie/Kerntechnik, vol. 43 (1983), pp. 42-46.

3. A. Gsponer, "New Nuclear Bombs" (in Italian) in A. Drago and G. Salio (Eds.), Science and War (Torino : Ed. Abele, 1983).

4. A. Gsponer, J. Grinevald, B. Vitale and M. Finger, Science and War (in German), (Zürich : VMP-VSETH, Universitätsstrasse 19, 1983), 94 pp.

5. A. Gsponer, B. Jasani and S. Sahin, "Emerging Nuclear Energy Systems and Nuclear Weapon Proliferation", Atomkernenergie/Kerntechnik, Vol. 43 (1983), pp. 169-174.

Collaboration with Foreign Study Centers

SIPRI on laser and particle beam weapons project and on military nuclear fuel cycle project.

DIRECTORY CODE NUMBER : 188

Name of Institution : International Civil Defence Organization
(ICDO)

Address : 10-12 chemin de Surville
1213 PETIT-LANCY/GENEVE

Telephone : (22) 93-44-33

Founding Date : 1931   Founding Place : Paris

Type of Organization : International Public

Objectives : To intensify and coordinate on a world-wide scale the development and improvement of organizations, means and techniques for preventing and reducing the consequences of natural disaster in peacetime and of the use of weapons in time of conflict.

Director : Dr. Milan Bodi

Total Staff : 12

Projects in Progress : Title

Data bank on disaster preparedness and civil protection.

Regular Periodicals : Title	Founding Date	Issues Annually
International Civil Defence (also appears in French, Spanish and Arabic editions)	1952	12

Other Publications (since January 1983)

Complete Records of Proceedings of World Civil Defence Conferences

Comments : The ICDO is an intergovernmental organization registered at the United Nations, and its Constitution is an international convention binding the High Contracting Parties. The organization was engaged in the preparation of the Additional Protocols to the Geneva Conventions in 1977. Georges Saint-Paul, the founder of the organization, originated the idea of the "Geneva Zones", well-demarcated, recognized localities where the civilian population could seek refuge in wartime.

DIRECTORY CODE NUMBER : 189

Name of Institution : Programme for Strategic and International Security Studies (PSIS)

Address : Institut Universitaire de Hautes Etudes Internationales
132, rue de Lausanne
C.P. 53
1211 GENEVE 21

Telephone : (22) 31-17-30

Founding Place : Genève

Type of organization : International University

Objectives : (1) research primarily on security in the developing countries and the changing environment of European security and its implications for neutral states;
(2) seminars and working-groups for graduate students on areas close to these research interests.

Director : Prof. Curt Gasteyger

Total Staff : 8

Number of researchers on security and defense issues : 5

Projects in Progress : Title   Name(s) of Researcher(s)

1. Arms control and the arms race.
                                      Curt Gasteyger

2. Comparative study of regional conflicts in the Third World.

3. Regional security and arms control in East Asia.

4. Contribution of small states (like Switzerland) to arms control and regional security.
                                      René Haug *et al*

5. Regional security in Northern Europe.

Regular Periodicals : Title   Founding Date   Issues Annually

PSIS Occasional Papers

Other Publications (since January 1983)

1. Fereidun Fesharaki, "The Oil Market and Western European Energy Security", PSIS Occasional Paper 1/83, 1983.

2. Neil MacFarlane, "Soviet Intervention in Third World Conflict", PSIS Occasional Paper 2/83, 1983.

3. Dilip Mukerjee, "Kampuchea : ASEAN Response to Great Power Rivalries", PSIS Occasional Paper 3/83, 1983.

4. David J. Blair and Paul A. Summerville, "Oil Import Security : the Cases of Japan and Great Britain", PSIS Occasional Paper 4/83, 1983.

5. Jessica Byron, "Regional Security in Latin America and Africa : the OAS and the OAU in the Light of Contemporary Security Issues", PSIS Occasional Paper 1/84, 1984.

6. Curt Gasteyger (Ed.), "The Security of Switzerland : the Challenges of the Future" (in French), PSIS Occasional Paper 2/84, 1984.

Library services provided for outside researchers : yes

Comments : The PSIS operates independently but within the framework of the Institut Universitaire de Hautes Etudes Internationales. It thus benefits from the advantages of a graduate teaching environment composed of many nationalities and several disciplines, and autonomy in its own research priorities.

DIRECTORY CODE NUMBER : 190

Name of Institution : Schweizerisches Institut für Auslandforschung

Address : Münstergasse 9
8001 ZURICH

Telephone : (1) 252-42-20

Founding Date : 1943   Founding Place : Zürich

Type of Organization : National Private Non-Profit

Objectives : To inform the Swiss public on problems of international politics and to produce confidential studies on security problems.

Director : Prof. Daniel Frei

Total Staff : 3

Number of researchers on security and defense issues : 1

Projects in Progress : Title
                           Name(s) of Researcher(s)

Issues of Swiss security policy.
                           Daniel Frei et al

Regular Periodicals : Title   Founding date   Issues Annually

Sozialwissenschaftliche   1953   1
Studien (yearbook)

Other Publications (since January 1983)

Daniel Frei (Ed.), The Free World : Balance Sheet and Perspective
(in German) (Zürich : Schulthess - Polygraphischer Verlag, 1983).

DIRECTORY CODE NUMBER : 191

Name of Institution : Schweizerisches Ost-Institut

Address : Jubiläumsstrasse 41
          3000 BERN 6

Telephone : (31) 43-12-12

Founding Date : 1959   Founding Place : Bern
Type of Organization : National Private Non-Profit
Director : Dr. Peter Sager

Regular Periodicals : Title	Founding Date	Issues Annually
ZeitBild (also appears in French edition, Etudes politiques)		

Library services provided for outside researchers : yes

DIRECTORY CODE NUMBER : 192

Name of Institution : Zentralstelle für Gesamtverteidigung

Address : 3003 BERN

Telephone : (31) 67-40-16

Founding Date : 1970   Founding Place : Bern

Type of Organization : National Public

Objectives : Planning, coordination and control of general defense policy.

Director : Dr. A. Wyser

Total Staff : 25

Number of researchers on security and defense issues : 2

Projects in Progress : Title	Name(s) of Researcher(s)

1. A comparative study on general defense policy in several European countries.
   Prof. A. Riklin

2. Possible long-term implications of global ecological and economic problems (as described in "Global 2000") on Switzerland and alternative strategies for meeting these problems.
   Dr. E. Ledergerber/Dr. S. Mauch

3. Plans for computerized support of crisis management on a governmental level.
   Prof. Kohlas/Dr. M. Walliser/ Dr. Kamber/Dr. de Rham

Regular Periodicals : Title	Founding Date	Issues Annually
General Defense : studies on problems of general defense	1975	2-3

Library services provided for outside researchers : yes

TURKEY

TURKEY

The major independent Turkish organization doing security and defense research is the Foreign Policy Institute, founded in 1974 in Ankara. The Institute publishes two quarterly journals (one in English) and occasional special studies; holds conferences and seminars; and sponsors long-term research projects on subjects like the Middle East, Turkey and NATO; Turkey and the European Community; and problems of terrorism. The European Community project is a collaborative effort with German, British, and Italian organizations. In addition, the Institute will soon be undertaking an in-depth study of Turkish security and defense policy from a civilian perspective.

Located in Istanbul, the Political and Social Studies Foundation (SISAV) is a private research organization reflecting an essentially conservative viewpoint. The SISAV is engaged in studies on NATO in the 1980s and on peace and disarmament movements. Both SISAV and the Foreign Policy Institute have strong links with the government in power.

In the words of one university faculty member : "As a result of extensive organizational and personnel changes in Turkish universities in the last two years, most research-oriented activities have come to a standstill". Some related work is being done by individuals at Istanbul University, Bogaziçi University, Ankara University, and the Middle East Technical University. But the academic research sector is not as strong as in other European countries.

The gradual re-introduction of civilian, democratic rule in Turkey should stimulate a greater public interest and a more extensive debate on security and defense questions. The sharpened tensions with Greece over Cyprus and the Aegean and the ramifications of Turkey's critical geopolitical role as a "bridge" between Europe, the Middle East, and the Soviet Union should be growing topics of concern for Turkish experts.

DIRECTORY CODE NUMBER : 193

Name of Institution : Foreign Policy Institute

Address : Mithatpasa Caddesi N° 28/16
Yenisehir
ANKARA

Telephone : (41) 33-31-31
(41) 33-31-32

Founding Date : 1974   Founding Place : Ankara

Type of Organization : National Private Non-Profit

Objectives : To publish original work based on individual research;
to provide intelligent analysis on current issues;
to fill long-term policy-oriented contracts;
to sponsor relevant seminars and conferences;
to promote better information on foreign policy and
strategy in Turkey and abroad.

Director : Seyfi Tashan

Total Staff : 6

Number of researchers on security and defense issues : 2

Projects in Progress : Title
                                 Name(s) of Researcher(s)

1. Turkey and the European Community.
                      Prof. Osman Okyar and others

2. Middle East, Turkey and the Atlantic Alliance.
                      Ali L. Karaosmanoglu and others

3. Terrorism.

4. Turkish security and defense policy.

Regular Periodicals : Title	Founding Date	Issues Annually
1. Foreign Policy (in English)	1971	4
2. Dis Politika	1982	4
3. Avrupa Konseyi Dergisi	1980	3

Other Publications (since January 1983)

1. Gen. Ihsan Gürkan, Turkish Foreign Policy and the Middle East, 1983.
2. Prof. Feyyaz Gölcüklü, Notes on the Turkish Constitution (in English), 1983.
3. Prof. Turhan Feyzioglu, Cyprus, Myths and realities (in French), 1983.

Collaboration with Foreign Study Centers

European Community project in cooperation with German, British and Italian institutes.

Library services provided for outside researchers : yes

DIRECTORY CODE NUMBER : 194

Name of Institution : Institute of International Relations

Address : Faculty of Political Sciences
University of Ankara
ANKARA

Telephone : (41) 19-77-20

Type of Organization : National Public University

Director : Prof. Mehmet Gönlübol

DIRECTORY CODE NUMBER : 195

Name of Institution : Political and Social Studies Foundation
(SISAV)

Address : Abdi Ipekçi Caddesi
Arzu Ap. N° 5/3
Nisantasi
ISTANBUL

Telephone : (1) 46-42-18
(1) 46-57-39

Founding Date : 1980   Founding Place : Istanbul

Type of Organization : National Private Non-Profit

Objectives : Conducting and encouraging research in social and
political problems of Turkey and publishing the findings
of such research in order to help the attainment of
solutions; organizing conferences and seminars and
participating with other organizations, both in Turkey
and abroad.

President : Prof. Memduh Yasa

Total Staff : 3

Projects in Progress : Title

1. NATO in the 1980s.
2. Peace and disarmament movements.

Publications (since January 1983)

<u>NATO in the 1980s</u> (symposium proceedings) (Istanbul : SISAV, 1983) 217 pp.

DIRECTORY CODE NUMBER : 196

Name of Institution : School of Administrative Sciences

Address : Middle East Technical University
          ANKARA

Projects in Progress : Title   Name(s) of Researcher(s)

1. Soviet strategy and Turkey.

                        Duygu Sezer

UNITED KINGDOM

UNITED KINGDOM

The state of British security and defense thinking is determined by the country's historical tradition as a great power and colonial empire, by its unique relationship with the U.S., by the geopolitical factors involved in its island situation (i.e., its physical separation from the continent), by the existence of a strong peace movement supported by one of the major political parties, and by the lingering economic crisis that Britain has faced since the end of the Second World War.

The British have long been ardent students of international politics, especially since Britain's self-proclaimed historical role as "balancer" on the European continent required astute analysis of political events and military capacities of the other powers. This analysis was largely accomplished by individual experts--politicians, diplomats, military men, historians, and journalists--while the formal study of international relations in universities has remained retarded vis-à-vis the United States. The major "think tanks" (International Institute of Strategic Studies, Royal Institute of International Affairs, Royal United Services Institute) are independent and operate outside the university environment. It is through these organizations that most of the interaction among elite groups takes place. The close relationship with the United States has, to a certain extent, diminished a sense of national identity among British analysts who often aim their research and writings toward policymakers across the Atlantic. Furthermore, the Official Secrets Act has imposed constraints on access to primary documentation and limited the interchange between the ministries, the institutes, and the universities.

The International Institute of Strategic Studies occupies a preeminent position as the most influential security research organization in Europe (if not the world). While the Institute emphasizes its international character (with 7000 members in 60 countries), its location in London has considerable impact on the orientations of British research. Strategic Survey and The Military Balance are standard references for strategists and are complemented by the bimonthly Survival and the Adelphi Papers special studies. The Royal Institute of International Affairs (at Chatham House) is the major private research group representing a national perspective on all aspects of foreign policy, including security and defense. Chatham House sponsors a number of national and international conferences and participated in recent collaborative studies on the future of the Atlantic Alliance and the European Community. Many of the conference proceedings are published by the Institute; its regular periodicals are the quarterly International Affairs and the monthly World Today.

The third major London research group, the Royal United Services Institute for Defence Studies (RUSI), emphasizes the study of military sciences and its close ties to the British defense establishment (it was founded by the Duke of Wellington in 1831). This year, the RUSI is undertaking an important research project on Soviet power and prospects. Its regular publications include the <u>Journal of the RUSI</u>, <u>Armed Forces</u>, and the <u>RUSI/Brassey's Defence Yearbook</u>.

Several smaller independent organizations in London reflect a distinctly pro-NATO, anti-pacifist point-of-view. Most active among these is the Institute for European Defence and Strategic Studies which produces a number of policy papers on East-West issues and now publishes <u>Survey</u> (still edited by Leo Labedz). The Institute for the Study of Conflict, the Foreign Affairs Research Institute, and the British Atlantic Committee also fall under this rubric. In terms of reference books, the Jane's series are regarded as authoritative in Western defense ministries.

On the other hand, peace research organizations are quite active, both as independent groups and university-affiliated institutions. The most respected peace research unit in Britain is the School of Peace Studies at the University of Bradford. The Bertrand Russell Peace Foundation publishes most of the position papers of the British disarmament movement and coordinates with other European Nuclear Disarmament (END) groups. University organizations include the Richardson Institute at Lancaster and the Armament and Disarmament Information Unit at Sussex. The Council for Arms Control is noteworthy for its efforts to establish some "middle ground" between the two conflicting schools of thought on defense issues.

British universities are making a growing contribution to the security and defense debate. Lawrence Freedman has recently been appointed Professor in the Department of War Studies, King's College, University of London. The program in war studies stresses the much neglected historical perspective on military and strategic questions. Researchers at the London School of Economics carry on their institution's commitment to policy-oriented work; two faculty members edit the new <u>Atlantic Quarterly</u>.

A great deal of the innovative university research is being done in provincial institutions. The Department of International Politics at Aberystwyth is in the forefront of strategic studies, as is the Centre for the Study of Arms Control and International Security at Lancaster and the Department of Politics at Southampton. David Greenwood has done pioneering work in defense economics at Aberdeen, while J.P. Perry Robinson, Mary Kaldor, and others are investigating the relationship between military technology and defense politics at Sussex's Science Policy Research Unit. Soviet and Eastern European studies are specialties at Edinburgh and Glasgow and also at the Sandhurst research center. The provincial universities are largely free of the persistent bias against policy-oriented work that one still finds at Oxford and Cambridge. Individual specialists--like

Michael Howard or Hedley Bull--predominate here, but these two prestigious universities have no real centers for this research. Budget cutbacks have greatly affected the expansion of research in all universities.

The high emotional level of the British disarmament campaign has made it all the more imperative for impartial, well-respected institutions to provide accurate information and realistic critiques on defense policy and strategy. The debate over the conduct of the Falklands war and the cost of the Trident modernization program has also underscored the need for more expert analysis. As Lawrence Freedman has noted : "Debate on defence issues either seems to be among a select few versed in the mysteries of weapons and strategies and who rarely challenge each other's underlying assumptions, or else it is broadly based but dependent upon mass demonstrations and the simplifications and confrontations that inevitably involves". The difficulty for the outside specialist, according to Freedman, is to maintain his independence and credibility and, at the same time, to raise the level of public discussion on these complicated problems ("The Development of the 'Think Tank'", Journal of the RUSI, March 1982, pp. 17-18).

DIRECTORY CODE NUMBER : 197

Name of Institution : Armament and Disarmament Information Unit
                      (ADIU)

Address : University of Sussex
          Mantell Building
          Falmer
          BRIGHTON, EAST SUSSEX BN1 9RF

Telephone : (273) 686758

Founding Date : 1978   Founding Place : Brighton

Type of Organization : National Public University

Objectives : To raise the level of debate on armament/disarmament
             through an information service and publications.

Director : Malcolm Spaven

Total Staff : 3

Number of researchers on security and defense issues : 2

Regular Periodicals : Title	Founding Date	Issues Annually
1. ADIU Report	1979	6
2. Occasional Papers	1980	
3. ADIU Fact Sheets		

Collaboration with Foreign Study Centers

Information cooperation with Institute for Defense and Disarmament Studies, Brookline, Mass., USA.

Library services provided for outside researchers : yes

Comments : The ADIU is a semi-autonomous element of the Science
Policy Research Unit of the University.

DIRECTORY CODE NUMBER : 198

Name of Institution : Bertrand Russell Peace Foundation

Address : Bertrand Russell House
Gamble Street
NOTTINGHAM NG7 4ET

Telephone : (602) 784504

Founding Date : Sept. 1963   Founding Place : London

Type of Organization : National Private Non-Profit

Objectives : To carry forward Bertrand Russell's work for peace,
human rights, and social justice through research,
publications, and special commissions of enquiry.

Director : Ken Coates

Total Staff : 7

Number of researchers on security and defense issues : 1

Projects in Progress : Title
                                Name(s) of Researcher(s)

1. European nuclear disarmament.

2. Situation in occupied territories of Palestine and Lebanon.

3. Falklands/Malvinas War : sinking of the General Belgrano and
   its implications for the peace process.

4. Carrying of nuclear weapons by British Falklands task force
   and its implications for Treaty of Tlatelolco and nuclear-free-
   zones.

Regular Periodicals : Title	Founding Date	Issues Annually
END Papers	1970	3

Other Publications (since January 1983)

1. Rudolf Steinke and Michel Vale (Eds.), <u>Germany Debates Defence</u>, 1983, 215 pp.

2. André Gunder Frank, <u>The European Challenge : From Atlantic Alliance to Pan-European Entente for Peace and Jobs</u>, 1983, 96 pp.

3. "Brick", <u>Beyond a Joke : Cold War Cartoons</u>, 1983, 72 pp.

4. Ken Coates, <u>Heresies : Resist Much, Obey Little</u>, 1983, 158 pp.

5. Johan Galtung, <u>Alternatives : Four Roads to Peace and Security</u>, 1984, 220 pp.

6. Carl G. Jacobsen, <u>The Nuclear Era : its History, its Implications</u>, 1983 ?, 143 pp.

7. Alva Myrdal et al, <u>Dynamics of European Nuclear Disarmament</u>, 1983 ?

Comments : <u>END Papers</u> incorporates <u>The END Bulletin</u>, <u>London Bulletin</u>, and <u>The Spokesman</u> (the latter founded by Bertrand Russell in 1970).

DIRECTORY CODE NUMBER : 199

Name of Institution : British Atlantic Committee

Address : 30A St. James' Square
LONDON SW1Y 4JH

Telephone : (1) 930-0555
930-0556

Founding Date : 1952   Founding Place : London

Type of Organization : National Private Non-Profit

Objectives : Promote public knowledge of NATO.

Director : Maj. Gen. C.J. Popham

Total Staff : 6

Publications (since January 1983)

---

1. Lord Cameron (Chairman), "Diminishing the Nuclear Threat : NATO's Defense and New Technology", 1984.

2. "Peace and Conflict Studies - A Syllabus in Peace Studies", 1983?

Collaboration with Foreign Study Centers

Coordination with other members of the Atlantic Treaty Organization.

DIRECTORY CODE NUMBER : 200

Name of Institution : Centre for the Analysis of Conflict (CAC)

Address : University of Kent
Rutherford College
CANTERBURY, KENT CT2 7NK

Telephone : (227) 66822

Founding Date : 1965   Founding Place : Kent

Type of Organization : National Public University

Director : Dr. J.W. Burton and Dr. A.J.R. Groom

Total Staff : 10

Number of researchers on security and defense issues : 7

Projects in Progress : Title
                       Name(s) of Researcher(s)

1. A Handbook of International Relations Theory.
            Light and Groom

2. Conflict in world society.
            Banks et al

3. Britain between East and West : a Concerned Independence.
            J.W. Burton et al

Library services provided for outside researchers : yes

DIRECTORY CODE NUMBER : 201

Name of Institution : Centre for Defense Studies

Address : University of Aberdeen
          Edward Wright Building
          Dunbar Street
          ABERDEEN AB9 2TY

Telephone : (224) 40241   x. 5414
                              5415

Founding Date : 1976   Founding Place : Aberdeen

Type of Organization : National Public University

Objectives : The Centre conducts a research effort on national and
             international security affairs, including problems of
             arms control and disarmament. There is a core program
             of studies, aimed at illuminating and informing British
             and European defense policy choices. The Centre also
             undertakes specifically-funded projects, especially in
             defense economics (on which contract research has been
             done for several bodies), on maritime topics, and on
             problems of security in northern Europe and northern
             waters.

Director : David Greenwood

Total Staff : 7

Number of researchers on security and defense issues : 4

Projects in Progress : Title
                       Name(s) of Researcher(s)

1. British defense priorities : an examination of the U.K.'s defense
   effort and issues likely to affect its evolution in the 1980s.
                       David Greenwood

2. Defense technology and industrial policy : options for EC policy
   in defense-related "hi-tech" industries, with particular reference to response to the Fergusson Report (1983).
                       David Greenwood

3. Alliance division of labor : a study of NATO countries' present
   provision and plans, margins for maneuver in planning national
   defense efforts, and of options and prospects for greater spe-
   cialization in the performance of key roles and missions.
                       David Greenwood, Clive Archer et al

4. Greenland and NATO : a study of the importance of Greenland for NATO, the perception of NATO by leading Greenlanders, the views of those at NATO headquarters and in national defense bureaucracies about Greenland, and the identification of factors that may place a strain on traditional Greenlandic links with the West.
Clive Archer

5. Northern waters study group : this study group of the Royal Institute of International Affairs (Scottish Branch) is examining security and resource issues in the northernmost part of the Atlantic.
Clive Archer, David Scrivener et al

6. Soviet arms control policy : domestic objectives and political factors.
David Scrivener

7. European security in the nuclear age (to be published in 1985).
James Wyllie

Regular Periodicals : Title	Founding Date	Issues Annually
1. Aberdeen Studies in Defence Economics (ASIDES)		occasional
2. CENTREPIECES		occasional

Other Publications (since January 1983)

1. C. Archer, International Organizations (London : George Allen and Unwin, 1983) 204 pp.

2. C. Archer (with D. Scrivener), "Frozen Frontiers and Resource Wrangles", International Affairs, Winter 1982/83, pp. 59-76.

3. D. Capitanchik (with R. C. Eichenberg), Defense and Public Opinion (London : Routledge and Kegan Paul, 1983) 98 pp.

4. P. Foot, "Western Security and the Third World", in L. Freedman (Ed.) The Troubled Alliance-Atlantic Relations in the 1980s (London : Heinemann, 1983) pp. 137-151.

5. D. Greenwood, "Economic Constraints and Political Preferences", in J. Baylis (Ed.), Alternative Approaches to Defence Policy, (London : Macmillan, 1983).

6. M. Sheehan, The Arms Race (London : Martin Robertson, 1983.

Library services provided for outside researchers : yes

DIRECTORY CODE NUMBER : 202

Name of Institution : Centre for the Study of Arms Control and International Security

Address : University of Lancaster
Fylde College, Bailrigg
LANCASTER LA1 4YF

Telephone : (524) 65201   x. 4890

Founding Date : 1979   Founding Place : Lancaster

Type of Organization : National Public University

Objectives : To carry out teaching and research in international security and arms control topics.

Director : Prof. Ian Bellany

Total Staff : 5

Number of researchers on security and defense issues : 4

Projects in Progress : Title
                              Name(s) of Researcher(s)

---

1. Indirect energy costs and the cost of defense.
                              Ian Bellany

2. West German armaments industry.
                              Regina Cowen

3. Recruitment, retention and wastage of officers in the British armed services.
   Ian Bellany

4. Nuclear proliferation risks arising from the commercial exploitation of nuclear energy.
   Joseph Gallacher/Ian Bellany

5. Theoretical aspects of arms control.
   Ian Bellany

6. Naval power in the Indian Ocean.
   W.L. Dowdy

7. British out-of-area operations : historical survey from Suez to the Falklands.

8. Impact of defense sector on industrial resources.

9. Offensive/defensive conventional weapons.

Regular Periodicals : Title	Founding Date	Issues Annually
1. *Arms Control*	1980	3
2. *Bailrigg Papers*	1980	occasional

Other Publications (since January 1983)

1. Ian Bellany (Ed.), *ABM Defense in the 1980s* (London : Frank Cass, 1983).

2. Ian Bellany (Ed.), *The Verification of Arms Control Agreements*, (London : Frank Cass, 1983).

3. Regina Cowen, "West German Arms Transfers to Sub-Saharan Africa", in *Arms for Africa*, Lexington Books, 1983.

4. Joseph Gallacher, "An Exercise in Pre-Emptive Verification", *Arms Control*, Vol. 4, N° 1, 1983.

5. W. L. Dowdy (with Russell B. Trood), "The Indian Ocean : an Emerging Geostrategic Region", International Journal, Vol. 37, N° 3, 1983.

6. Regina Cowen, "Consensus in NATO : Past Experience and Present Problems", Arms Control, Vol. 4, N° 2, 1983.

7. Ian Bellany, "Why Men Enlist : the Navy and the Air Force", Bailrigg Paper N° 6, Nov. 1983.

8. G. M. Dillon, "Regional Conflicts and Public Opinion : Policy and Public Opinion in the United Kingdom during the Falklands/Malvinas Crisis, April-June 1982", Bailrigg Paper N° 7, 1984.

Collaboration with Foreign Study Centers

1. Cooperation with Stanford University to publish Arms Control.

2. Possible cooperative project on nuclear proliferation with University of Lille (France).

Library services provided for outside researchers : yes

Comments : The Centre offers a new one-year M.A. degree in Science, Technology and International Affairs. The program is designed for persons with qualifications in the natural sciences who wish to develop an expertise in international relations, with a particular emphasis on peace and security issues.

DIRECTORY CODE NUMBER : 203

Name of Institution : Centre of International Studies

Address : University of Cambridge
          CAMBRIDGE

Founding Date : Aug. 1967   Founding Place : Cambridge

Type of Organization : National Private University

Objectives : Encourage interdisciplinary research and teaching in
            international studies.

Director : Prof. F. H. Hinsley
Deputy Director : Dr. Philip Towle

Comments : The Centre offers a one-year M. Phil. course in international relations.

DIRECTORY CODE NUMBER : 204

Name of Institution : Council for Arms Control

Address : Faraday House
          8-10 Charing Cross Road
          LONDON WC2H OHG

Telephone : (1)-240-0419

Founding-Date : 1981   Founding Place : Windsor

Type of Organization : National Private Non-Profit

Objectives : Research into problems of arms control and dissemination of the results in publications, lectures, seminars, etc. with particular focus on educational institutions.

Director : Peter Foster

Total Staff : 4

Number of researchers on security and defense issues : 1

Regular Periodicals : Title	Founding Date	Issues Annually
Bulletin	Feb. 1982	6

Other Publications (since January 1983)

1. Neville Brown, An Unbreakable Nuclear Stalemate, 1983.
2. Peter Blomley, The Arms Trade and Arms Conversion, 1983
3. Coral Bell, Communication Strategies : an Analysis of International Signalling Patterns, 1983.
4. Josephine O'Connor-Howe (Ed.), Armed Peace (London : Macmillan, to be published Autumn 1984) -- a collection of essays on security problems.

Comments : The Council provides an advisory service for the press and private enquiries.

DIRECTORY CODE NUMBER : 205

Name of Institution : Department of International Politics

Address : University College of Wales
          Llandinam Building
          Penglais
          ABERYSTWYTH DYFED SY23 3DB, WALES

Telephone : (970) 3111   x. 3234

Founding Date : 1919   Founding Place : Aberystwyth

Type of Organization : National Public University

Objectives : To pursue research in the field of international politics and to teach international politics at the undergraduate and postgraduate levels.

Director : Prof. John C. Garnett

Total Staff : 10

Number of researchers on security and defense issues : 3

Projects in Progress : Title
                                          Name(s) of Researcher(s)

1. Regional navies in the Indian Ocean (to be published in 1985 by Macmillan).
                               K. Booth/L. Dowdy/J. Davis

2. Study of naval strategy (to be published in 1985 by Harvester Press).
                               K. Booth

3. Ethical theories and international politics.
                               M. Wright

4. Britain and the formation of NATO.
                               J. Baylis

5. Origins of the Arab-Israeli wars.
                               R. Ovendale

6. Sir Francis Bertie and his embassies.
                               K. Hamilton

7. Spain in international relations 1898-1914.
                               K. Hamilton

Other Publications (since January 1983)

1. Ken Booth, <u>Law, Force and Diplomacy at Sea</u> (London : Allen and Unwin, 1984).

2. Ken Booth et al, <u>Contemporary Strategy : Theories and Policies</u> (New York : Holmes and Meier, 1984, revised edition).

3. John Baylis (Ed.), <u>Alternative Approaches to British Defense Policy</u> (London : Macmillan, 1983).

4. John C. Garnett, <u>Common Sense and the Theory of International Politics</u> (London : Macmillan, 1984)

5. R. Ovendale, <u>The Origins of Modern Wars : the Arab-Israeli Wars</u> (London : Longman, 1983).

6. R. Ovendale (Ed.), <u>The Foreign Policy of the British Labour Government</u> (Leicester : Leicester University Press, 1984).

7. Ken Booth, "Strategy and Conscription", in <u>Alternative Defense Policies</u>, (London : Macmillan, 1984).

8. Ken Booth, "Naval Strategy and the Spread of Psycho-legal Boundaries at Sea", <u>International Journal</u>, Vol. 38, N° 3, Summer 1983.

9. Ken Booth, "Soviet Security Interests in the Indian Ocean", in D. R. Jones (Ed.), <u>Soviet Armed Forces Review Annual</u>.

Library services provided for outside researchers : yes

Comments : The Department offers the only undergraduate degree scheme in International Politics and Strategic Studies in Britain. It also offers Master's, Diploma and Ph.D. Programs in Strategic Studies.

DIRECTORY CODE NUMBER : 206

Name of Institution : Department of International Relations

Address : Keele University
STAFFS ST5 5BG

Telephone : 621111

Founding Date : 1973   Founding Place : Keele

Type of Organization : National Public University

Objectives : Teaching international relations.

Director : Prof. A. M. James

Total Staff : 6

Number of researchers on security and defense issues : 2

Projects in Progress : Title   Name(s) of Researcher(s)

---

1. British multilateral nuclear disarmers.
B. Keohane

2. Nuclear weapons and international relations.
R.J. Vincent

Publications (since January 1983)

1. D. Keohane, "British Policy on Nuclear Proliferation and Trident", in J. Simpson and A. McGrew (Eds.). <u>Nuclear Proliferation</u> (London : FCO, 1984).

Library services provided for outside researchers : yes

DIRECTORY CODE NUMBER : 207

Name of Institution : Department of International Relations

Address : London School of Economics
Houghton Street
LONDON WC 2A 2AE

Telephone : (1) 405-7686

Founding Date : 1920s   Founding Place : London

Type of Organization : University

Objectives : Teaching and research.

Director : Prof. Susan Strange

Total Staff : 14

Number of researchers on security and defense issues : 3

Projects in Progress : Title   Name(s) of Researcher(s)

1. The future of arms control negotiations.
     Hugh Macdonald

2. The control of chemical weapons.
     Nicholas Sims

3. Security and the Middle East conflict.
     Philip Windsor

4. Warsaw Pact out-of-area operations.
     Christopher Coker

5. European defense community.
     Christopher Hill

6. Security of East Asia and the special role of China.
     Michael Yahuda

Regular Periodicals : Title	Founding Date	Issues Annually
1. Atlantic Quarterly	1983	4
2. Millenium	1974	4

Library services provided for outside researchers : yes

Comments : The Atlantic Quarterly is edited by two faculty members (Christopher Coker and Andrew Smith) and published by Longman.

DIRECTORY CODE NUMBER : 208

Name of Institution : Department of Politics

Address : University of Edinburgh
          31 Buccleuch Place
          EDINBURGH EH8 9JT, SCOTLAND

Telephone : (31)-667-1011

Projects in Progress : Title
                                    Name(s) of Researcher(s)

Soviet strategy.
                            John Erickson/David Holloway

DIRECTORY CODE NUMBER : 209

Name of Institution : Department of Politics

Address : University of Southampton
          SOUTHAMPTON SO9 5NH

Telephone : (703) 559122   x. 2522
                               2512

Founding Date : 1963   Founding Place : Southampton

Type of Organization : National Public University

Objectives : Teaching at undergraduate and postgraduate level and research into politics and international relations.

Director : Prof. Par Calvert

Total Staff : 15

Number of researchers on security and defense issues : 6

— 340 —

Projects in Progress : Title   Name(s) of Researcher(s)

1. Bibliography of nuclear non-proliferation sources.
                          P. Lomas/J. Simpson/A. Brier

2. Bibliography of arms control and disarmament.
                          P. Lomas/J. Simpson/A. Brier

3. Into the 1990s : an agenda for North-South security relations.
                          P. Calvert/K. Dawisha/J. Simpson/
                          C. Thomas/P. Williams

Publications (since January 1983)

1. J. Simpson, <u>The Independent Nuclear State : The United States, Britain and the Military Atom</u> (London : Macmillan, 1983).

2. Par Calvert, <u>Politics, Power and Revolution : an Introduction to Comparative Politics</u> (Brighton : Harvester, 1983).

Collaboration with Foreign Study Centers

University of Montpellier, France (in negotiation) for a joint project on comparative U.K./French perspectives on Third World security problems and out-of-area operations.

<u>Library services provided for outside researchers</u> : yes

<u>Comments</u> : The Department has just established a Centre for International Policy Studies.

DIRECTORY CODE NUMBER : 210

Name of Institution : Department of War Studies

Address : King's College
University of London
Strand
LONDON WC2R 2LS

Telephone : (1) 836-5454

Founding Date : 1953   Founding Place : London

Type of Organization : University

Objectives : Educational-concerned with the historical, political, technical, economic, and social problems which arise out of the preparation for and conduct of war, including questions of arms control and disarmament.

Director : Prof. Lawrence Freedman

Total Staff : 8

Number of researchers on security and defense issues : 8

Projects in Progress : Title
                                   Name(s) of Researcher(s)

1. The Falklands and the Media.
                        Valerie Adams

2. Teaching and research in technology and military affairs.
                        B. Reid

3. Role of military history in officer training.
                        Suzanne Marsh

Other Publications (since January 1983)

The Department will soon be establishing a series of King's College Studies in Military History with Macmillan's.

Library services provided for outside researchers : yes

Comments : The Department offers research courses for the M. Phil.
and te Ph.D.

DIRECTORY CODE NUMBER : 211

Name-of Institution : The European-Atlantic Movement (TEAM)

Address : 7 Cathedral Close
         EXETER, DEVON

Telephone : (392)-74908

Founding Date : 1958   Founding Place : London

Type of Organization : International Private Non-Profit

Objectives : (1) communicate Western values to youth
             (2) improve knowledge about European-Atlantic institutions, their functions, cooperation and problems.

Director : J.W. Heard

Total Staff : 6

Number of researchers on security and defense issues : 1

Projects in Progress : Title
                              Name(s) of Researcher(s)

Keeping the Peace : progress in European cooperation towards a defense alliance and policy that will "keep the peace in Europe".

                              Mary Nightingale

DIRECTORY CODE NUMBER : 212

Name of Institution : European Centre for Political Studies

Address : Policy Studies Institute
1/2 Castle Lane
LONDON SWIE 6DR

Telephone : (1) 828-7055

Director : Dr. Roger Morgan

DIRECTORY CODE NUMBER : 213

Name of Institution : Foreign Affairs Research Institute

Address : Arrow House
27-31 Whitehall
LONDON SW1A 2BX

Telephone : (1) 8319-5987

Founding Date : 1976   Founding Place : London

Type of Organization : International Private Non-Profit

Objectives : Political education on the world balance of power, and information in defense of the Free World, especially the security of the West.

Director : Geoffrey Stewart-Smith

Total Staff : 3

Number of researchers on security and defense issues : 1

Regular Periodicals : Title	Founding date	Issues Annually
Papers		24

DIRECTORY CODE NUMBER : 214

Name of Institution : Graduate School of European and International
                      Studies (GSEIS)

Address : University of Reading
          Whiteknights
          READING RG6 2AH

Founding Date : 1965   Founding Place : Reading

type of Organization : National Public University

Objectives : To encourage teaching and research in the field of
             European and international studies (of a multi-
             disciplinary character).

Director : G.N. Yannopoulos

Number of researchers on security and defense issues : 5

Projects in Progress : Title
                              Name(s) of Researcher(s)

French defense policies in the 1980s.
                              N.W. Waites

Other Publications (since January 1983)

1. A. Shlaim, the United States and the Berlin Blockade 1948-1949 :
   a Study in Crisis Decision Making (Berkeley : university of
   California Press, 1983).

2. N.W. Waites, D.L. Hanley and A.P. Kerr, Contemporary France :
   Politics and Society Since 1945 (London : Routledge and Kegan
   Paul, 1984, 2nd ed.). Chap. 5 : Foreign and Defense Policies.

3. N.W. Waites, "Problems of French Defense Policy in their
   Historical Context", in J. Howarth and P. Chilton (Eds.),
   Defence and Dissent in Contemporary France (London : Croom
   Helm, 1983) Chap. 1.

Library services provided for outside researchers : yes

DIRECTORY CODE NUMBER : 215

Name of Institution : History Faculty

Address : Oxford University
Broad Street
OXFORD OX1 3BD

Telephone : 240043

Type of Organization : National Private University

Projects in Progress : Title
                      Name(s) of Researcher(s)

Tactical doctrines of European armies immediately before and during the First World War.
                      Michael Howard

DIRECTORY CODE NUMBER : 216

Name of Institution : Institute for European Defence and Strategic Studies

Address : 13/14 Golden Square
LONDON W1R 3AF

Telephone : (1) 439-8719
            439-8710

Founding Date : 1979   Founding Place : London

Type of Organization : International Private Non-Profit

Objectives : To assess the impact of political change in Europe and North America upon defense and strategic issues, with particular reference to the Atlantic Alliance. Its field of study includes changes occurring in the domestic

— 346 —

political situations of the Alliance members, in the relations between the Alliance and the Warsaw Pact, and between Alliance member states.

Director : Gerald Frost

Total Staff : 3

Number of researchers on security and defense issues : 3

Projects in Progress : Title
                             Name(s) of Researcher(s)

1. Western propaganda and the Soviet bloc.
   Leonard Vladimirov

2. The United Nations Organization : does it serve Britain's interests ?
   Martin Ivens

3. Deterring chemical warfare.
   Manfred Hamm

4. West Germany's role in the Alliance.
   George Szamuely

5. Communist propaganda and the Soviet army.
   Edward Williams

6. Changing attitudes to military life.
   Dennis O'Keefe

7. The Helsinki process.
   Jonathan Luxmore

8. Britain's naval role in NATO.
   Desmond Wettern

9. Interpretations of the Central American Conflict.
   Alfred Sherman

10. Northern Ireland : policy options.
    Various

11. Peace studies.
    Roger Scruton/Caroline Cox

12. Europe and America : the Crumbling Alliance.
    Stephen Haseler

13. Turkey's role in the Alliance.
                              Kenneth Mackenzie
14. Yugoslavia : the prospects for democratic reform.
                              Various
15. A space-launched defense system.
                              Werner Kaltefleiter

Regular Periodicals : Title	Founding Date	Issues Annually
1. Occasional Papers	1982	about 6
2. Survey : a Journal of East and West Affairs	1955	4

Other Publications (since January 1983)

1. Philip Towle, Iain Elliot and Gerald Frost, Protest and Perish : A Critique of Unilateralism (London : Alliance Publishers, 1983).

Collaboration with Foreign Study Centers

Informal research cooperation with Heritage Foundation, Washington, D.C.

DIRECTORY CODE NUMBER : 217

Name of Institution : Institute for the Study of Conflict

Address : 12/12A Golden Square
LONDON W1R 3AF

Telephone : (1) 439-7381

Founding Date : June 1970   Founding Place : London

Type of Organization : National Private Non-Profit

Objectives : To research into the causes, manifestations and likely trends of political instability world-wide; to identify and analyze threats posed by Soviet expansionism; to highlight terrorist and subversive activities.

Director : Michael Goodwin

Regular Periodicals : Title	Founding Date	Issues Annually
1. Conflict Studies		12
2. Conflict Bulletin	1983	4

DIRECTORY CODE NUMBER : 218

Name of Institution : Institute of Civil Defence

Address : P.O. Box N° 229
3 Little Montague Court
LONDON EC1P 1HN

Telephone : (1) 600-0579

Founding Date : 1938   Founding Place : London

Type of Organization : International Private Non-Profit

Objectives : An educational, technical and professional body devoted to the interests of civil defense in all its phases.

Regular Periodicals : Title	Founding Date	Issues Annually
The Journal of the Institute of Civil Defence	1938	4

Comments : The Institute is primarily engaged in "disaster studies" and offers a diploma in civil defense.

DIRECTORY CODE NUMBER : 219

Name of Institution : International Institute for Strategic Studies

Address : 23 Tavistock Street
LONDON WC2E 7NQ

Telephone : (1) 379-7676

Founding Date : 1958   Founding Place : London

Type of Organization : International Private Non-Profit

Objectives : An international and independent center for research, information, and debate on the problems of security, conflict and conflict control, arms and arms control in the modern world.

Director : Dr. Robert O'Neill

Total Staff : 40

Number of researchers on security and defense issues : 14

Projects in Progress : Title
                              Name(s) of Researcher(s)

1. Warsaw Pact, NATO and conflict in Southern Africa.
                              K. Campbell

2. French military role in Africa and African security.
                              J. Chipman

3. NATO and battlefield nuclear weapons : deployments and arms control.
                              E. Fischer

4. Politics of conventional deterrence in Europe : domestic factors influencing NATO force planning in the 1980s.
                              S. Flanagan

5. Soviet theater nuclear forces : the short-range dimension.
                              D. Gormley

6. Technology transfer.
                              I. Portny

7. Space-based command and control.
                              R.R. Russell

8. Soviet policy towards West Germany
                              R. Smith

9. Japan-U.S. relations : a Japanese perspective.
                              A. Tokinoya

10. Soviet decision-making in conventional forces.
                              L. Carrel

11. Role of Britain, France, and Germany in the maintenance of European security.
                              S. May

12. Sino-Soviet relations.
                              G. Segal

Regular Periodicals : Title	Founding Date	Issues Annually
1. Survival	1959	6
2. Adelphi Papers	1964	8-10
3. Strategic Survey		1
4. The Military Balance		1
5. Studies in International Security		1-2

Collaboration with Foreign Study Centers

1. Council on Foreign Relations, New York, on the effectiveness of stronger conventional forces for NATO.
2. Brookings Institution on "no-first-use" issues.

Library services provided for outside researchers : yes

Comments : In addition to individual research topics, the IISS is engaged in three long-term studies : (1) East-West relations, focusing mainly on politico-strategic issues; (2) arms control, focusing on the qualitative aspects of new weapons and their control; and (3) regional studies, focusing in 1984 on Central America.

DIRECTORY CODE NUMBER : 220

Name of Institution : Richardson Institute for Conflict and Peace Research

Address : Department of Politics
University of Lancaster
LANCASTER LA1 4YF

Telephone : (524) 65201 x. 4568

Founding Date : 1959   Founding Place : Lancaster

Type of Organization : National Public University

Objectives : To carry on the work of Lewis Fry Richardson in the field of peace and conflict research.

Director : Paul Smoker

Projects in Progress : Title
                      Name(s) of Researcher(s)

---

1. Alternative work for military industries in the North West U.K.
   Barbara Munske

2. Computer-based peace studies packages.
   Paul Smoker

3. Crises and crisis management.
   Jonathan Roberts

4. Politics of nuclear power.
   Ian Welsh

5. History of British direct action protest against nuclear weapons.
   Andy Skelhorn

6. Technologies of political control.
   Steve Wright

Other Publications (since January 1983)

Hanns-Fred Rathenow and Paul Smoker, *Peace Education in Great Britain*, Lancaster, Workshop Report N° 1, Nov. 1983, 28 pp.

DIRECTORY CODE NUMBER : 221

Name of Institution : Royal Institute of International Affairs

Address : Chatham House
           10 St. James' Square
           LONDON SW1Y 4LE

Telephone : (1) 930-2233

Founding Date : 1920   Founding Place : London

Type of Organization : National Private Non-Profit

Objectives : To provide and maintain means of information upon international questions and promote the study and investigation of international questions by means of lectures and discussions and by the preparation and publication of books, records, reports or other works, or otherwise as may seem desirable.

Director : Admiral Sir James Eberle

Total Staff : 60

Number of researchers on security and defense issues : 2

Projects in Progress : Title
                              Name(s) of Researcher(s)

---

1. European defense cooperation (prospects).
       Trevor Taylor

2. Future of British defense policy.
       John Roper

3. Domestic roots of Soviet foreign policy.
       Curtis Keeble

4. Soviet economic interests in the Third World.
       Robert Cassen

5. Evolution of detente in the 1970s.
       Phil Williams

6. Japan's relations with the Middle East.
       Kunio Katakura

7. Geopolitics of international natural gas trade.
       Jonathan Stern

Regular Periodicals : Title	Founding Date	Issues Annually
1. International Affairs	1922	4
2. The World Today	1945	12

Other Publications (since January 1983)

1. Simon Lunn, Burden Sharing in NATO (Chatham House Paper, May 1983).
2. Phil Williams, U.S. Troops in Europe (Chatham House Paper, 1984).
3. The European Community : Progress or Decline ? (jointly with French, German, Dutch and Italian Institutes of international affairs), April 1983.
4. Gerald Segal (Ed.), The Soviet Union in East Asia.
5. James Piscatori (Ed.), Islam in the Political Process, March 1983.
6. Adeed Dawisha (Ed.), Islam in Foreign Policy, 1983.
7. Stewart Harris and Brian Bridges, European Interests in ASEAN, 1983.
8. Robert Belgrave (Ed.), Energy : Two Decades of Crisis, May 1983.
9. Wilfrid Kohl, International Institutions for Energy Management, May 1983.
10. Nigerian Foreign Policy, 1983.
11. The Uneasy Relationship : Britain and South Africa, 1983.

Library services provided for outside researchers : yes

Comments : Chatham House sponsors regular bilateral conferences with the Deutsche Gesellschaft für Auswärtige Politik and the Institut Français des Relations Internationales. The Institute also holds conferences in cooperation with the Council on Foreign Relations (New York), IMEMO (Moscow), the Istituto Affari Italiani, NUPI (Oslo), and others.

DIRECTORY CODE NUMBER : 222

Name of Institution : Royal Naval College

Address : Greenwich
LONDON SE10 9NN

Founding Date : 1873

Type of Organization : National Public

Objectives : (1) to train and educate officers of the services, principally Royal Navy officers, towards staff and general policy employment;
(2) to train Royal Navy officers in the design, operation, maintenance and safe handling of nuclear propulsion systems.

Director : Prof. P. Nailor

Total Staff : 67

Number of researchers on security and defense issues : 9

Projects in Progress : Title
                                  Name(s) of Researcher(s)

1. Future of British seapower.
                        G. Till

2. Maritime defense of the West.
                        G. Till

3. European nuclear-weapons-sharing.
                        W. H. Park

4. The Carrier debate : a case study of U.S. Defense Policy Formulation (1976-1980).
                        J. Day

Regular Periodicals : Title	Founding Date	Issues Annually
1. Journal of Strategic Studies	1979	4

Other Publications (since January 1983)

1. G. Till and B. Melranft, The Sea in Soviet Strategy (London : Macmillan, 1983).

Library services provided for outside researchers : yes

Comments : The British seapower project represents the proceedings of a conference to be turned into a book. The results of the maritime defense project will be published in 1985-1986.

DIRECTORY CODE NUMBER : 223

Name of Institution : Royal United Services Institute for Defence Studies (RUSI)

Address : Whitehall
LONDON SW1A 2ET

Telephone : (1) 930-5854

Founding date : 1831   Founding Place : London

Type of Organization : National Private Non-Profit

Objectives : The promotion and advancement of the military sciences. The distinguishing feature of the RUSI is its close ties to the armed forces and, in the widest sense, to the defense establishment. As an independent organization, it is able to act as a bridge between different constituencies and disciplines concerned with defense policy and planning in Britain as well as abroad.

Director : Group Capt. David Bolton

Total Staff : 19

Number of researchers on security and defense issues : 6

Projects in Progress : Title   Name(s) of Researcher(s)

1. "The Vulnerable Society".
                               Lt. Col. Pope

2. Military implications of emerging technologies.
                               Farooq Hussain/Kenneth Freeman

3. Soviet power and prospects (1983-1984 RUSI Main Theme Study).

Regular Periodicals : Title	Founding Date	Issues Annually
1. Journal of the Royal United Services Institute for Defence Studies	1857	4
2. RUSI News Sheet	1981	12
3. Armed Forces	1982	12
4. RUSI/Brassey's Defence Yearbook	1886	1

Other Publications (since January 1983)

1. Nuclear Attack : Civil Defence. Aspects of Civil Defence in the Nuclear Age : a Symposium.

2. Christopher Coker, <u>U.S. Military Power in the 1980's</u> (RUSI/ Macmillan's Defence Studies Series).

3. <u>The Realities of Soviet Power</u> (to be published by Macmillan).

Library services provided for outside researchers : yes

Comments : The RUSI study program is organized around "desks" (for NATO, USSR and Eastern Europe, Intelligence and Terrorism, and Defence Technology), each supervised by a research fellow.

DIRECTORY CODE NUMBER : 224

Name of Institution : School of Law

Address : University of Essex
Wivenhoe Park
COLCHESTER, ESSEX CO4 3SQ

Telephone : (206)-862286

Type of Organization : National Public University

Director : Prof. A. D. Yates

Total Staff : 12

Number of researchers on security and defense issues : 1

Projects in Progress : Title
                       Name(s) of Researcher(s)

---

1. Recent developments in international law and their impact on NATO and SHAPE.
   Françoise J. Hampson

2. Mercenaries in international law.
   Françoise J. Hampson

3. International law of armed conflicts, humanitarian law and human rights.
   Françoise J. Hampson

DIRECTORY CODE NUMBER : 225

Name of Institution : School of Peace Studies

Address : University of Bradford
Richmond Road
BRADFORD BD7 1DP

Telephone : (274) 33466

Founding Date : 1974   Founding Place : Bradford

Type of Organization : National Public University

Objectives : Teaching and researching on the maintenance and repair of peace.

Director : Prof. James O'Connell

Total Staff : 12

Number of researchers on security and defense issues : 6

Projects in Progress : Title
                              Name(s) of researcher(s)

1. British civil defense and nuclear war.
            George Crossley

2. Falklands war and the future of the British Navy.
            Andrew Kelly

3. British defense policy.
            Malcolm Chalmers

4. U.S. nuclear policy.
            Andrew White

5. U.S.S.R. nuclear policy.
            Pat Litherland

6. Nuclear proliferation.
            Charles Dakubo

Regular Periodicals : Title	Founding Date	Issues Annually
1. Peace Studies Papers	1980	4
2. Peace Research Reports	1983	3
3. Background Briefing Documents	1982	6

Other Publications (since January 1983)

1. Alan Litherland, a Short Guide to Disarmament.
2. Ken Wilson, a Global Peace Study Guide.

Library services provided for outside researchers : yes

DIRECTORY CODE NUMBER : 226

Name of institution : Science Policy Research Unit (SPRU)

Address : University of Sussex
Mantell Building
Falmer
BRIGHTON, EAST SUSSEX BN1 9RF

Telephone : (273) 686758

Founding Date : 1966   Founding Place : Brighton

Type of Organization : National Public University

Objectives : The primary aim of SPRU is to contribute through its research to the advancement of knowledge of the complex social processes of research, invention, innovation and diffusion of innovations, and thereby to a deeper understanding of policy for science and technology. One of six main research areas is on Military Technology and Arms Limitation.

<u>Director</u> : Prof. C. H. G. Oldham

<u>Total Staff</u> : 40

<u>Number of researchers on security and defense issues</u> : 5

Projects in Progress : Title
                                    Name(s) of Researcher(s)

1. The Weapons Succession Process : studies in military innovation.
   J.P.P. Robinson/M.H. Kaldor/ M.M. Graham

2. Characteristics of European technology culture in relation to politico-military organization (part of an international collaborative research program through the United Nations University).
   M.H. Kaldor/S.M. Phillips

3. Approaches to the restructuring of manufacturing industry for conversion from defense production.
   M.H. Kaldor

4. Possible structures of an international chemical-warfare disarmament regime, with particular reference to the chemical industry.
   J.P.P. Robinson

5. Potentially significant differences in war with and without chemical weapons (an international collaborative project mediated through SIPRI).
   J.P.P. Robinson

Publications (since January 1983)

1. M. H. Kaldor, <u>The Baroque Arsenal</u>.

2. About 40 scholarly articles and 6 submissions to parliamentary and other investigating bodies.

Collaboration with Foreign Study Centers

1. SIPRI on chemical warfare project.
2. U.N. University on European technology culture project.

Library services provided for outside researchers : yes

Comments : SPRU is part of the University's interdisciplinary approach, in which a number of research organizations have been set up to complement the teaching departments.

DIRECTORY CODE NUMBER : 227

Name of Institution : Soviet Studies Research Centre

Address : Royal Military Academy
Sandhurst
CAMBERLEY, SURREY

Telephone : Camberley 63344   x. 346

Founding Date : 1973   Founding Place : Camberley

Type of Organization : National Public

Objectives : To achieve an understanding of the U.S.S.R. and the Soviet military system and to pass on that understanding to U.K. and NATO military personnel and other interested parties.

Director : Christopher N. Donnelly

Total Staff : 8

Number of researchers on security and defense issues : 7

Regular Periodicals : Title   Founding Date   Issues Annually

Unpublished reports (private)

Other Publications (since January 1983)

Contributions to numerous defense journals and books.

Library services provided for outside researchers : yes

DIRECTORY CODE NUMBER : 228

Name of Institution : Welsh Centre for International Affairs

Address : Temple of Peace
          Cathays Park
          CARDIFF CF1 3AP

Telephone : (222) 28549

Founding Date : 1970   Founding Place : Cardiff

Type of Organization : National Private Non-Profit

Objectives : Welsh forum on international issues.

Director : W. R. Davies

Total Staff : 8

Number of researchers on security and defense issues : 1

Library services provided for outside researchers : yes

INSTITUTIONS INDEX

(Note : The numbers here refer to the Directory Code Number and not the page number).

Aarhus (Univ.), Institute of Political Science (Denmark), 30.
Aberdeen (Univ.), Centre for Defence Studies (U.K.), 201.
Abo Academy, Dept. of Political Science (Finland), 34.
Amsterdam (Univ.), Vakgroep Internationale Betrekkingen en
    Volkenrecht (Netherlands), 148.
Amsterdam (Vrije Univ.), Werkgroep Polemologie (Netherlands), 151.
Ankara (Univ.), Institute of International Relations (Turkey), 194.
Archivio Disarmo : Centro Studi e Documentazione sulla Pace e sul
    Disarmo (Italy), 113.
Association pour la Coordination des Etudes et Recherches de
    Défense et de Stratégie (France), 43.
Association pour les Recherches et les Etudes de Défense (France), 44.
Associazione Italiana Studi di Politica Estera (Italy), 114.
Atlantic Institute for International Affairs (France), 45.
Austrian Institute for Peace Research, 1.
Austrian Society for Foreign Affairs and International Relations, 2.
Barcelona (Univ. Autonoma), Dept. of Political Science (Spain), 165.
Berghof Stiftung für Konfliktforschung (FRG), 75.
Berlin (Freie Univ.), Institut für Internationale Politik und
    Regionalstudien (FRG), 95.
Berliner Projektverbund der Berghofstiftung für Konfliktforschung
    (FRG), 76.
Bertrand Russell Peace Foundation (U.K.), 198.
Bologna Center, The Johns Hopkins Univ. (Italy), 115.
Bonn (Univ.), Seminar für Politische Wissenschaft (FRG), 102.
Bradford (Univ.), School of Peace Studies (U.K.), 225.
British Atlantic Committee (U.K.), 199.
Brussels (Univ. Libre), Centre de Sociologie de la Guerre
    (Belgium), 12.
Brussels (Vrije Univ.), Centrum voor Polemologie (Belgium), 14.
Bundesinstitut für ostwissenschaftliche und internationale
    Studien (FRG), 77.
Cambridge (Univ.), Centre of International Studies (U.K.), 203.
Centre d'Etudes de Défense Nationale (France), 47.
Centre d'Etudes et de Documentation sur l'URSS, la Chine et l'Europe
    de l'Est (France), 48.
Centre d'Etudes et de Recherches Internationales, Fondation Nationale
    des Sciences Politiques (France), 49.
Centre d'Etudes Pratiques de la Négociation Internationale
    (Switz.), 183.
Centre d'Etudes Prospectives et d'Informations Internationales
    (France), 53.
Centre de Formation aux Réalités Internationales (France), 54.
Centre de Recherches sur la Défense et la Sécurité (France), 56.
Centre de Sociologie de la Défense Nationale (France), 57.

Centre d'Informacio i Documentacio Internacionals a Barcelona,
    Fundacio (Spain), 166.
Centre for European Policy Studies (Belgium), 13.
Centre for the Study of International Relations (Sweden), 172.
Centre Interdisciplinaire sur la Paix et d'Etudes Stratégiques
    (France), 58.
Centro Alti Studi Difesa (Italy), 116.
Centro de Estudios Constitucionales (Spain), 163.
Centro de Estudios Superiores de Defensa Nacional, Instituto
    Espanol de Estudios Estrategicos (Spain), 169.
Centro di Studi Strategici, Libera Univ. Internazionale di Studi
    Sociale (Italy), 118.
Centro Internazionale di Cultura Scientifica "Ettore Majorana"
    (Italy), 119.
Centro Studi Manlio Brosio (Italy), 122.
Centro Studi Politica Internazionale (Italy), 123.
Cercle d'Etudes de Stratégie Totale (France), 60.
Cercle Renaissance (France), 61.
Christian Albrechts Univ., Institut für Internationales Recht
    (FRG), 96.
Christian Albrechts Univ., Institut für Politische Wissenschaft
    (FRG), 98.
Comité International pour la Sécurité et la Coopération Européennes
    (Belgium), 17.
Copenhagen (Univ.), Institute of Political Studies (Denmark), 31.
Copenhagen (Univ.), Working Group for Peace and Conflict Research
    (Denmark), 33.
Council for Arms Control (U.K.), 204.
Danish Commission on Security and Disarmament Affairs, 25.
Danish Institute of International Studies, 26.
Danish Peace Research Association, 27.
Deutsch-Franzosisches Institut (FRG), 78.
Deutsche Atlantische Gesellschaft (FRG), 79.
Deutsche Friedensgesellschaft - Vereinigte Kriegsdienstgegner
    (FRG), 80.
Deutsche Gesellschaft für Auswärtige Politik, Forschungsinstitut
    (FRG), 84.
Deutsche Strategie-Forum (FRG), 81.
Deutsches Orient-Institut (FRG), 82.
Edinburgh (Univ.), Dept. of Politics (U.K.), 208.
Eidgenössische Technische Hochschule Zürich, Dept. of Military
    Science (Switz.), 184.
Essex (Univ.), School of Law (U.K.), 224.
European-Atlantic Movement (U.K.), 211.
European Centre for Political Studies, Policy Studies Institute
    (U.K.), 212.
European Institute for Security Matters (Luxembourg), 136.
Europese Beweging in Nederland (Netherlands), 138.
Finnish Institute of International Affairs, 37.
Finnish Peace Research Association, 38.
Firenze (Univ.), Centro Analizi Relazioni Internazionali (Italy), 117.
Fondation du Futur (France), 62.

Fondation Nationale des Sciences Politiques, Centre d'Etudes et de
    Recherches Internationales (France), 49.
Fondation pour les Etudes de Défense Nationale (France), 63.
Foreign Affairs Research Institute (U.K.), 213.
Foreign Policy Institute (Turkey), 193.
Foreign Policy Society (Denmark), 28.
Forschungsinstitut für Internationale Politik und Sicherheit,
    Stiftung Wissenschaft und Politik (FRG), 85.
Forschungsstätte der Evangelischen Studiengemeinschaft (FRG), 87.
Foundation for Mediterranean Studies (Greece), 105.
Fridtjof Nansen Foundation (Norway), 152.
Friedrich-Ebert Stiftung (FRG), 88.
Friedrich-Naumann Stiftung (FRG), 89.
Führungsakademie der Bundeswehr (FRG), 90.
Fundacio Centre d'Informacio i Documentacio Internacionals a
    Barcelona (Spain), 166.
Geneva International Peace Research Institute (Switz.), 186.
Genova (Univ.), Centro Studi sulla Difesa (Italy), 124.
Gothenburg (Univ.), Dept. of Peace and Conflict Research
    (Sweden), 173.
Gothenburg (Univ.), Dept. of Political Science (Sweden), 176.
Graz (Univ.), Institut für Völkerrecht und Internationale
    Beziehungen (Austria), 4.
Grenoble (Univ.), Centre d'Etudes de Défense et de Sécurité
    Internationale (France), 46.
Groningen (Univ.), Polemologisch Instituut (Netherlands), 144.
Groupe de Recherche et d'Information sur la Paix (Belgium), 19.
Hamburg (Univ.), Institut für Friedensforschung und Sicherheits-
    politik (FRG), 94.
Hanns-Seidel Stiftung (FRG), 91.
Hans Rissen : Internationales Institut für Politik und
    Wirtschaft (FRG), 92.
Heidelberg (Univ.), Arbeitgemeinschaft für Konflikt -und
    Friedensforschung (FRG), 73.
Hellenic Institute for Defense Studies (Greece), 106.
Hellenic Society of International Law and Relations (Greece), 107.
Helsinki (Univ.), Dept. of Political Science (Finland), 35.
Hessische Stiftung Friedens- und Konfliktforschung (FRG), 93.
Iceland (Univ.), Faculty of Social Sciences, 109.
Icelandic Commission on Security and International Affairs, 110.
Independent Scientific Research Institute (Switz.), 187.
Institut d'Etudes Politiques d'Aix-en-Provence (France), 64.
Institut d'Histoire des Relations Internationales Contemporaines
    (France), 66.
Institut du Droit de la Paix et du Développement, Centre d'Etudes
    et de Recherches sur la Défense et la Sécurité (France), 51.
Institut Européen pour la Paix et la Sécurité (Belgium), 20.
Institut Français de Polémologie (France), 67.
Institut Français des Relations Internationales (France), 68.
Institut für Strategische Grundlagenforschung an der Landes-
    verteidigungsakademie (Austria), 3.
Institut International de Géopolitique (France), 70.

Institut Universitaire de Hautes Etudes Internationales, Programme
    for Strategic and International Security Studies (Switz.), 189.
Institute for Alternative Development Research (Norway), 154.
Institute for European Defence and Strategic Studies (U.K.), 216.
Institute for Military Science (Finland), 39.
Institute for the Study of Conflict (U.K.), 217.
Institute of Civil Defence (U.K.), 218.
Institute of Social Studies (Netherlands), 139.
Instituto da Defesa Nacional (Portugal), 161.
Instituto de Cuestiones Internacionales (Spain), 167.
Instituto de Estudos Estratégicos e Internacionais (Portugal), 162.
Instituto Espanol de Estudios Estrategicos, Centro de Estudios
    Superiores de Defensa Nacional (Spain), 169.
International Civil Defence Organization (Switz.), 188.
International Institute for Strategic Studies (U.K.), 219.
International Peace Information Service (Belgium), 21.
International Peace Research Institute (Norway), 156.
International School on Disarmament and Arms Control (Italy), 126.
Internationales Institut für Vergleichende Gesellschaftsforschung
    (FRG), 99.
Istituto Affari Internazionali (Italy), 127.
Istituto di Ricerca per il Disarmo, lo Sviluppo e la Pace
    (Italy), 128.
Istituto Italiano di Polemologia e di Ricerche sui Conflitti
    (Italy), 129.
Istituto Italiano Ricerca sulla Pace (Italy), 130.
Istituto per gli Studi di Politica Internazionale (Italy), 131.
Istituto per le Relazioni tra l'Italia e i Paesi dell'Africa,
    America Latina e Medio Oriente (Italy), 132.
Istituto Studi e Richerche Difesa (Italy), 133.
John F. Kennedy Institute, Center for International Studies
    (Netherlands), 141.
Johns Hopkins Univ., Bologna Center (Italy), 115.
Keele (Univ.), Dept. of International Relations (U.K.), 206.
Kent (Univ.), Centre for the Analysis of Conflict (U.K.), 200.
King's College, Univ. of London, Dept. of War Studies (U.K.), 210.
Köln (Univ.), Forschungsinstitut für Politische Wissenschaft
    und Europäische Fragen (FRG), 86.
Koninklijke Vereniging ter Beogfening van de Krijgswetenschap
    (Netherlands), 142.
Konrad-Adenauer Stiftung, Sozialwissenschaftliches Forschungs-
    institut (FRG), 100.
Konstanz (Univ.), Fachbereich Politische Wissenschaft (FRG), 83.
Lancaster (Univ.), Centre for the Study of Arms Control and
    International Security (U.K.), 202.
Lancaster (Univ.), Richardson Institute for Conflict and Peace
    Research (U.K.), 220.
Leiden (Univ.), Instituut voor Internationale Studien
    (Netherlands), 140.
Leuven (Catholic Univ.), Centrum voor Strategische Studies
    (Belgium), 15.
Leuven (Catholic Univ.), Centrum voor Vredesonderzoek (Belgium), 16.

Libera Univ. Internazionale di Studi Sociale (Roma), Centro di
   Studi Strategici (Italy), 118.
London School of Economics, Dept. of International Relations
   (U.K.), 207.
London (Univ. - King's College), Dept. of War Studies (U.K.), 210.
Lund (Univ.), Dept. of Peace and Conflict Research (Sweden), 174.
Lyon-III (Univ.), Centre Lyonnais d'Etudes de Sécurité Internationale
   et de Défense (France), 59.
Madrid (Univ. Autonoma), Dept. of International Public Law
   (Spain), 164.
Madrid (Univ. Autonoma), Instituto de Economia Aplicada (Spain), 168.
Madrid (Univ. Complutense) (Spain), 171.
Max Planck Institut für Sozialwissenschaften, Arbeitsgruppe
   Afheldt (FRG), 101.
Middle East Technical Univ., School of Administrative Sciences
   (Turkey), 196.
Milano (Univ. Cattolica), Gruppo di Studio su Armi e Disarmo
   (Italy), 125.
Montpellier (Univ.), Centre d'Histoire Militaire et d'Etudes de
   Défense Nationale (France), 55.
National Defence College, Research Centre for Defence History
   (Norway), 159.
National Defense Research Institute, Division for International
   Studies (Sweden), 178.
NATO Defense College (Italy), 134.
Nederlands Instituut voor Internationale Betrekkingen
   (Clingendael), 143.
Nijmegen (Univ.), Studiecentrum voor Vredesvraagstukken
   (Netherlands), 146.
Nordic Cooperation Committee for International Politics (Sweden), 179.
North Atlantic Assembly (Belgium), 22.
Norwegian Defence Research Establishment, 157.
Norwegian Institute of International Affairs, 158.
Odense (Univ.), Institute of Social Science (Denmark), 32.
Oesterreichische Gesellschaft für Aussenpolitik und Internationale
   Beziehungen (Austria), 6.
Oesterreichische Gesellschaft für Politische-Strategische Studien
   (Austria), 7.
Oesterreichische Gesellschaft zur Förderung der Landesverteidigung
   (Austria), 8.
Oesterreichisches Institut für Internationale Politik (Austria), 9.
Oesterreichisches Ost- und Südosteuropa-Institut (Austria), 10.
Oslo (Univ.), Institute of Political Science (Norway), 153.
Oxford (Univ.), History Faculty (U.K.), 215.
Paris-I (Univ.), Institut National Supérieur d'Etudes de Défense
   et de Désarmement (France), 71.
Paris-Sorbonne (Univ.), Centre d'Etudes et de Recherches sur les
   Stratégies (France), 52.
Paris-Sud (Univ.), Institut International d'Etudes Diplomatiques
   (France), 69.
Paris-X (Univ.), Institut de Politique Internationale et Européenne
   (France), 65.

Peace Forum of the Swedish Labour Movement, 180.
Pisa (Univ.), Centro Interuniversitario di Studi e Ricerche
    Storico-Militari (Italy), 120.
Policy Studies Institute, European Centre for Political Studies
    (U.K.), 212.
Political and Social Studies Foundation (Turkey), 195.
Programme for Strategic and International Security Studies, Institut
    Universitaire de Hautes Etudes Internationales (Switz.), 189.
Reading (Univ.), Graduate School of European and International
    Studies (U.K.), 214.
Research Centre for Defence History, National Defence College
    (Norway), 159.
Richardson Institute for Conflict and Peace Research, Lancaster
    (Univ.) (U.K.), 220.
Royal Higher Institute for Defense, Defense Studies Center
    (Belgium), 18.
Royal Institute for International Relations (Belgium), 23.
Royal Institute of International Affairs (U.K.), 221.
Royal Irish Academy, International Relations Committee, 112.
Royal Military Academy, Soviet Studies Research Centre (U.K.), 227.
Royal Naval College (U.K.), 222.
Royal United Services Institute for Defence Studies (U.K.), 223.
Saarlandes (Univ.), Institut für Politikwissenschaft (FRG), 97.
Schweizerisches Institut für Auslandforschung (Switz.), 190.
Schweizerisches Ost-Institut (Switz.), 191.
Science Policy Council of Norway, 160.
Sociedad de Estudios Internacionales (Spain), 170.
Società Italiana per l'Organizzazione Internazionale (Italy), 135.
Soviet Studies Research Centre, Royal Military Academy (U.K.), 227.
South Jutland (Univ. Centre), Institute of East-West Research
    (Denmark), 29.
Southampton (Univ.), Dept. of Politics (U.K.), 209.
Sozialwissenschaftlichen Instituts der Bundeswehr (FRG), 103.
Stichting Atlantische Commissie (Netherlands), 145.
Stiftung Wissenschaft und Politik, Forschungsinstitut für
    Internationale Politik und Sicherheit (FRG), 85.
Stockholm International Peace Research Institute (Sweden), 181.
Stockholm (Univ.), Dept. of Political Science (Sweden), 177.
Studiengesellschaft für Friedensforschung (FRG), 104.
Stuttgart (Univ.), Arbeitsgemeinschaft für Friedensforschung
    und Europäische Sicherheitspolitik (FRG), 72.
Sussex (Univ.), Armament and Disarmament Information Unit
    (U.K.), 197.
Sussex (Univ.), Science Policy Research Unit (U.K.), 226.
Swedish Institute of International Affairs, 182.
Tampere Peace Research Institute (Finland), 40.
Tampere (Univ.), Institute of Political Science (Finland), 41.
Thessaloniki (Univ.), Institute of Public International Law and
    International Relations (Greece), 108.
Torino (Univ.), Centro Studi e Documentazione Internazionale
    (Italy), 121.
Toulouse (Univ.), Centre d'Etudes et de Recherches sur l'Armée
    (France), 50.

Transnational Institute (Netherlands), 147.
Trinity College, Dept. of Political Science (Ireland), 111.
Tromso (Univ.), Institute for Social Sciences (Norway), 155.
Tübingen (Univ.), Arbeitsgruppe Friedensforschung (FRG), 74.
Turku (Univ.), Dept. of Political Science (Finland), 36.
Twente (Technische Hogeschool), Center for Studies on Problems of Science and Society (Netherlands), 137.
Universitätszentrum für Friedensforschung (Austria), 11.
Université de Paix (Belgium), 24.
Uppsala (Univ.), Dept. of Peace and Conflict Research (Sweden), 175.
Wales (University College-Aberystwyth), Dept. of International Politics (U.K.), 205.
Welsh Centre for International Affairs (U.K.), 228.
Western European Union, Assembly (France), 42.
Wetenschappelijk Instituut voor het CDA (Netherlands), 149.
Wiardi Beckman Stichting (Netherlands), 150.
Wien (Univ.), Institut für Volkerrecht und Internationale Beziehungen (Austria), 5.
Zentralstelle für Gesamtverteidigung (Switz.), 192.
Zürich (Eidgenössische Technische Hochschule), Dept. of Military Science (Switz.), 184.
Zürich (Univ.), Forschungstelle für Politische Wissenschaft (Switz.), 185.

SUBJECT INDEX

(<u>Note</u> : The numbers here refer to the Directory Code Number and <u>not</u> the page number).

<u>Africa</u> : 40,71,82,84,85,86,132,143,162,167,174,181,189,202,219,221.
<u>Alternative Defense (and Non-Violence)</u> : 21,24,31,33,52,72,74,77,80, 87,94,130,149,166,174,198,205.
<u>Arms Control and Disarmament</u> : 16,19,25,36,37,40,42,46,68,71,72,74, 80,84,85,88,93,94,95,96,98,110,113,118,123,125,126,128,130,131,135, 137,144,154,156,158,170,174,180,181,185,187,189,197,198,201,202,204, 206,207,209,219,225,226.
<u>Arms Race</u> : 31,87,93,113,128,133,137,139,140,144,146,156,174,175, 189,201,226.
<u>Arms Transfers (and Sales)</u> : 19,21,46,85,94,140,181,185,202,204.
<u>Austria</u> : 1,2,3,6,7,9,11,30.
<u>Belgium</u> : 12,14,15,18,19,21,23,45,86,148.
<u>Bibliographies</u> : 15,31,37,46,65,86,120,160,179,209.
<u>Biological and Chemical Warfare</u> : 25,72,85,118,181,207,216,226.
<u>China</u> : 48,49,57,63,85,97,123,141,181,182,207,219.
<u>Civil Defense</u> : 20,85,188,218,223,225.
<u>Conference on Security and Cooperation in Europe</u> : 17,22,88,93, 165,216.
<u>Confidence-Building Measures</u> : 9,37,71,77,84,85,88,93,94,95,96,111, 156,158,180,181,182.
<u>Conflict (Theory and Resolution</u> : 15,33,67,76,93,99,135,144,156,174, 175,181,186,189,200,217,219,224.
<u>Crisis Management</u> : 16,35,85,185,192,204,214,219,220.
<u>Decision-Making</u> : 12,30,50,57,103,113,122,133,140,153,158,177,201, 214,219,222.
<u>Defense Budgets and Expenditures</u> : 12,19,113,128,133,169,174,178, 181,201,202,219,221,223.
<u>Denmark (and Greenland)</u> : 25,26,28,30,32,45,174,201.
<u>Deterrence (and "Flexible Response")</u> : 52,68,81,85,88,93,95,127,146, 156,184,221.
<u>Domestic Factors</u> : 55,86,93,100,107,113,122,133,140,158,177,201,219.
<u>East-West Relations (including Detente)</u> : 9,13,22,25,31,45,54,61,62, 70,81,84,85,86,88,93,94,95,97,100,110,133,139,141,144,158,159,176, 177,178,181,185,190,200,213,216,219,221,222,223.
<u>Eastern Europe</u> : 10,21,25,31,45,48,49,77,85,143,154,178,182,191,207, 216,223.
<u>Economic Relations and Development</u> : 16,22,30,31,37,48,49,53,68,71, 84,85,86,93,94,95,127,132,137,139,141,144,146,151,154,156,158,168, 173,174,178,180,181,182,192,201,202,221.
<u>Energy Policy and Dependency</u> : 33,82,84,85,87,93,152,175,182,186,189, 201,202,221.
<u>Environmental Destruction</u> : 80,86,181,192.
<u>Ethical Issues</u> : 11,15,18,21,81,86,87,93,103,104,140,141,151,159, 175,205.

Euromissiles (and INF Negotiations) : 19,22,25,30,63,72,77,81,85,88,
94,95,98,100,113,123,127,158,175,182,219.
European Community (Integration) : 9,31,49,68,84,85,86,92,111,135,
138,158,162,167,183,193,201,221.
European Security and Defense Cooperation : 13,15,16,18,19,20,22,23,
31,36,40,42,45,46,56,58,65,68,70,72,74,81,85,86,87,88,93,94,95,97,
100,124,127,135,136,137,138,141,143,151,154,158,162,165,166,169,181,
185,189,198,201,207,211,216,219,221,222.
Falklands Conflict : 30,198,202,210,225.
Far East (includes Japan) : 49,85,95,178,181,189,207,219,221.
Finland : 34,36,37,40.
Force Comparisons (and Posture) : 19,71,81,85,93,94,95,128,133,161,
166,181,182,184,192,201,219,223.
France : 15,43,46,47,50,52,54,55,57,63,67,68,78,84,85,86,98,178,
214,219.
Germany (Democratic Republic) : 84,85,93,97,176,178.
Germany (Federal Republic) : 50,63,65,67,72,77,84,85,86,88,94,95,97,
100,103,156,176,182,198,202,214,216,219.
Greece : 50,106,107,108.
Human Rights : 21,22,80,84,113,128,135,143,156,183,198,224.
Iceland : 109,110.
Industrial Conversion : 94,113,128,156,180,204,220,226.
Intelligence Capabilities (and Verification) : 42,85,174,187,202,223.
International Law : 3,18,94,96,107,164,205,224.
International Relations (Theory) : 23,31,35,40,49,66,86,97,99,107,
117,131,135,139,161,172,177,185,200,205,206.
Iran-Iraq War : 68,71,82,85,132.
Ireland : 111,112,216.
Italy : 50,113,116,118,120,122,124,127,128,130,131,132,133,134.
Latin America : 46,49,67,74,85,132,154,166,167,170,189,216,219.
Law of the Sea : 32,85,123,152,205.
Luxembourg : 23,136.
Manpower (Military) : 12,22,50,55,57,85,202,205,224.
Media and Communications : 14,18,21,30,40,50,57,80,113,133,158,197,
198,210,216.
Mediterranean (and Southern Flank) : 22,55,65,105,106,124,127,156,
165,166,167,169,193.
Middle East : 9,34,46,49,52,68,71,82,84,85,127,132,141,143,156,158,
166,175,193,198,205,207,221.
Military (as Profession) and Militarism : 50,55,57,80,87,93,103,133,
134,154,156,161,169,174,182,187,210,216,222,223,226.
Military Bases : 109,156,162.
National Security : 15,16,24,28,46,50,63,68,72,77,85,93,95,99,101,
122,133,149,157,159,161,169,170,174,178,182,184,190,192,193,219,221.
NATO : 14,15,20,22,30,45,50,72,79,81,84,85,86,88,93,94,95,100,101,
109,110,116,122,127,134,141,145,146,148,151,154,158,159,162,164,182,
184,193,195,199,201,202,205,216,219,221,223,224.
Naval Strategy : 68,85,94,158,162,167,181,201,202,205,216,222,225.
Netherlands : 21,45,140,142,143,145,146,148.
Neutrality : 1,3,9,40,50,111,174,182,189.
Neutron (ERW) Weapons : 98,187.
No-First-Use (Nuclear) : 86,88,101,110,158,181,219.

North-South Relations : 13,85,87,93,94,123,128,132,139,140,156,173,
178,183,189,201,209,221.
Norway : 45,152,153,156,157,158,159.
Nuclear Proliferation (and Nuclear Energy) : 13,36,37,74,87,93,95,
137,164,181,187,202,206,209,220,225.
Nuclear-Weapon-Free Zones : 18,37,46,74,80,85,94,98,100,109,154,156,
158,180,198.
Offensive vs. Defensive Weapons : 101,151,202.
Out-of-Area Operations (Intervention) : 22,85,116,127,175,181,182,
189,202,207,209,219.
Peace Movements (Pacifism) : 12,21,46,50,68,86,94,97,109,113,134,146,
151,156,162,169,195,198,206,216,220.
Peace Research and Education : 1,3,11,14,16,19,21,24,27,33,38,40,58,
73,74,75,80,86,87,91,93,94,96,104,113,119,128,129,130,144,145,146,151,
156,160,173,174,175,180,181,186,198,199,216,220,225.
Poland : 174,178.
Portugal : 50,161,162.
Public Opinion (and Polls) : 13,22,40,45,50,99,109,110,140,158,162,
201,202.
Research and Development (Military) : 14,25,55,85,94,113,124,128,151,
156,159,174,175,178,181,202.
SALT/START : 100.
Scandinavia (and Northern Flank) : 25,30,32,34,37,45,85,154,155,156,
158,174,175,179,189,201.
Small States (Dependency) : 158,189.
South Asia (includes India) : 49,85,181,202,205.
Space Warfare (and ABMs) : 20,22,42,55,72,84,85,100,164,181,187,202,
216,219.
Spain : 50,162,164,165,166,167,169,170,205.
Strategy (Conventional) : 22,72,81,84,85,86,88,93,95,122,127,145,156,
181,199,201,205,219,223.
Strategy (Nuclear) : 56,72,81,84,85,86,87,88,93,94,95,98,101,110,122,
139,145,156,184,185,198,199,201,204,205,206,219,222,225.
Sweden : 9,31,174,178,182.
Switzerland : 9,184,186,189,190,192.
Technology Transfer : 22,74,84,85,219.
Terrorism (and Low-Level Conflicts) : 50,67,174,193,217,223.
Threat Perceptions : 14,85,123,146,181,185.
Turkey : 82,85,94,106,107,108,139,193,195,196,216.
U.S.S.R.-Defense Policy : 13,29,31,33,45,52,63,68,71,77,81,85,93,100,
110,123,131,143,146,158,175,178,181,182,184,185,189,201,205,207,208,
216,217,219,222,223,225,227.
U.S.S.R.-Foreign Policy : 9,10,13,16,25,29,30,31,32,33,37,45,48,49,
77,85,93,98,100,143,152,176,178,182,191,196,201,208,217,219,221,222,223,
227.
United Kingdom : 50,95,111,155,159,182,189,198,200,201,202,205,206,
209,210,216,219,220,221,222,223,225.
United Nations : 25,34,80,84,85,94,135,143,156,158,216.
United States - Defense Policy : 31,57,58,81,85,88,93,95,123,124,154,
158,162,181,184,185,209,214,221,222,223,225.
United States - Foreign Policy : 29,30,31,35,46,49,82,84,85,86,93,95,
97,108,127,141,143,148,154,162,182,214,219,221.

War (History and Theory) : 9,11,39,50,52,55,65,67,86,120,142,143,144,
156,159,170,174,175,205,210,215.
Weapons Technology : 22,25,55,85,110,127,139,146,151,174,181,187,201,
210,220,223,226.
World War II : 63,184.

THE EDITORS :

Luc Reychler is Professor of International Relations and Strategic Studies at the Catholic University of Leuven. He is the author of Patterns of Diplomatic Thinking (Praeger, 1979) and is currently working on Belgian defense policy and methodological aspects of comparative strategic analysis.

Robert Rudney is Research Associate, Division of International Relations (Center for Strategic Studies), Catholic University of Leuven. His major fields of interest include French strategic and political issues and European diplomatic history. He is now engaged in a comparative study of European-American security research.